# PEARSON EDUCATION TEST PREP SERIES

# FOR

# AP® UNITED STATES GOVERNMENT AND POLITICS

### Cathy Griffin

*To accompany:*

**EDWARDS/WATTENBERG/HOWELL, *GOVERNMENT IN AMERICA: PEOPLE, POLITICS, AND POLICY***

SEVENTEENTH EDITION, AP® EDITION

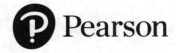 Pearson

330 Hudson Street, New York, NY 10013

D1530653

Printed in the United States of America

 Pearson

1  18
ISBN 10:     0-13-461165-9
ISBN 13: 978-0-13-461165-5
PearsonSchool.com/Advanced

# Contents

# 1 Introducing Government in America

## Chapter Overview

Politics and government matter-that is the single most important message of this book. Consider, for example, the following list of ways that government and politics may have already impacted your life:

- Chances are pretty good that you or someone in your family has recently been the recipient of one of the 80 million payments made to individuals by the federal government every month. In 2016, nearly 20 percent of the money that went into Americans' wallets was from government payments like jobless benefits, food stamps, Social Security payments, veterans' benefits, and so on.

- Any public schools you attended were prohibited by the federal government from discriminating against females and minorities and from holding prayer sessions led by school officials. Municipal school boards regulated your education, and the state certified and paid your teachers.

- The ages at which you could get your driver's license, drink alcohol, and vote were determined by state and federal governments.

- Before you could get a job, the federal government had to issue you a Social Security number, and you have been paying Social Security taxes every month that you have been employed. If you worked at a low-paying job, your starting wages were likely determined by state and federal minimum-wage laws.

- As a college student, you may be drawing student loans financed by the government. The government even dictates certain school holidays.

- Even though gasoline prices have risen substantially in recent years, federal policy continues to make it possible for you to drive long distances relatively cheaply compared to citizens in other countries. In many other advanced industrialized nations, such as England and Japan, gasoline is twice as expensive as in the United States because of the high taxes their governments impose on fuel.

- If you apply to rent an apartment, by federal law landlords cannot discriminate against you because of your race or religion.

This list could, of course, be greatly extended. And it helps explain the importance of politics and government. As Barack Obama said when he first ran for public office in 1993, "Politics does matter. It can make the difference in terms of a benefits check. It can make the difference in terms of school funding. Citizens can't just remove themselves from that process. They actually have to engage themselves and not just leave it to the professionals."

It is our hope that after reading this book, you will be persuaded that paying attention to politics and government is important. Government has a substantial impact on all our lives. But it is also true that we have the opportunity to have a substantial impact on government. Involvement in public affairs can take many forms, ranging from simply becoming better informed by browsing through political Web sites to running for elected office. In between are countless opportunities for *everyone* to make a difference.

# Study Outline

 **Learning Objective 1.1: Identify the key functions of government and explain why they matter. (p. 7)**

## *Government*

- The institutions through which public policy is made are collectively known as government. The key functions of government are:
  - **Maintain a national defense:** A government typically maintains armed forces to protect its sovereignty.
  - **Provide public goods and services:** The government provides **collective goods**, those goods and services which cannot be denied to anyone, as well as other goods and services which may be provided by both the government and the private sector, such as college and medical care.
  - **Preserve order:** The government is responsible for maintaining public order, sometimes using extreme measures, if needed.
  - **Socialize the young:** The government pays for public education as a means of instilling knowledge and pride in the nation's young.
  - **Collect taxes:** The government uses tax money to fund the public goods and services it provides.

**1.2** **Learning Objective 1.2: Define politics in the context of democratic government. (p. 8)**

- **Politics** is the process by which government leaders and policies are selected.
- The activities in which citizens engage in order to influence that selection are known as **political participation**, which may take the form of voting, running for office, or getting involved in political action groups.
- **Single issue groups** include members who are uncompromisingly committed to a particular issue.

**1.3** **Learning Objective 1.3: Assess how citizens can have an impact on public policy and how policies can impact people. (p. 9)**

- The **policymaking system** is the process by which the people shape public policy.
- The political processes and channels through which the concerns of the people are translated into public policy are **linkage institutions**, such as political parties, elections, interest groups and the media.
- Through these linkage institutions, concerns reach the **policy agenda** from which the policymaking institutions select issues to be addressed.
- A **political issue** is an issue that arises when people disagree about a problem and how to fix it.
- **Policymaking institutions** are established by the Constitution and are the branches of government charged with taking action on political issues. These institutions are Congress, the presidency, and the courts.
- **Public policy** is a choice that government makes in response to a political issue.
- **Policy impacts** are the effects a policy has on people and problems.

**1.4** **Learning Objective 1.4: Identify the key principles of democracy and outline theories regarding how it works in practice and the challenges democracy faces today. (p. 12)**

### *Democracy in America: Traditional Democratic Theory*

- Traditional democratic theory suggests that five characteristics are needed in order to make a political system democratic:
  - **Equality in voting:** The public has the right to **vote** for government representatives, and the principle of one person, one vote is generally respected.
  - **Effective participation:** Citizens must have equal opportunities to express their **political views** by such means as voting or joining political groups such as **political parties**.

- □ **Enlightened understanding:** The public should be informed about various political and social issues to formulate judgments and make **informed decisions**.
- □ **Citizen control of the agenda:** The issues taken up by the government should reflect those issues that are of concern to the people.
- □ **Inclusion:** All people subject to the laws of a nation must have the opportunity to become citizens and to possess all the **rights of citizenship**.
- In addition, democratic political systems must balance two principles that often conflict:
  - □ **Majority rule:** Decisions are made by a vote of the **majority** to reflect the will of the largest percentage of citizens.
  - □ **Minority rights:** The American political system protects some rights of the **minority** against the majority.
  - □ Freedom of speech and of petition, for example, allows the minority to express its opinions despite **majority rule**.
  - □ **Representation** is also a basic principle of traditional democratic theory that describes the relationship between the few leaders and the many followers.

## Three Contemporary Theories of American Democracy

- Traditionally, two main competing theories describe contemporary American politics: pluralist theory and elite theory. A third, hyperpluralist theory, has been developed more recently.

## Pluralism

- The political system is composed of groups representing **competing interests**.
- The existence of such groups indicates that the government allows sufficient access to policymaking.
- The interests of the public may be more widely represented in government.
- Power is **decentralized** so that no one body or group has too much influence over policymaking.

## Elitism

- Government favors only a narrow percentage of the public, primarily the **wealthy**. Wealth is the main cause of political influence.

- Many political groups may exist, but the distribution of government resources among them is not necessarily equal. The more wealth and influence a group has, the more it benefits from the government.

- Groups do not have equal access to policymaking or equal power; **big business** plays a prominent role in politics because corporations that have money also have power.

- Businesses have tremendous advantages in their ability to organize, both through the concentration of their interests and through the interlocking relationships among the people who run business and the government, and therefore out-compete other groups.

## Hyperpluralism

- The proliferation of political groups has weakened the government.

- Policies are often made by "subgovernments" or "iron triangles" composed of interest groups, the bureaucracies that regulate these groups, and the congressional committees that oversee these bureaucracies.

- With so many interests vying for political influence and so many points of access in government, power is decentralized, and, ultimately, policies become muddled and therefore less effective.

## Challenges to Democracy

- Modern democracies face numerous challenges from a variety of sources:
  - **Increased complexity of issues:** An increase in the knowledge base makes it difficult for average citizens to make informed decisions.
  - **Limited participation in government:** Citizens do not take full advantage of participation opportunities, as demonstrated by poor voter turnout.

- **Escalating campaign costs:** An increase in the costs of running for office makes candidates increasingly dependent on PACs and further removed from democratic theory.
- **Diverse political interests:** Diversity of population can lead to weak coalitions, which may result in policy gridlock.

### American Political Culture and Democracy

- American democracy is held together by a unifying political culture, a common set of political values that are widely shared in the nation, which includes liberty, egalitarianism, individualism, belief in a free market, laissez faire economics, and populism.
- In recent years, some scholars have worried that a polarization has taken place within the nation—a so-called culture war—threatening a division that might jeopardize the nation's health. Other scholars disagree, saying there is little evidence of irreconcilable differences among groups, especially outside of political elites.

## 1.5 Learning Objective 1.5: Outline the central arguments of the debate in America over the proper scope of government. (p. 19)

### The Scope of Government in America

- Politicians constantly debate whether the scope of government responsibilities is too vast, just about right, or not comprehensive enough.

### How Active is American Government?

- In terms of dollars spent, government in America is vast. Altogether, the national, state, and local governments consume about a third of the **gross domestic product** (the total value of goods and services produced annually by the United States).

## For Additional Review

To understand more fully the important ideas of the government in America, review the relevant vocabulary terms in the chapter. To aid in your review, create flash cards or make sentences using the vocabulary terms. Review these vocabulary study aids in preparation for the test.

To understand more fully the important ideas of the government in America, develop and use effective strategies for taking notes on readings. Create a system of note-taking which allows you to write quickly and get down the basic concepts. Use the structure of the textbook as the structure of your notes. Review these notes in preparation for the test.

# Review Questions

## Multiple-Choice Questions

1.  Which of the following best illustrates elite theory?
    a.  The idea that large interest groups such as AARP (American Association of Retired Persons) dominate government decision-making.
    b.  The idea that a small group of wealthy individuals dominate government policy-making.
    c.  The idea that contending interests are so strong within the United States that government is often weakened.
    d.  The fact that more than 20,000 special interest groups lobby Congress each year.

2.  All of the following are characteristic beliefs associated with American political culture EXCEPT
    a.  liberty.
    b.  equality of opportunity.
    c.  individualism.
    d.  government regulation of the economy.

**Questions 3-4 refer to the following graph below.**

Age and Political Knowledge, 1972 and 2012

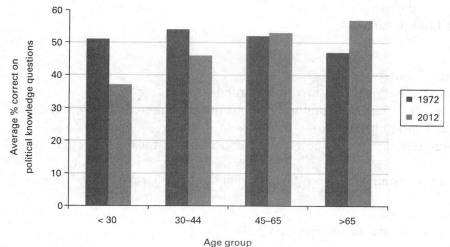

*Authors' analysis of 1972-2012 American National Election Studies data.*

3.  Which of the following is reflected in the graph?
    a.  In 1972, the relationship between age and political knowledge was basically flat.
    b.  In 2012, the relationship between age and political knowledge remained basically flat.
    c.  In 2012, young people were correct 57 percent of the time.
    d.  In 2012, people over 65 were correct 37 percent of the time.

4.  Which of the following is a possible consequence of the trend illustrated in the graph?
    a.  People over 65 will become less involved in the political process.
    b.  Young people will become much more informed and involved participants in the political process.
    c.  Young people will be less likely to be able to identify policies which could benefit them.
    d.  Young people will be more likely to be able to identify policies which could benefit them.

5.  All of the following are examples of public policy EXCEPT
    a.  The president issues an executive order requiring corporations doing business with the government to have affirmative action hiring plans.
    b.  Congress writes a law requiring lobbyists to disclose which interest groups employ them.
    c.  The Supreme Court upholds the death penalty for a murder conviction.
    d.  The American Association of Retired Persons passes a rule giving access to their insurance policies only to dues-paying members.

6.  Democratic theory includes which of the following?
    a.  "one person, one vote"
    b.  freedom of religion
    c.  majority rule
    d.  a bicameral Congress

7.  Basic functions common to all national governments include all of the following EXCEPT
    a.  collecting taxes.
    b.  maintaining a national defense.
    c.  providing universal health care.
    d.  preserving order.

8.  Members of single interest groups
    a.  work to limit the bias in national laws favoring married couples.
    b.  lobby the government to enact laws limiting the percentages that credit card companies can charge to finance monthly balances.
    c.  regulate the discount rate that the government charges to banks for the loans that they choose to make.
    d.  are reluctant, usually, to compromise on the issue that defines their narrowly defined goal.

9.  All of the following can create public policies EXCEPT
    a.  Congress.
    b.  the president.
    c.  an interest group.
    d.  the courts.

10. Which characteristic of American politics is concerned with the rights of the minority?
   a. the election process
   b. the congressional policymaking process
   c. interest group bargaining and compromising on political issues
   d. the Bill of Rights guarantee of civil liberties

11. All of the following are core political ideas in the United States EXCEPT
   a. liberty.
   b. individualism.
   c. socialism.
   d. self-government.

12. One effect of the American political system's use of checks and balances is
   a. the fact that the three branches operate independently of one another.
   b. that policy mistakes are completely avoided.
   c. the absolute guarantee that governmental power will not be abused.
   d.. severe fragmentation of the governing authority.

13. Which of the following is an output of the American political system?
   a. the judiciary appointment process
   b. a general election
   c. law passed by Congress and presidential decision in foreign policy
   d. a primary election

14. Politics
   a. is a process created by the Constitution.
   b. is a process based on the tyranny of the majority.
   c. is a process which exists only in the United States.
   d. is a process that determines the leaders selected and the policies they choose.

15. Which of the following statements provides the most accurate description of democracy as practiced in the United States?
   a. The will of the majority always prevails.
   b. The will of the people is checked by nothing.
   c. The people govern through elected officials.
   d. The people govern through mandates.

16. The characteristics and beliefs of a particular people about government and politics is known as
   a. scientific socialism.
   b. political culture.
   c. elitism.
   d. pluralism.

17. The United States operates under a system of
    a. totalitarianism.
    b. judicial activism.
    c. executive superiority.
    d. constitutional democracy.

18. All of the following statements about majoritarianism in the United States are true EXCEPT
    a. policy makers often ignore the opinion of the majority when making policy decisions.
    b. the majority of the public supports general statements about civil liberties but are less likely to support specific applications.
    c. public policy tends to change with the changes in majority opinion on major issues.
    d. the public is interested in and well-informed on all policy issues.

19. Government
    a. includes citizens, interest groups, the media, and other actors in society.
    b. is the procedures and institutions by which a people govern and rule themselves.
    c. was initially conceived by Thomas Hobbes as a means to ensure control of society by aristocrats.
    d. is defined as the study of "who gets what, when, and how."

20. All of the following are considered inputs into the American political system EXCEPT
    a. the activities of interests groups.
    b. the activities of political parties.
    c. laws passed by Congress.
    d. voting in elections.

## Free-Response Questions

1.  Page 16 of the text states "As Ronald Inglehart and Christian Welzel argue in their book on cultural change and democracy, 'Democracy is not simply the result of clever elite bargaining and constitutional engineering. It depends on deep-rooted orientations among the people themselves…Genuine democracy is not simply a machine that, once set up, functions by itself. It depends on the people.'" This common set of values is known as a political culture.

    a.  Identify three elements of American political culture.

    b.  Describe two of these elements.

    c.  Explain why citizens might espouse these values but object to specific applications.

2.  Page 8 of the text states, "In 2015, after rioting broke out in Baltimore, Maryland, after the tragic death of Freddie Gray, the National Guard had to be called in to restore peace in the city… Once order was restored, it was possible for peaceful protests to resume."

*Barbara Haddock Taylor/Baltimore Sun/AP Image*

    a.  In the context of this scenario, which function of government was being described?

    b.  Describe three additional functions government serves.

    c.  Provide two explanations why people might choose to use government to pursue these functions.

# Answers and Explanations

## Multiple-Choice Questions

1. B   The elite theory holds that a small group of wealthy and well-placed individuals dominate government decision making.
*Page reference: 17, AP Big Idea: CON*

2. D   Americans generally believe that a largely unregulated economy, similar to a laissez faire system, would be in the national interest.
*Page reference: 16-19, AP Big Idea: CON*

3. A   In 1972, the relationship between age and political knowledge was basically flat.
*Page reference: 3-14, AP Big Idea: MPA*

4. C   Young people will be less likely to be able to identify policies which could benefit them.
*Page reference: 3-14, AP Big Idea: MPA*

5. D   The AARP is an interest group and therefore cannot make policies that would be binding on all citizens, but rather are limited to making rules that apply only to members of their organization on issues over which they have control.
*Page reference: 9-12, AP Big Idea: PMI*

6. C   A democracy is founded on the needs and wants of the people and the closest representation of the whole populace is the majority; therefore, in a theoretical democracy, decisions are made by majority rule.
*Page reference: 12-15, AP Big Idea: CON*

7. C   While universal medical care might be desirable, and while all governments provide some social services, not all governments can afford universal coverage.
*Page reference: 7-8, AP Big Idea: PMI*

8. D   Single interest groups tend to be associated with hyperpluralism, and because they are formed around one narrowly defined issue, they rarely engage in the compromises characteristic of pluralistic bargaining.
*Page reference: 9, AP Big Idea: PMI*

9. C   Interest groups can affect public policies, but do not have the power or authority to create public policies.
*Page reference: 9-12, AP Big Idea: PMI*

10. D   The Bill of Rights was added to the Constitution to protect the expression of unpopular ideas, among other things, and these rights are not dependent on majoritarian concerns, but are designed to protect the rights of the minority.
*Page reference: 17, AP Big Idea: CON*

11. C   Socialism is an economic system where there is government ownership and management of the economy and that is not a core political idea of the United States.
*Page reference: 16-19, AP Big Idea: CON*

12. D   Even though checks and balances limit government's power by requiring each branch to obtain the consent of the others for its actions, it also results in severe fragmentation in the American political system.
*Page reference: 9-11, AP Big Idea: CON*

13. C   Laws passed by Congress and decisions made by the President are products of the United States government and therefore fit the definition of an output.
*Page reference: 9-11, AP Big Idea: PMI*

14. D   The process of politics is the method of determining the leaders we select and the policies they pursue.
*Page reference: 8-9, AP Big Idea: CON*

15. C   Democracy in the United States is a system of electing policymakers and of organizing government so that policy represents and responds to the public's preferences.
*Page reference: 12-19, AP Big Idea: CON*

16. B   Political culture is an overall set of values and beliefs widely shared within a society.
*Page reference: 16-19, AP Big Idea: CON*

17. D   The United States operates under a system of constitutional democracy.
*Page reference: 12-13, AP Big Idea: CON*

18. D   Majoritarianism is the traditional political philosophy which asserts that the majority has the right to make the decisions in the government.
*Page reference: 13, AP Big Idea: CON*

19. B   Government is a very broad term that encompasses the different institutions in which the politicians function.
*Page reference: 7, AP Big Idea: CON*

20. C   Laws passed by Congress constitute an output, not an input.
*Page reference: 8-12, AP Big Idea: CON*

# Free-Response Questions

*This rubric provides examples of many, but not all, of the possible correct responses to the free-response questions.*

1.  There is a common set of values generally espoused by United States citizens—a political culture.

    a.  Identify three elements of American political culture.

        ■ Identification of any three of the following would earn credit.
        - Liberty
        - Political equality
        - Popular rule/populism
        - Individualism
        - Laissez-faire economics

    b.  Describe two of these elements.

        ■ Liberty generally implies freedom, either from government or to engage in chosen activities or to abstain from certain activities.
        ■ Political equality implies an equal chance to participate in politics if one chooses to do so.
        ■ Popular rule/populism is an expression of popular sovereignty/majority rule/government "by the people."
        ■ Individualism is the general idea that persons should take responsibility for their own advancement and that rights inherent in persons, not groups.
        ■ Laissez-faire economics espouses limited government in market activities.

    c.  Explain why citizens might espouse these values but object to specific applications.

        ■ There is a well-known difference between diffuse and specific support for principles. Thus, individuals voice support for liberty but are quite willing to support regulation of behavior of which they disapprove. Likewise, they voice support for political participation—as long as the participation supports positions they support. The same caveat applies to popular rule. And, individuals often ignore the extent to which they benefit from collective actions. Similarly, advocates of "getting the government out of the marketplace" generally find it useful to have a stable monetary system, to have contracts enforced, to have law and order, to have their fellow citizens educated, to have their food free of adulteration, to have roads on which to drive, etc.—much of which is provided by government.

2. Page 8 of the text states, "In 2015, after rioting broke out in Baltimore, Maryland, after the tragic death of Freddie Gray, the National Guard had to be called in to restore peace in the city… Once order was restored, it was possible for peaceful protests to resume."

   a. In the context of this scenario, which function of government was being described?

      ■ Preserve Order

   b. Describe three functions government serves.

      ■ Identification of any three of the following would earn credit.
         □ Dispensing justice
         □ Ensuring "domestic tranquility"/order
         □ Providing for national defense
         □ Promoting general welfare
         □ Providing "public goods"
         □ Political socialization
         □ Collecting taxes

   c. Provide two explanations why people might choose to use government to pursue these functions.

      ■ Having government perform any of these functions divides labor and allows the development of expertise. For example, instead of each person having to provide for personal safety or to dispense justice for crimes committed against them, we can call police, have prosecutors act, and have governments incarcerate. Thus, people may choose government because it allows them to simplify their lives.

      ■ Second, engaging in collective action allows for the achievement of economies of scale. Thus, people might choose to have government build roads, for example, because it is cheaper for all concerned to do this collectively rather than individually.

# 2

# The Constitution

## Chapter Overview

A **constitution** is a nation's basic law. It creates political institutions, assigns the powers of government, and provides guarantees to citizens. Constitutions can be either written or unwritten. The Constitution supersedes statutory law, even when the law represents the wishes of the majority of citizens. The Constitution not only guarantees individual rights but also decentralizes power. Power is not concentrated efficiently in the hands of one person, such as the president. Instead, there are numerous checks on the exercise of power and many obstacles to change. Some complain that this system is inefficient and too often produces stalemate, while others praise the way in which it protects minority views. Both positions are correct. Our theme of the scope of government runs throughout this chapter, which focuses on what the national government can and cannot do. A nation that prides itself on being "democratic" must evaluate the Constitution according to democratic standards, the core of our other theme. To understand government and to answer questions about how we are governed and what government does, we must first understand the Constitution.

# Study Outline

 **2.1** Learning Objective 2.1: Describe the ideas behind the American Revolution and their role in shaping the Constitution. (p. 26)

## *The Origins of the Constitution*

### *The Road To Revolution*

- The French and Indian War led to the passage of numerous taxes and trade laws that were designed to benefit England.

- The colonists lacked direct representation in Parliament, which led to colonial protest.

### *Declaration of Independence (1776)*

- The document lists grievances against the king of England.
- The document justifies revolution.
- The document is based on the idea of **natural rights**.

### *The English Heritage, The Power of Ideas*

- John Locke built his powerful philosophy on a belief in **natural rights.**

    - **Natural Rights**: Rights inherent in human beings, not dependent on governments, which include life, liberty and property.

    - **Consent of the governed:** The idea that government derives its authority from the people (social contract).

    - **Limited government:** The idea that certain restrictions should be placed on government to protect the natural rights of citizens.

    - Government should protect people's property.

*The American Creed*

- There are remarkable parallels between Locke's thought and the language of the Declaration of Independence.
- No government had ever been based on these principles.

*Winning Independence*

- In 1783, The American colonies won their independence.

*The Conservative Revolution*

- American colonists did not feel the need for great social, economic, or political upheavals.
- The Revolution did not create great class conflicts.

**2.2** **Learning Objective 2.2: Analyze how the weaknesses of the Articles of Confederation led to its failure. (p. 30)**

## The Government That Failed: 1776–1787

*The Articles of Confederation*

- The Articles established the first government of the United States (enacted in 1781).
- The Articles were designed to preserve the independence of the states.
- The Articles created a national government without any centralized power; proves to be ineffectual.

*Key Provisions of the Articles of Confederation*

- **Unicameral** national legislature
- No executive or judicial institutions
- Most power rests with state legislatures
- No power to tax
- No regulation of foreign or interstate trade
- No national currency
- No national defense

## Weaknesses of the Articles

- Without the power to **collect taxes**, the national government had few financial resources with which to repay its war debts.
- The development of a national economy was inhibited also by the government's inability to establish and **regulate trade**.
- The Articles **prevented the formation of a unified nation** out of a collection of states with different political, economic, and social concerns.
- States retained full sovereignty.

## Changes in the States

- Most states adopted bills of rights to protect freedoms, abolish religious qualifications for holding office, and liberalize requirements for voting.
- The structure of the government in the states also became more responsive to the people.

## Economic Turmoil

- **Shays' Rebellion** was not easily quelled, because the government had no power to raise a militia. The incident provided the final proof that the Articles were not a sufficient plan of government.

## The Aborted Annapolis Meeting

- **Annapolis Convention** in 1786 attempted to suggest reforms of the Articles, but it was determined instead to ask Congress to schedule a convention for 1787.

**Learning Objective 2.3: Describe the delegates to the Constitutional Convention and the core ideas they shared. (p. 33)**

## Making a Constitution: The Philadelphia Convention

- Many issues were hotly debated during the writing of the **Constitution**. In effect, the framers faced the momentous task of defining the nature of government. They did, however, agree on some basic principles:
  - The government should check the self-interest of the people yet protect their individual liberties and advance natural rights such as equality.
  - Factions should not be allowed to create political conflict and thereby undermine the government.
  - No one faction should have the opportunity to prevail upon the others.

### Gentlemen in Philadelphia

- Although the 55 founders at the Constitutional Convention were almost all wealthy and well educated, they had divergent views about major issues.

### Philosophy into Action

- The 55 delegates did not share the same political philosophy, yet the Founders shared a common core of ideas. The group agreed on the critical questions of:
  - Human nature
  - Political conflict and the nature of **factions**
  - Purposes of government
  - Nature of government

**2.4**

## Learning Objective 2.4: Categorize the issues at the Constitutional Convention and outline the resolutions reached on each type of issue. (p. 35)

### Critical Issues at the Convention

#### The Equality Issues

- Two plans were proposed to ensure **equal representation** of the people in the legislature: the Virginia Plan (representation in the national Congress should be determined by the **population** of each state) and the New Jersey Plan (each state should be allowed the same number of representatives in the national Congress).

- The **Connecticut Compromise**, or Great Compromise, established a **bicameral legislature**. The **Senate** would include two representatives from each state as per the New Jersey Plan, and representation in the **House** would be determined by the population of each state.

- The **Three-Fifths Compromise** mandated that only three-fifths of slaves be counted in determining state representation (this was repealed by the **Fourteenth Amendment** in 1868).

#### The Economic Issues

- The authors identified interstate tariffs, worthless paper money, and economic recession as serious problems of the American economy.

- These concerns led the Philadelphia delegates to strengthen the economic powers of the new national government to address these problems.

#### The Individual Rights Issues

- The **writ of habeas corpus** cannot be suspended.
- **Bills of attainder**, which punish people without a trial, cannot be passed.
- **Ex post facto laws**, which are retroactive criminal laws, are prohibited.
- **Religious qualifications** cannot be used as a prerequisite for public office.
- All citizens are entitled to a **trial by jury** in a criminal case.

## Learning Objective 2.5: Analyze how the components of the Madisonian system addressed the dilemma of reconciling majority rule with the protection of minority interests. (p. 40)

### *The Madisonian System*

#### *Thwarting the Tyranny of the Majority*

- James Madison warned that both the majority (poorer and less-educated Americans) and minority (the wealthy elite) factions could pose a threat to the stability of a government.

- To protect government from the will of the majority, the president would be chosen by the **Electoral College** and, until the Seventeenth Amendment in 1913, senators would be chosen by states' legislatures, not directly by the people.

- Madison proposed that the national government be divided into three branches: the **executive**, **legislative**, and **judicial**. Each branch would have its own powers and responsibilities.

- A system of **checks and balances** would ensure that no branch could become more powerful than the others. The majority or the minority might be able to take control of any one branch but not necessarily the whole political system.

- Establishing a **federal** system of government allowed power to be shared between the national and state levels of government.

### *Checks and Balances*

#### *Legislative Branch*

- The House and the Senate can veto a bill of the other house.
- The Senate approves presidential nominations for judges and other officials.
- The legislative branch can impeach the president (House impeaches, Senate removes).
- The legislative branch controls the budget.
- The legislative branch can pass laws over a president's veto with a two-thirds majority.

### Executive Branch

- The president can veto bills passed by Congress.
- The president can nominate judges and other government officials.

### Judicial Branch

- The judicial branch can declare laws passed by Congress to be unconstitutional.
- The judicial branch can declare acts of the president to be unconstitutional.
- The Constitution did not grant courts the power to check the other branches.
- The Supreme Court did not assert its authority to declare laws **unconstitutional** until the case of **Marbury v. Madison** in 1803.

### The Constitutional Republic

- The Constitution established that the government would be one of elected representatives.

## Learning Objective 2.6: Compare and contrast the Federalists and Anti-Federalists in terms of their background and their positions regarding government. (p. 44)

### Ratifying the Constitution

- The approval of at least nine states was needed to ratify the Constitution, and it did not come easily.

### Anti-Federalists

- Anti-Federalists feared that the Constitution favored an elite minority.
- Anti-Federalists believed that the Constitution failed to protect too many individual freedoms.
- Anti-Federalists believed that a strong central government would limit the power of the states.
- Anti-Federalists published scathing articles and political cartoons denouncing the Constitution as a tool of the aristocracy.

## Federalists

- Federalists published a series of articles called the *Federalist Papers* to defend the Constitution.
- Federalists asserted that the Constitution would benefit the growing middle class of tradesmen as well as the wealthy plantation owners.
- Federalists promised to add a **bill of rights** to guarantee individual liberties.
- The Constitution was ratified in 1787, largely because the authors promised to add a bill of rights.
- The Constitution established the United States as a **federal republic** in which power would be divided among levels of government.
- The Constitution is considered a "**living document**" because it can be amended as the United States grows and changes.

## 2.7 Learning Objective 2.7: Explain how the Constitution can be formally amended and how it changes informally. (p. 46)

### Changing the Constitution

#### The Formal Amendment Process

- Amendments can be proposed by Congress with a 2/3 vote in each House or by National Convention called by 2/3 of states.
- Amendments can be ratified by 3/4 of state legislatures or by Conventions in 3/4 of the states.
- Some amendments have not been ratified by the states. The best known of these is the **Equal Rights Amendment (ERA).** It was passed by Congress in 1972 stating that "equality of rights under the law shall not be denied or abridged by the United States or by any state on account of sex."

#### The Informal Processes of Constitutional Change

- **The Constitution can be informally amended through judicial interpretation,** known as **judicial review** (established in *Marbury v. Madison*).

- The Constitution can be informally amended by changing political practice, technology, and increased demands on policymakers.
- Over the years, the Constitution has become **more democratic** than the authors intended.

### The Importance of Flexibility

- The Constitution was not meant to be static.
- The authors created a flexible system of government that could adapt to the needs of times without sacrificing personal freedom.

## Learning Objective 2.8: Assess whether the Constitution establishes a majoritarian democracy and how it limits the scope of government. (p. 52)

### The Constitution and Democracy

- The Constitution did not establish a majoritarian democracy because majorities do not always rule in America.
- There has, however, been a gradual democratization of the Constitution.

### The Constitution and the Scope of Government

- The Constitution limits the scope of government by protecting individual rights and by dispersing power among institutions.

## For Additional Review

Create a "storyboard" to trace the events leading up to the establishment of the Constitution through the ratification process. List all events/ideas from the Declaration of Independence through the ratification of the Bill of Rights. For each event, write a brief statement describing the importance of the event/idea. Use this storyboard when reviewing and studying for the unit test.

Make a chart comparing and contrasting the Articles of Confederation and the Constitution. How did they organize government differently? In what ways did the Constitution amend the failures of the Articles? Use this chart when reviewing and studying for the unit test.

# Review Questions

## Multiple-Choice Questions

1. Under America's first constitution, the Articles of Confederation,
   a. the national government dominated state governments.
   b. the executive branch had more power than Congress.
   c. Congress was a unicameral body.
   d. states were represented in Congress proportionally according to population.

2. Which of the following founders was the "principal architect" of the Constitution?
   a. Edmund Randolph
   b. George Washington
   c. Thomas Jefferson
   d. James Madison

3. The Three-Fifths Compromise at the Constitutional Convention
   a. allowed cloture to be invoked, ending a filibuster in the Senate, with the support of 60 senators.
   b. prescribed the proportion of states required to ratify a constitutional amendment.
   c. provided a formula by which slaves would be counted for apportioning the House of Representatives.
   d. established the percentage of votes necessary for electors to be chosen under the original provisions of the Electoral College system.

4. Any law passed by a legislature that punishes an individual without a trial, under the Constitution, violates the constitutional concept of
   a. a bill of attainder.
   b. an ex post facto law.
   c. double jeopardy.
   d. eminent domain.

5. The idea of limiting the role of government to protecting "life, liberty, and property" is generally attributed to
   a. Karl Marx.
   b. Thomas Jefferson.
   c. Thomas Hobbes.
   d. John Locke.

6. Granting supremacy to the national government was done in part to
   a. protect the rights of minorities.
   b. promote the economic interests of those at the Constitutional Convention.
   c. prevent the people from instituting the ideas of John Locke.
   d. protect debtors from abusive creditors.

**Questions 7-8 refer to the following chart.**

Separation of Powers and Checks and Balances in the Constitution

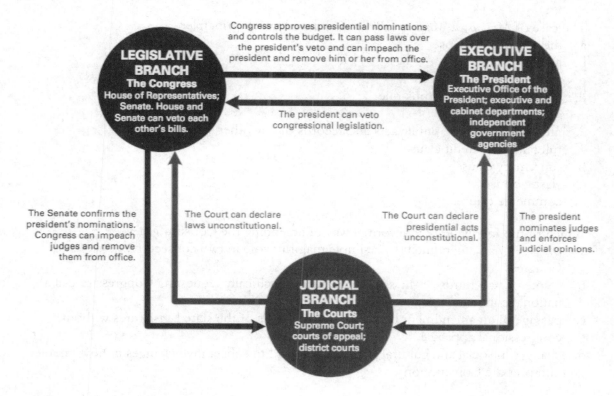

7. The Founding Fathers designed a system of checks and balances for the national government. Which of the following best illustrates that concept?
   a. Congress passes a law.
   b. The Supreme Court declares a law unconstitutional.
   c. The president issues an executive order reducing the size of the bureaucracy.
   d. The House and Senate cannot agree on a Conference Committee report.

8. An important effect of Checks and Balances is
   a. it allows the government to be easily dominated by one group.
   b. it makes it easier for a president to gain more power than the other two branches.
   c. it makes it difficult for either a minority or a majority to easily dominate the government.
   d. it makes it less difficult to pass legislation over which there is an agreement.

9. Which plan proposed at the Constitutional Convention called for a bicameral legislature with one chamber having members from states calculated proportionally based upon population and the other having two members per state?
   a. Connecticut Compromise
   b. Virginia Plan
   c. Annapolis Convention Plan
   d. Philadelphia Plan

10. The case of *Marbury v. Madison* (1803) established which principle?
    a. the supremacy clause
    b. judicial review
    c. natural rights of citizens
    d. the writ of habeas corpus rule

11. A state must honor the public acts and records of any other state under the
    a. full faith and credit clause.
    b. supremacy clause.
    c. elastic clause.
    d. commerce clause.

12. Which of the following is an informal way of amending the Constitution?
    a. passage of an amendment by a simple majority vote in two consecutive sessions of Congress
    b. a vote of two-thirds of the state legislatures specifically requesting Congress to call a national convention to propose amendments
    c. passage of an amendment by a vote of two-thirds of the state legislatures without congressional approval
    d. changes in social and cultural attitudes that lead to substantive changes in how people interpret the Constitution

13. The outcome of a conflict between the Constitution and the states is determined by
    a. the Great Compromise.
    b. the supremacy clause.
    c. *Federalist* No. 10.
    d. judicial review.

14. The Articles of Confederation failed for all of the following reasons EXCEPT
    a. The national government lacked the power to tax.
    b. The national government lacked the ability to regulate trade.
    c. There was no national judiciary.
    d. There was no provision to amend the Articles.

15. Which of the following was stipulated in Article III of the Constitution?
    a. creation of the Supreme Court
    b. executive powers
    c. powers of Congress
    d. full faith and credit clause

16. The significance of Shays' Rebellion was that
    a. it demonstrated that the Articles of Confederation was weak and unable to adequately respond to a crisis.
    b. it exposed the flaws in the Constitution.
    c. it demonstrated the superiority of the national standing army.
    d. it demonstrated the effectiveness of the national court system.

17. The original Constitution provided that U.S. senators were to be elected by
    a. the Supreme Court.
    b. direct vote of the people.
    c. the House of Representatives.
    d. state legislatures.

18. The issue of representation in Congress was dealt with by
    a. the Slave Trade Compromise.
    b. the Voter Registration Compromise.
    c. the Commerce Compromise.
    d. the Great or Connecticut Compromise.

19. Individuals who supported the new Constitution were known as
    a. Anti-Federalists.
    b. States' Righters.
    c. Federalists.
    d. Philosophes.

20. The series of essays that encouraged the ratification of the Constitution was known as
    a. *Common Sense.*
    b. *The Spirit of the Laws.*
    c. *The Social Contract.*
    d. *The Federalist Papers.*

# Free-Response Questions

1.  The Constitution has had 17 formal amendments since the adoption of the Bill of Rights, yet there are basic elements that have changed because of informal processes as well.

    a.  Describe the most common process of formally amending the Constitution.

    b.  Identify one formal amendment and describe how it has changed the meaning of the Constitution.

    c.  Identify one informal change in the Constitution, and describe how it has changed the meaning of the Constitution even without formal amendment.

2.  When James Madison proposed a new constitution, he tried to "unite a proper energy in the Executive and a proper stability in the Legislative departments, with the essential characters of Republican Government."

    *--James Madison, Letter to Jefferson, October 24, 1787*

    a.  Identify two features Madison proposed for keeping any branch of government from becoming too powerful.

    b.  Explain how each feature identified in (a) balances the need for strong government with a need for limited government.

    c.  Identify one feature Madison proposed for dividing powers between national and state governments.

    d.  Explain how this feature balanced the need for a strong central government while assuring the states of adequate power.

# Answers and Explanations

## Multiple-Choice Questions

1.  C   The Articles of Confederation had a unicameral legislature.
        *Page reference: 30-31, AP Big Idea: CON*

2.  D   James Madison provided the intellectual impetus for the Constitution, arriving at the convention with the Virginia Plan and as a result, in terms of his impact on the Constitution, Madison was known as "the Father of the Constitution."
        *Page reference: 40-43, AP Big Idea: CON*

3.  C   Although all of the options could provide for a 3/5 ratio, only the treatment of the slaves was specified in the Constitution.
        *Page reference: 36, AP Big Idea: CON*

4.  A   One of the civil liberties issues addressed in the original Constitution attempted to limit the practice of passing laws that singled out individuals. Therefore, the idea in the United States was that such bills of attainder were unfair, and that laws should apply to all citizens equally.
        *Page reference: 39, AP Big Idea: CON*

5.  D   Locke believed in a representative democracy with limited powers, concepts that underscore the Constitution.
        *Page reference: 28, AP Big Idea: CON*

6.  B   Those at the Constitutional Convention were primarily merchant and manufacturing elites, and the Constitution gives the national government powers to further the development of a national economy of merchants and manufacturing at the expense of the states and agrarians.
        *Page reference: 34, AP Big Idea: CON*

7.  B   The Supreme Court declaring a law unconstitutional is an example of checks and balances.
        *Page reference: 42, AP Big Idea: CON*

8.  C   Checks and Balances make it difficult for either a minority or a majority to easily dominate the government.
        *Page reference: 42, AP Big Idea: CON*

9.  A   The "great compromise" that led to a Senate based upon equal state representation and a House allocated proportionally based upon population was the Connecticut Compromise.
        *Page reference: 36, AP Big Idea: CON*

10. B  The case of *Marbury v. Madison* was the landmark decision of the Supreme Court declaring that it was an inherent duty of the judicial branch to "determine what the law is," thus establishing judicial review.
*Page reference: 50, AP Big Idea: CON*

11. A  The full faith and credit clause, found in Article IV of the Constitution, guarantees that the legal records, laws, and judicial proceedings of one state will be honored by another state.
*Page reference: 39, AP Big Idea: CON*

12. D  An informal method of amending the Constitution would be a practice or development that led to a change in how the Constitution was applied, even with no direct changes to the document through the formal amendment process.
*Page reference: 49-52, AP Big Idea: CON*

13. B  The supremacy clause requires all states to adopt laws that conform to the limits of the U.S. Constitution.
*Page reference: 43-44, AP Big Idea: CON*

14. D  The Articles of Confederation could be amended with unanimous consent of all of the states.
*Page reference: 30-33, AP Big Idea: CON*

15. A  Article III of the Constitution established the judicial branch of the new federal government.
*Page reference: 40-42, AP Big Idea: CON*

16. A  The government under the Articles did not have the power to raise a military and therefore could not deal with the crisis.
*Page reference: 33, AP Big Idea: CON*

17. D  The original Constitution limited the participation of the people by having state legislatures elect senators.
*Page reference: 35-41, AP Big Idea: CON*

18. D  The Great Compromise, also known as the Connecticut Compromise, settled the dispute over representation between the Virginia and New Jersey plans.
*Page reference: 35-36, AP Big Idea: CON*

19. C  The supporters of the Constitution who worked for ratification were known as Federalists.
*Page reference: 44-45, AP Big Idea: CON*

20. D  The collection of essays written in support of the Constitution is known as *The Federalist Papers*.
*Page reference: 44, AP Big Idea: CON*

# Free-Response Questions

*This rubric provides examples of many, but not all of the possible correct responses to the free-response questions.*

1.  The Constitution has had 17 formal amendments since the adoption of the Bill of Rights, yet there are basic elements that have changed because of informal processes as well.

    a.  Describe the most common process of formally amending the Constitution.

        - The Constitution is the cornerstone of American democracy. It was written by the Founding Fathers to guarantee that American democracy would survive for all times. The Constitution can be amended either formally or informally.

        - The process for formal amendments begins with the proposal of an amendment. This comes either by a two-thirds vote of each house of Congress or by the vote of two-thirds of the states in a national convention. The proposed amendment must be ratified by three-fourths of the states in either votes of the state legislatures or a ratifying convention in each state.

    b.  Identify one formal amendment and describe how it has changed the meaning of the Constitution.

        - The Fourteenth Amendment to the Constitution followed the Civil War. Before that, the Bill of Rights only applied to acts of the federal government. But the Fourteenth Amendment specifies that no state shall deprive anyone of life, liberty, or property without due process. This gave the federal government power over many areas that had been left to the states in 1787, such as state court procedures.

    c.  Identify one informal change in the Constitution, and describe how it has changed the meaning of the Constitution even without formal amendment.

        - The constitution can be amended informally in a number of ways. That means that the Constitution might have changed meaning without having a formal amendment added. Often, this involves custom and usage. For example, a president can issue an executive order or negotiate an executive agreement with other nations. These are not part of the Constitution, but presidents have learned to use them anyway, and as a result have gained powers that the founders originally gave to Congress. As a result, they are, in a way, the same as formal amendments to the Constitution.

2.  When James Madison proposed a new constitution, he tried to "unite a proper energy in the Executive and a proper stability in the Legislative departments, with the essential characters of Republican Government."

    *--James Madison, Letter to Jefferson, October 24, 1787*

    a.  Identify two features Madison proposed for keeping any branch of government from becoming too powerful.

    b.  Explain how each feature identified in (a) balances the need for strong government with a need for limited government. Both a. and b are answered below

    - In order for any branch to be kept from being too powerful, Madison designed a government that included the twin concepts of separation of powers and checks and balances. In a system such as that, power is divided among three branches of government—the legislative, the executive, and the judicial. Each branch has a specific grant of power and each one is given checks over the other. For example, Congress must approve presidential treaties and can override a president's veto. Congress can even impeach and remove a president from power. The president can veto a bill of Congress. And the Supreme Court can declare acts of the president or laws of Congress unconstitutional. In other words, this is a Madisonian design that is intended to limit the powers of each of the branches of government, preventing any one branch from becoming too powerful by allowing other branches to stop them.

    c.  Identify one feature Madison proposed for dividing powers between national and state governments.

    d.  Explain how this feature balanced the need for a strong central government while assuring the states of adequate power. Both c and d are answered below.

    - In order to keep the federal government from gaining too much power, the Constitution created a system of federalism, that is, a system that divided power between the national government and the state governments. The powers of the national government are listed in Article I of the Constitution, and the Tenth Amendment makes it clear that powers not listed in Article I are reserved for the states. As a result, the concept of federalism was designed to keep the national government from becoming too strong.

- In recent years, many observers have argued that the national government has become too strong. As a result, the federal design has been seen as under siege. But President Reagan designed a "new federalism," consisting of changing categorical grants to block grants that devolved power from the national government to the states. Also, Congress passed a law that outlawed "unfunded mandates." So, the powers of the national government and the states have come more into balance.

# 3

# Federalism

## Chapter Overview

"Federalism" refers to the division of power between the national government and the states. Under our federal system, significant government powers are divided between the central government and small governmental units; neither completely controls the other, and each has some room for independent action. In exploring American federalism, we will be especially attentive to our themes of democracy and the scope of government. Does federalism, the vertical division of power, enhance democracy in the United States? Does the additional layer of policymakers at the state level make government more responsive to public opinion or merely more complicated? Does it enhance the prospects that a majority of Americans will have their way in public policy? And what are the implications of federalism for the scope of the national government's activities? Why has the national government grown so much relative to state governments, and has this growth been at the expense of the states?

# Study Outline

 **Learning Objective 3.1: Define federalism and contrast it with alternative ways of organizing a nation. (p. 59)**

## *Defining Federalism*

- **Federal government:** Government is **divided into more than one level**. Different bodies share power over the same group of people.
- **Unitary government:** Only one **central government** has authority over a nation. There are no levels of government that share power.
- **Confederation:** An association of states with some authority delegated to a national government. The states in such a system retain most of the power.
- Intergovernmental relations **become especially important in a federal system because of the elaborate communication necessary to share power.**

 **Learning Objective 3.2: Characterize the type of nation typically associated with federalism. (p. 60)**

## *Why Federalism*

- Only 11 of the 190 nations of the world have federal systems

- Countries large in size tend to have federal systems, which decentralize the administration of government services.

- All countries with federal systems are democracies, although most democracies are not federal systems. Authoritarian regimes do not wish to disperse power away from the central government.

**Learning Objective 3.3: Outline the constitutional basis for the division of power between national and state governments, the establishment of national supremacy, and states' obligations to each other. (p. 61)**

## *The Constitutional Basis of Federalism*

### *The Division of Power*

- Framers favored a stronger national government but still made states vital components in the machinery of government.

- States are responsible for state and national elections and they have the power to ratify constitutional amendments.

- The states and national government have overlapping responsibilities for important matters, such as establishing courts, maintaining law and order, protecting citizens' health and safety, and regulating financial institutions.

### *National Supremacy*

- The Supremacy Clause is located in Article VI.
- The Supremacy Clause asserts the authority of the national government over the states.
- In cases of discrepancy, federal laws usually supersede state laws.

### *Tenth Amendment*

- The tenth amendment is located in the Bill of Rights.
- The tenth amendment grants all powers not specifically reserved for the national government to the states.
- The tenth amendment is often cited in arguments in favor of states' rights.

### *Eleventh Amendment*

- The eleventh amendment gives states immunity from certain prosecution.

### *Enumerated Powers*

- Enumerated powers are located in Article I, Section 8 of the Constitution.

- Enumerated powers are granted to the national government, and specifically to Congress.

## Implied Powers

- Implied powers were established in *McCulloch v. Maryland*, an 1819 Supreme Court case in which the states battled the formation of a national bank.
- The Supreme Court, under Chief Justice John Marshall, ruled against the states, thereby reinforcing the supremacy of the national government.
- The constitutional basis for implied powers is Article I, Section 8. This is known as the elastic clause, also called the necessary and proper clause.
- Implied powers give Congress the authority to pass any laws necessary to carry out its duties as enumerated in the Constitution.
- The elastic clause, as interpreted in *McCulloch v. Maryland*, allows Congress to act on implied powers that are not specifically defined in the Constitution.
- The case of *Gibbons v. Ogden* in 1824 expanded congressional power to regulate commerce.

# States' Obligations to Each Other

## Full Faith and Credit Clause

- The full faith and credit clause is located in Article IV, Section 1.
- Full faith and credit requires each state to formally recognize the documents and judgments handed down by courts in other states.
- Full faith and credit helps coalesce the state laws under a national umbrella.

## Extradition

- Extradition is located in Article IV, Section 2.
- Requires the return (**extradition**) of fugitive criminals arrested in one state to the state in which the crime was committed for prosecution.

## Privileges and Immunities Clause

- The privileges and immunities clause is located in Article IV, Section 2.

- The privileges and immunities clause helps unify the states by assuring that all citizens are treated equally when they travel from state to state.

 **Learning Objective 3.4: Characterize the shift from dual to cooperative federalism and the role of fiscal federalism in intergovernmental relations today. (p. 68)**

## Intergovernmental Relations

### From Dual to Cooperative Federalism

- **Dual federalism:** Each level of government has distinct responsibilities that do not overlap.
- **Cooperative federalism:** Levels of government share responsibilities.
- Shared costs: To receive federal aid, states must pay for part of a program.
- Federal guidelines: To receive funding, state programs must follow federal rules and regulations.
- Shared administration: Though programs must adhere to basic federal guidelines, they are administered according to the state's directives.

### Devolution?

- Devolution: Transferring responsibility for policies from the federal government to state and local governments.
- In recent years, some political leaders have called not only for a smaller national government in general but also for devolving the principal responsibility for policies such as health care and income security to the states.

### Fiscal Federalism

- **Fiscal federalism:** The system of distributing federal money to state governments.
- About a quarter of states' fiscal spending is derived from federal aid.
- Money is distributed through relatively restrictive **categorical grants** and **block grants**, which allow states more spending discretion.
- **Project grants** are categorical grants given for specific purposes and awarded on the basis of the merits of application.

- **Formula grants** are categorical grants distributed according to a formula specified in legislation or in administrative regulations.
- **Mandates**, however, can create economic hardships for states when Congress creates financial obligations for the states without providing funding for those obligations.

 **Learning Objective 3.5: Explain the consequences of federalism for diversity in public policies among the states. (p. 76)**

- States have certain powers which allow them to adopt policies different from other states.
- Federalism facilitates state innovations in policy, and it allows states to move beyond the limits of national policy.
- However, federalism also leaves states dependent upon the resources within their borders to finance public services, and it may discourage states from providing some services.

 **Learning Objective 3.6: Assess the impact of federalism on democratic government and the scope of government. (p. 78)**

## Understanding Federalism

### Federalism and Democracy

- Federalism contributes to democracy by increasing access to the government at all levels, but it also creates disadvantages due to differences in the resources of individual states.
- These differences can lead to inequities among the states in areas such as education.

### Federalism and the Scope of the National Government

- The United States has grown in response to the demands of Americans for public services it can best provide, but it has not in any way supplanted the states.

# For Additional Review

To understand more fully the idea of federalism, create a "Taking Stock" table for federalism. The table should have three columns:

1. What do I know about federalism? (fill in this column at the beginning of the unit)
2. What do I not know about federalism? (fill in this column at the beginning of the unit)
3. What have I learned about federalism? (fill this in upon completion of each section of the chapter)

Use this table to guide your reading and note-taking as well as a study tool for the topic of federalism.

To understand more fully the idea of federalism, create a chart or Venn diagram identifying the major powers of the federal, state, and current powers. Use this diagram to serve as a useful study tool for the topic of federalism.

# Review Questions

## Multiple-Choice Questions

1. Which of the following forms of fiscal federalism allow the states the broadest financial discretion?
   a. categorical grants
   b. block grants
   c. mandates
   d. foreign assistance

2. The Constitution grants Congress the power to establish post offices and post roads. This is an example of
   a. enumerated powers.
   b. implied powers.
   c. reserved powers.
   d. concurrent powers.

3. In a confederation,
   a. power is divided between a central government and regional governments.
   b. the sovereignty within a nation is held entirely by the central government.
   c. sovereignty is shared at the national, state, and local levels.
   d. power is held at the regional level, with the central government exercising only such influence as the regional governments give it.

4. The fiscal relationship between the national and state governments involves complex relationships. Which would *least* likely be favored by state governments?
   a. unfunded mandates
   b. categorical grants
   c. block grants
   d. revenue sharing

5. "Enumerated" powers are those given to
   a. the Supreme Court.
   b. the federal bureaucracy.
   c. state governments.
   d. the national government.

6. The system of federalism that allowed states to do most of the fundamental governing from 1789 to 1937 was
   a. home rule.
   b. regulated or "marble cake" federalism.
   c. dual federalism.
   d. shared powers.

7. The case of *McCulloch v. Maryland* (1809) ruled that
   a. The federal government could exercise only the enumerated powers of the Constitution.
   b. The implied powers in Article I of the Constitution allowed Congress to create a nationally chartered bank.
   c. The state governments could levy taxes on national government institutions.
   d. The state courts had sole jurisdiction over regulatory affairs within their boundaries.

8. "Dual federalism" refers to the fact that
   a. the Constitution provides two layers of government in the nation—the national and the state.
   b. there are two major forms of aid from the national government to the states—categorical and block grants.
   c. both the national and state governments can levy taxes on citizens.
   d. there are two distinct eras in American history—the era before cooperative federalism and the era since the development of cooperative federalism.

9. The power of the national government to regulate interstate commerce was expanded in the landmark case of
   a. *Marbury v. Madison.*
   b. *Plessy v. Ferguson.*
   c. *McCulloch v. Maryland.*
   d. *Gibbons v. Ogden.*

10. The notion that when state and federal laws conflict, the national laws will prevail, is the
    a. necessary and proper clause.
    b. supremacy clause.
    c. extradition clause.
    d. full faith and credit clause.

**Questions 11-12 refer to the following graph.**

Fiscal Federalism: Federal Grants to State and Local Governments

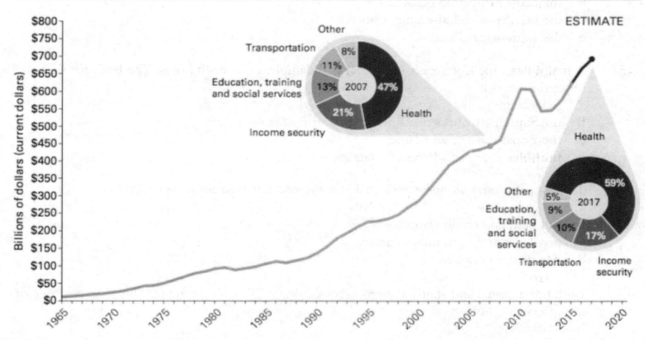

*Office of Management and Budget, Budget of the United States Government, Fiscal Year 2017: Historical Tables (Washington, DC: U.S. Government Printing Office, 2016), Tables 12.1 and 12.2.*

11.    Which of the following statements reflects the data in the chart?
    a.    The number of federal mandates has grown since 1965.
    b.    The number of grants has declined in recent years.
    c.    The number of grants has increased in recent years.
    d.    The number grants had its greatest increase in 1990.

12.    Fiscal Federalism
    a.    allows the national government to aid, but not influence state governments.
    b.    allows the state governments to aid and influence the national government.
    c.    allows the national government to influence, but not aid state governments.
    d.    allows the national government to both aid and influence state governments.

13.    Federalism as a form of government helps accommodate
    a.    differences across states.
    b.    governments in small geographic areas.
    c.    citizens who want a strong government.
    d.    citizens who want uniform policies across their political system.

14. National policies override state policies when there is a conflict and the Constitution gives the national government power in that policy area. This is a statement of
    a. the due process clause.
    b. the equal protection clause.
    c. the privileges and immunity clause.
    d. the supremacy clause.

15. A major basis for Congressional power is the implied powers it holds. The basis for these implied powers is
    a. federalism.
    b. the Supreme Court's decision in *Marbury v. Madison*.
    c. the Equal Protection Clause.
    d. the "Necessary and Proper" Clause.

16. The constitutional provision that makes same-sex marriage controversial is
    a. judicial review.
    b. full faith and credit clause.
    c. privileges and immunities clause.
    d. due process clause.

17. Both the national and states' governments can establish court systems. This is an example of
    a. reserved powers.
    b. a mandate.
    c. concurrent powers.
    d. full faith and credit clause.

18. The Constitution provides for the power of extradition. Extradition is an example of
    a. states' taxing powers.
    b. grants-in-aid.
    c. formula grants.
    d. interstate relations.

19. A power delegated to the national government is the power to
    a. regulate foreign and interstate commerce.
    b. police citizens.
    c. establish educational systems.
    d. establish the drinking age.

20. An example of a concurrent power is
    a. declare war.
    b. establish educational systems.
    c. establish the drinking age.
    d. tax.

# Free-Response Questions

1.  The Constitution designed a system in which various types of powers were assigned to different levels of government. Those types of powers are variously described as:

    - enumerated powers
    - reserved powers
    - concurrent powers
    - implied powers

    Select three of the types of powers listed above.

    a.  Define each of the chosen types of powers.

    b.  Explain how each of the chosen types of powers affects the distribution of powers between national and state governments.

2.  Cooperative federalism is a term often used to describe the complex fiscal relationship between the national and state governments. Develop an essay which outlines the shift from dual to cooperative federalism and compare the advantages and disadvantages of this system. In your essay you must:

    a.  Define categorical grants and block grants, and describe the differences between them.

    b.  Identify an advantage and a disadvantage of categorical grants.

    c.  Identify an advantage and a disadvantage of block grants.

# Answers and Explanations

## Multiple-Choice Questions

1. B  Block grants are given to the states with only general spending guidelines.
   *Page reference: 73, AP Big Idea: PMI*

2. A  Enumerated powers are listed in Article I, Sec. 8 and one example is the establishment of post offices and roads.
   *Page reference: 17, AP Big Idea: CON*

3. D  It is the only correct definition of a confederation provided.
   *Page reference: 60, AP Big Idea: CON*

4. A  Mandates allow the states no discretion in spending money. From the state's position, the least liked of mandates are "unfunded mandates" that require states to spend money without any financial assistance from the national government.
   *Page reference: 74-75, AP Big Idea: PMI*

5. D  It is the definition of enumerated powers which are the powers given to the national government.
   *Page reference: 65, AP Big Idea: CON*

6. C  Before the creation of cooperative federalism with the passing of "New Deal" programs in the mid–1930s, federalism generally conformed to the dual federalism model allowing the states to do most of the fundamental governing.
   *Page reference: 68-69, AP Big Idea: PMI*

7. D  the *McCulloch* case is a landmark decision that had two major findings, that state and national governments could not destroy one another by taxing, and that the implied powers allowed the establishment of a national bank even though that was not explicitly mentioned in Article I, Section 8.
   *Page reference: 64-65, AP Big Idea: CON*

8. A  Dual federalism is used to describe the original view of the relationship between the levels of government as clearly separated, or layered.
   *Page reference: 68, AP Big Idea: PMI*

9. D  *Gibbons v. Ogden* had to do with expanding the national government's power to regulate interstate commerce.
   *Page reference: 66, AP Big Idea: CON*

10. B    The supremacy clause assures that states comply with guiding provisions of the national government. Where the Constitution is silent, states have a great deal of discretion in their decision making. But where there is a constitutional requirement, states cannot have laws that are at variance with the national requirement.
*Page reference: 62-63, AP Big Idea: CON*

11. C    The number of grants has increased in recent years.
*Page reference: 722, AP Big Idea: CON*

12. D    Fiscal Federalism allows the national government to both aid and influence state governments.
*Page Reference: 722, AP Big Idea: CON*

13. A    Federalism, by providing for state governments, makes allowances for differences that occur across states.
*Page reference: 61-67, AP Big Idea: CON*

14. D    The supremacy clause is the correct term for the description provided in the question.
*Page reference: 62-63, AP Big Idea: CON*

15. D    The "Necessary and Proper" clause found in Article I, Section 8 of the Constitution provides the basis for the implied powers of Congress.
*Page reference: 64-65, AP Big Idea: CON*

16. B    Full faith and credit is the provision of the Constitution that requires each state to recognize the public acts, records, and judicial proceedings of all other states, including marriages.
*Page reference: 67, AP Big Idea: CON*

17. C    Concurrent powers are those powers which can be exercised by both the national government and the states, such as the power to establish court systems.
*Page reference: 78-82, AP Big Idea: CON*

18. D    Extradition is an example of a Constitutional power that deals with relations between the states.
*Page reference: 67-68, AP Big Idea: CON*

19. A    Delegated powers are those given to the national government by the Constitution, and regulating foreign and interstate commerce is an example of a delegated power.
*Page reference: 65-66, AP Big Idea: CON*

20. D    Concurrent powers are those that belong to both the national and state governments, and the power to tax is an example of a concurrent power.
*Page reference: 61-62, AP Big Idea: CON*

# Free-Response Questions

*This rubric provides examples of many, but not all of the possible correct responses to the free-response questions.*

1. The Constitution designed a system in which various types of powers were assigned to different levels of government. Those types of powers are variously described as:

   - enumerated powers
   - reserved powers
   - concurrent powers, and
   - implied powers

   Select three of the types of powers listed above.

   a. Define each of the chosen types of powers.

   b. Explain how each of the chosen types of powers affects the distribution of powers between national and state governments.

   - The Constitution provides for several types of powers that are given to the federal government or kept away from it, including enumerated powers, reserved powers, concurrent powers, and implied powers. In this essay, I will discuss enumerated powers, concurrent powers, and implied powers. These are all powers that governments have.

   - The enumerated powers are specific powers listed in the Constitution as given to the federal government. The reserved powers are powers reserved to the state governments. Implied powers are powers that are implied but not expressly discussed in the Constitution. The implied powers were given to the national government by the Supreme Court case of *McCulloch v. Maryland*. In this case, the state of Maryland tried to tell the Supreme Court that the national government couldn't do anything unless the Constitution specifically said that they could do it. But the Supreme Court took a loose interpretation of the Constitution and said that if the powers were "necessary and proper," the national government could use them. This allowed the national government to establish a national bank.

- The reason that these powers are important in politics these days is that Republicans think that state governments should have more powers while Democrats think that the national government should have more power. A narrow vision of implied powers will limit the federal government to only its enumerated powers and give states much more authority than just the reserved powers.

2. Cooperative federalism is a term often used to describe the complex fiscal relationship between the national and state governments. In your essay, do the following:

   a. Define categorical grants and block grants, and describe the differences between them.

   b. Identify an advantage and a disadvantage of categorical grants.

   c. Identify an advantage and a disadvantage of block grants.

      - In American politics, the priorities of government are set by the ways government spend money. A further issue concerns which level of government has the power to set those priorities by making decisions about how to spend money. These issues, where money is spent and which level of government makes decisions about where money is spent, form the basis for understanding the issues surrounding categorical and block grants.

      - Categorical grants are grants from the national government to the state government for specific purposes and they have strings attached. In contrast, block grants are moneys given by the national government to the states for more general purposes. Usually, categorical grants give money to states to spend with almost no discretion— if the states agree to receive categorical grants they agree to spend the money in specific ways. With block grants, states will often have choices to make on how to spend money.

      - One advantage of a categorical grant is that it allows the national government to have greater fiscal responsibility for the money that it collects. Members of Congress may feel that since they are ultimately responsible for the money collected from their constituents, they should exercise specific control over how that money is spent. For example, the Interstate Highway Act is a categorical grant. As a result, if states accept money under that act, Congress knows that it will be spent for building and maintaining the interstate highways. However, a disadvantage of categorical grants is that the states can be blackmailed by the national government. The Interstate Highway Act illustrates that as well. In order to receive that money, states must comply with all of the provisions of the grant. So, as a result, when the national government stipulated that in order to receive this grant, states would have to raise their drinking age to 21, all 50 states complied. So, although the national government does not have authority to raise the drinking age, it can make the states do that with categorical grant money.

■ One advantage of block grants is that it allows the states, which are closer to the people, the ability to channel the use of that money to the specific needs of the state. Northern states might have needs that are different from Southern states, and urban states might have needs that are different than rural states. For example, if the national government wants to improve science and math education, needs might be different in a state like Texas, where many students speak Spanish, than in a state like Minnesota, where language barriers are not as big an issue. The disadvantage of block grants is that the national government does not have as much control over the money, and states might "waste" the free money that the federal government gave them. That would mean that the national government was not a good steward of its money.

■ In all, the politics of intergovernmental relations is fascinating and reflects partisan differences as well as policy preferences. Categorical and block grants illustrate those differences very well.

# 4

# Civil Liberties and Public Policy

## Chapter Overview

This chapter explores the nature of **civil liberties**—those individual legal and constitutional protections against the government—afforded in the United States. Americans' civil liberties are set down in the **Bill of Rights.** Deciding complex questions about civil liberties requires balancing competing values, such as maintaining an open system of expression while protecting individuals from the excesses that such a system may produce. Civil liberties are essential to democracy. How could we have free elections without free speech, for example? And who should decide the extent of our liberty? Should it be a representative institution such as Congress or a judicial elite such as the Supreme Court? The role of government in resolving civil liberties controversies is the subject of much debate. Disputes about civil liberties often end up in court. The Supreme Court of the United States is the final interpreter of the content and scope of our liberties. By the end of the chapter, students should understand the scope and nature of their rights under the U.S. Constitution and how these rights have evolved over time.

# Study Outline

 **Learning Objective 4.1: Trace the process by which the Bill of Rights has been applied to the states. (p. 87)**

## *The Bill of Rights – Then and Now*

- The **Bill of Rights,** the first 10 amendments to the U.S. Constitution, protects freedoms at a national level, but these freedoms were not necessarily guaranteed in some state constitutions.
- Because few rights are absolute, we cannot avoid the difficult questions of how to balance civil liberties with other individual and societal values.

## *The Bill of Rights and the States*

- The **First Amendment** established the four great liberties: freedom of the press, of speech, of religion, and of assembly.
- In the case of *Barron v. Baltimore* (1833), the Supreme Court ruled that the Bill of Rights did not protect individuals against state governments.
- In *Gitlow v. New York* (1925), the Court reversed its earlier decision, citing the due process clause of the **Fourteenth Amendment** as reason to protect individuals' free speech and free press rights, found in the **First Amendment**, against state government incursions.
- *Gitlow* began a tradition called the selective **incorporation doctrine**, by which the Supreme Court has gradually, on a case-by-case basis, ensured the protection of most freedoms listed in the Bill of Rights from state infringement by means of the due process clause of the Fourteenth Amendment.

## Learning Objective 4.2: Distinguish the two types of religious rights protected by the First Amendment and determine the boundaries of those rights. (p. 89)

### *Freedom of Religion*

- **Establishment Clause:** A part of the First Amendment that prohibits Congress from making laws establishing any religion in conjunction with the government.

  - Some critics interpret the clause loosely: The government should not favor one religion over another in its policies. Others, including Thomas Jefferson, argue that the establishment clause endorses the **separation of church and state**.

  - The establishment clause is at the center of the debate over prayer in school and over federal funding to private religious schools.

  - *Lemon v. Kurtzman* (1971): The Supreme Court allowed federal funding of parochial schools, provided that the money neither advances nor inhibits religious teaching, but instead is used for administrative purposes. In 2002, the Supreme Court also permitted state vouchers to be used for parochial schools in *Zelman v. Simmons-Harris*.

  - *Engel v. Vitale* (1962) and *School District of Abington Township, Pennsylvania v. Schempp* (1963): Forbade the practice of prayer in school as a violation of the establishment clause and a breaching of the separation of church and state.

  - Federal funds may be used to construct school buildings and to provide administrative and academic supplies, but not to endorse religious teaching.

  - Student religious groups cannot be denied access to school buildings for the purpose of meeting or worship if other groups are also allowed access.

  - Lower courts have begun to also rule that requiring teachers to present intelligent design as an alternative to evolution is a constitutionally unacceptable promotion of religion in the classroom.

  - Government may support religious activities that have a secular purpose if doing so does not foster its excessive entanglement with religion.

- **Free Exercise Clause:** A First Amendment right that guarantees the freedom to practice or not practice any religion.
    - The Court has upheld that the government cannot infringe on people's beliefs, but it can regulate religious behavior to some degree.
    - State laws can ban religious practices that conflict with other laws, but they cannot forbid religious worship itself.

 **Learning Objective 4.3: Differentiate the rights of free expression protected by the First Amendment and determine the boundaries of those rights. (p. 95)**

## Freedom of Expression

### Speech

- Courts grapple with the definition of "speech." Political protests and picketing are protected by the First Amendment, but **libel**, **slander**, and **obscenity** are not.
- Fraud and incitement to violence are considered action, not speech, and are not protected.
- The Constitution forbids **prior restraint**, or government censorship of the press. This policy was strengthened by the case of *Near v. Minnesota* (1931), in which the Court ruled in favor of the press.
- Prior restraint is granted in situations where **national security** might be compromised.
- As decided in *Schenck v. United States* (1919), freedom of speech may be curtailed when it threatens **public order**.
- Acts of symbolic speech, such as protesting and flag burning (*Texas v. Johnson*, 1989), are protected under the First Amendment.
- **Commercial speech**, such as advertising, is closely regulated by the **Federal Trade Commission**.
- Commercial speech on radio and television is regulated by the **Federal Communications Commission**.
- The broadcast media have significantly less freedom than do print media (*Red Lion Broadcasting Company v. Federal Communications Commission*, 1969), though they are not

required to print replies from candidates they have criticized (*Miami Herald Publishing Company v. Tornillo*, 1974).

- In *Buckley v. Valeo* the Court ruled that spending money to influence elections is a form of constitutionally protected speech.

## The Press

- Freedom of the press can conflict with the **right to a fair trial**, but the press does have a right to report on any criminal proceeding, and all trials must be open to the public.
- However, in *Branzburg v. Hayes* (1972), the Supreme Court ruled in favor of fair trial over a reporter's right to protect sources, and in *Zucher v. Stanford* (1978) the Court sided with the police over the press.
- ***Roth v. United States*** (1957): The Court asserted that obscenity is not protected under the First Amendment. However, the definition of "obscenity" continues to be a point of controversy.
- ***Miller v. California*** (1973): Allowed community standards, varying in different parts of the country, to be used in determining if material is obscene.
- Cases of libel are usually difficult to win because public figures must prove that the insults were intentionally malicious, as mandated in **New York Times v. Sullivan** (1964).

## Learning Objective 4.4: Describe the rights to assemble and associate protected by the First Amendment and their limitations. (p. 105)

## Freedom of Assembly

- **The Right to Assemble** includes, first, the right to protest, picket, or hold a demonstration within reasonable limits called "time, place, and manner restrictions" and with virtually no limitations on the content of a group's message.
- In *NAACP v. Alabama* (1958), the Supreme Court held that the right to establish groups of people with similar political interests, from political parties to the Ku Klux Klan, was also protected under freedom of assembly.

## Learning Objective 4.5: Describe the right to bear arms protected by the Second Amendment and its limitations. (p. 107)

### *Right to Bear Arms*

- The right to keep and bear arms is protected by the Second Amendment, but it has rarely been the subject of Supreme Court review.
- States have generally had wide latitude in restricting firearms as the Second Amendment has not been incorporated.
- In ***District of Columbia v. Heller*** (2008), however, the Supreme Court ruled that the Second Amendment did protect an individual's right to possess a firearm unconnected with service in a militia, and to use that firearm for traditionally lawful purposes, such as self-defense within the home.
- This was extended to state and local laws (Washington, D.C. is governed by Congress and is not a state) in *McDonald v. Chicago* (2010).

## Learning Objective 4.6: Characterize defendants' rights and identify issues that arise in their implementation. (p. 109)

### *Defendants' Rights*

- As with free speech, the courts must continually interpret the vague language of the Constitution to apply it to today's issues and events.
- **Searches and seizures:** The **Fourth Amendment** protects citizens from **unreasonable searches and seizures**.
  - Police investigators cannot search private property without a **search warrant** issued by a court unless there is reason to believe that the evidence will disappear or be destroyed or removed in the meantime.
  - The police cannot arrest someone unless there is **probable cause** to believe that he or she is guilty.
  - The **exclusionary rule** prevents prosecutors from using evidence acquired through unreasonable search and seizure. ***Mapp v. Ohio*** (1961) extended the exclusionary rule to state as well as federal cases.

- In recent years, the Supreme Court has made exceptions to the exclusionary rule; for example, when police are thought to have acted in "good faith," even if their actions technically violate the rule, the Court has allowed use of the evidence seized (*Herring v. U.S. 2009*)

- The **U.S.A. Patriot Act** (2001) and the 2008 revisions to the **Foreign Intelligence Surveillance Act** that followed revelations about warrantless eavesdropping by federal agencies expanded the government's right to investigate terrorism suspects without warrants.

- **Self-incrimination:** The **Fifth Amendment** protects people from being forced to supply evidence against themselves.

  - Because a person is innocent until proven guilty, the prosecution is responsible for proving a defendant's guilt.

  - *Miranda v. Arizona* (1966): Established that suspects must be informed of their constitutional rights before they are questioned by the police.

- **Right to counsel:** The **Sixth Amendment** guarantees that all accused persons tried in a federal court have the right to be represented by an attorney.

  - *Gideon v. Wainwright* (1963): Extends this privilege to cases tried in state courts as well.

  - Most cases are settled by **plea bargaining** between lawyers instead of by a trial.

  - The Sixth Amendment requires a trial by a jury of 12 people in federal cases; in state cases this number may be fewer, and a conviction does not require a unanimous vote.

- **Cruel and unusual punishment** is prohibited by the **Eighth Amendment**, though the term is not clearly defined in the Bill of Rights.

  - In *Gregg v. Georgia* (1976) and *McCleskey v. Kemp* (1987), the Supreme Court confirmed that the death penalty does not violate the Bill of Rights— that is, it is not considered "cruel and unusual."

  - The Supreme Court has, however, placed an increasing number of restrictions on who can be executed, such as the mentally ill (*Ford v. Wainwright*, 1986), mentally retarded persons (*Atkins v. Virginia*, 2002), those under the age of 18 when they committed their crimes (*Roper v. Simmons*, 2005), and those who committed individual crimes where the victim's life was not taken (*Kennedy v. Louisiana*, 2008).

- ☐ The Court has also required that a jury, not just a judge, find an aggravating circumstance necessary for imposition of the death penalty (*Ring v. Arizona*, 2002) and that lawyers for defendants in death penalty cases make reasonable efforts to fight for their clients at a trial's sentencing phase (*Rompilla v. Beard*, 2005).

- ☐ Debate over the death penalty continues. DNA tests sometimes prove the innocence of inmates on death row, leading some states to declare moratoria on executions. The number of executions has generally been declining.

## 4.7 Learning Objective 4.7: Outline the evolution of a right to privacy and its application to the issue of abortion. (p. 121)

### *Right to Privacy*

- ■ The right to privacy is not specifically guaranteed by the Bill of Rights, but the Supreme Court has interpreted the first ten amendments to imply this right.
  - ☐ ***Griswold v. Connecticut*** (1965) asserted the right to privacy, which became more controversial when the principle was applied, in ***Roe v. Wade*** (1973), to forbid states from controlling abortions during the first trimester of pregnancy.
  - ☐ ***Webster v. Reproductive Health Services*** (1989): The Supreme Court upheld a Missouri law that prevented the use of state funds for abortion clinics and that prohibited state employees from performing abortions.
  - ☐ The Supreme Court, while allowing abortions, has increasingly permitted regulation of them (***Planned Parenthood v. Casey***, 1992).
  - ☐ The Court has ruled, however, that some restrictions violate the Constitution by creating an undue burden on abortion access (*Whole Woman's Health v. Hellerstedt 2016*).
  - ☐ Medical technology also causes debate over the right to privacy in cases of surrogate parenthood and physician-assisted suicide.

**4.8**  **Learning Objective 4.8: Assess how civil liberties affect democratic government and how they both limit and expand the scope of government. (p. 124)**

## *Understanding Civil Liberties*

### *Civil Liberties and Democracy*

- When the Bill of Rights, including defendants' rights, conflicts with majority rule, rights prevail.

### *Civil Liberties and the Scope of Government*

- Civil liberties limit the scope of government action, yet substantial government effort may be necessary to protect the exercise of those rights.

## For Additional Review

Make a three-column table. In the first column, write all of the civil liberties discussed in this chapter. In the second column, list all Supreme Court cases that have addressed each liberty, including the date, the chief justice, and a brief synopsis of the case. In the third column, list the corresponding amendment or any previous court cases on which the Supreme Court based its decisions about each civil liberty. Use this chart when studying and reviewing the information for the unit test.

Make a chart describing the paradox about civil liberties and the scope of government. In one column, list the ways that civil liberties expand the scope of government. In the other column, list the ways that civil liberties limit the scope of government. Be sure to include specific examples of both. Use this chart when studying and reviewing the information for the unit test.

# Review Questions

## Multiple-Choice Questions

1. *Roe v. Wade* (1973) ruled that a woman's right to an abortion came from the
   a. right of symbolic speech.
   b. right of the people to "be secure in their persons, houses, papers, and effects."
   c. "right to remain silent."
   d. right to privacy.

2. In *Engel v. Vitale* (1962), the Supreme Court ruled that
   a. the reciting of a state-required prayer in public school constituted an impermissible establishment of religion under the First Amendment.
   b. the Gideon Society could distribute Bibles in public schools under the free exercise clause of the First Amendment.
   c. the eminent domain clause of the Fifth Amendment prevents government from taking religious property for public purposes.
   d. public school children may wear crosses as necklaces as a permissible mode of symbolic speech under the First Amendment.

3. The "exclusionary rule" means
   a. the Senate has removed a member from voting membership because of a violation of ethics rules.
   b. the House Rules Committee has refused to schedule a debate on a bill.
   c. the bureaucracy has failed to enforce unpopular legislation.
   d. evidence gathered in violation of the Fourth Amendment has not been allowed to be introduced during a trial.

4. Which of the following cases made decisions regarding the establishment of religion?
   a. *Mapp v. Ohio* (1965)
   b. *Texas v. Johnson* (1989)
   c. *School District of Abington Township, Pennsylvania v. Schempp* (1963)
   d. *Miranda v. Arizona* (1966)

5. Which of the following forms of expression is protected by the First Amendment?
   a. obscenity
   b. libel
   c. fighting words
   d. symbolic speech

6. Which of the following rights is protected by the Fifth Amendment?
   a. the right to privacy
   b. protection against self-incrimination
   c. the right to bear arms
   d. the right to counsel

7. The Bill of Rights begins with the words "Congress shall make no law. . ." telling the reader that the Bill of Rights is intended to protect citizens only from the national government. Yet, most of the provisions of the Bill of Rights now limit the states as well. Which of the following provisions is most relevant in explaining that change?
   a. equal protection clause of the Fourteenth Amendment
   b. double jeopardy clause of the Fifth Amendment
   c. rights "retained by the people" in the Ninth Amendment
   d. due process clause of the Fourteenth Amendment

**Questions 8-9 refer to the following figure.**

The Constitution and the Stages of the Criminal Justice System

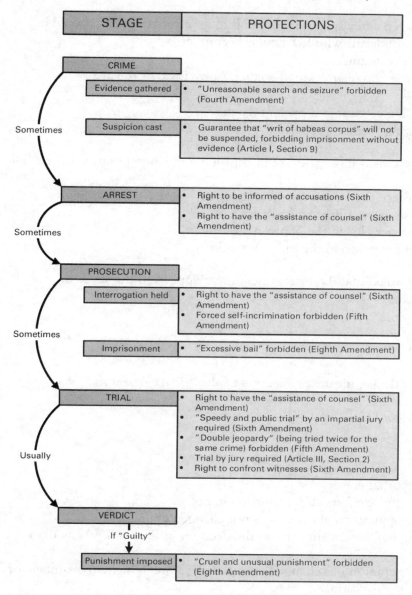

*United States Constitution*

8.   The right of citizens to be made aware of their constitutional guarantees against self-incrimination and to be represented by counsel was established in
   a.   *Gitlow v. New York* (1925).
   b.   *Mapp v. Ohio* (1965).
   c.   *Miranda v. Arizona* (1966).
   d.   *Gideon v. Wainwright* (1963).

9.   All of the following concepts are guaranteed to a citizen accused of a crime EXCEPT
   a.   a speedy and public trial by an impartial jury.
   b.   security against unreasonable search and seizures.
   c.   protection from capital punishment.
   d.   a citizen will not be put in jeopardy of life or limb twice for the same offense.

10.   The right of government to keep a newspaper from publishing information that would be harmful to the reputation of politicians who led a military conflict
   a.   would be denied as "prior restraint."
   b.   would be allowed under the "no quartering of soldiers" provision of the 3rd Amendment.
   c.   would be denied as entailing a "clear and present danger."
   d.   would be allowed as denying "seditious speech."

11.   Which of the following provisions is most relevant in explaining the incorporation of the Bill of Rights against the states?
   a.   the equal protection clause of the Fourteenth Amendment
   b.   the double jeopardy clause of the Fifth Amendment
   c.   the rights "retained by the people" in the Ninth Amendment
   d.   the grand jury indictment provision in the Fifth Amendment

12.   The Supreme Court, in 1925, ruled that the First Amendment applied to the states in
   a.   *New York Times Co. v. Sullivan.*
   b.   *Miranda v. Arizona.*
   c.   *Benton v. Maryland.*
   d.   *Gitlow v. New York.*

13.   The Supreme Court case that dealt with the publication of the "Pentagon Papers" was
   a.   *Gitlow v. New York.*
   b.   *New York Times v. The United States.*
   c.   *Schenck v. U.S.*
   d.   *Miranda v. Arizona.*

14.   Select the following statement that is true.
   a.   It is very difficult to identify opinions about abortion in polls.
   b.   Since *Roe v. Wade*, public opinion on abortion has not changed dramatically.
   c.   A much higher percentage of Americans oppose the decision in *Roe v. Wade* now than when it was rendered.
   d.   Since the decision, public opinion has changed dramatically; a much higher percentage of Americans now support the decision.

15. Cruel and unusual punishment and excessive bail and fine are forbidden by which Amendment?
    a. First Amendment
    b. Eighth Amendment
    c. Sixth Amendment
    d. Eleventh Amendment

16. Which Supreme Court case, in 1973, in an attempt to redefine obscenity, ruled that local standards might affect the assessment of obscenity?
    a. *Roe v. Wade*
    b. *Miller v. California*
    c. *Lemon v. Kurtzman*
    d. *Roth v. United States*

17. Civil liberties, the personal guarantees and freedoms that the government cannot abridge by law
    a. are not absolute and must be balanced against other considerations.
    b. are all guaranteed by state constitutions.
    c. are also known as civil rights.
    d. are in the core of the original Constitution.

18. A false written statement that defames the character and reputation of an individual is known as
    a. symbolic speech.
    b. libel.
    c. hate speech.
    d. obscenity.

19. The "Right to Privacy" is
    a. in Amendment I of the Constitution.
    b. in Article I of the Constitution.
    c. in Amendment V of the Constitution.
    d. not specifically mentioned in the Constitution.

20. The individual right considered to be the most fundamental of all of the rights in the Bill of Rights is
    a. freedom of religion.
    b. right to an attorney.
    c. right to bear arms.
    d. freedom of expression.

# Free-Response Questions

1.　Use the following table to answer the questions below.

The Incorporation of the Bill of Rights

| Date of Incorporation | Amendment | Right | Case |
|---|---|---|---|
| 1925 | First | Freedom of speech | Gitlow v. New York |
| 1931 | First | Freedom of the press | Near v. Minnesota |
| 1937 | First | Freedom of assembly | De Jonge v. Oregon |
| 1940 | First | Free exercise of religion | Cantwell v. Connecticut |
| 1947 | First | Establishment of religion | Everson v. Board of Education |
| 1958 | First | Freedom of association | NAACP v. Alabama |
| 1963 | First | Right to petition government | NAACP v. Button |
| 2010 | Second | Right to bear arms | McDonald v. Chicago |
| Not incorporated[a] | Third | No quartering of soldiers | |
| 1949 | Fourth | No unreasonable searches and seizures | Wolf v. Colorado |
| 1961 | Fourth | Exclusionary rule | Mapp v. Ohio |
| 1897 | Fifth | Guarantee of just compensation | Chicago, Burlington, and Quincy RR v. Chicago |
| 1964 | Fifth | Immunity from self-incrimination | Mallory v. Hogan |
| 1969 | Fifth | Immunity from double jeopardy | Benton v. Maryland |
| Not incorporated | Fifth | Right to grand jury indictment | |
| 1932 | Sixth | Right to counsel in capital cases | Powell v. Alabama |
| 1948 | Sixth | Right to public trial | In re Oliver |
| 1963 | Sixth | Right to counsel in felony cases | Gideon v. Wainwright |
| 1965 | Sixth | Right to confrontation of witnesses | Pointer v. Texas |
| 1966 | Sixth | Right to impartial jury | Parker v. Gladden |
| 1967 | Sixth | Right to speedy trial | Klopfer v. North Carolina |
| 1967 | Sixth | Right to compulsory process for obtaining witnesses | Washington v. Texas |
| 1968 | Sixth | Right to jury trial for serious crimes | Duncan v. Louisiana |
| 1972 | Sixth | Right to counsel for all crimes involving jail terms | Argersinger v. Hamlin |
| Not incorporated | Seventh | Right to jury trial in civil cases | |
| 1962 | Eighth | Freedom from cruel and unusual punishment | Robinson v. California |
| Not incorporated | Eighth | Freedom from excessive fines or bail | |
| 1965 | Ninth | Right of privacy | Griswold v. Connecticut |

[a]The quartering of soldiers has not occurred under the Constitution.

　　a.　Define the incorporation of the Bill of Rights.

　　b.　Describe the importance of *Gitlow v. New York* to the incorporation doctrine.

　　c.　There are four unincorporated sections of the Bill of Rights. Explain why these might not have been incorporated.

2.   Under the Constitution, the Supreme Court has the right of judicial review.

    a.   Define judicial review.

    b.   Describe the application of judicial review to the decisions in two of the following cases:

- *Brown v. Board of Education* (1954)
- *Engel v. Vitale* (1962)
- *Texas v. Johnson* (1989)
- *Roe v. Wade* (1973)

    c.   Explain how each selected decision could be seen as an "activist" decision.

# Answers and Explanations

## Multiple-Choice Questions

1. D  In Roe v. Wade, the Supreme Court extended the right to privacy to include a right to abortion.
*Page reference: 122, AP Big Ideas: LOR, PMI*

2. A  The *Engel* decision was based on the establishment clause of the Constitution.
*Page reference: 91, AP Big Ideas: LOR, PMI*

3. D  The exclusionary rule prohibits police from using illegally seized evidence at trial.
*Page reference: 112, AP Big Ideas: LOR, PMI*

4. C  *School District of Abington Township, Pennsylvania v. Schempp* (1963) did relate to the establishment of religion.
*Page reference: 90, AP Big Ideas: LOR, PMI*

5. D  Freedom of speech is subject to almost no limits regarding symbolic acts like flag burning.
*Page reference: 95-102, AP Big Ideas: LOR, PMI*

6. B  The most famous provision of the Fifth Amendment is that no one is required to provide testimony against himself or herself in court.
*Page reference: 114-115, AP Big Ideas: LOR, PMI*

7. D  The Bill of Rights has largely been incorporated by the states through the due process clause of the Fourteenth Amendment; that amendment, adopted after the Civil War, has been ruled to make states comply with provisions of the national constitution.
*Page reference: 88-89, AP Big Ideas: LOR, PMI*

8. C  *Miranda v. Arizona* extended the rights of the accused to those who did not know the Constitution. In that case, the Supreme Court said that knowing that the rights existed was as fundamental as having the rights.
*Page reference: 110, AP Big Idea: LOR*

9. C  Capital punishment has never been ruled to violate the cruel and unusual provision of the Eighth Amendment.
*Page reference: 110, AP Big Idea: LOR*

10. A  Under the First Amendment, banning of prior restraint of publication is a very strong rule.
*Page reference: 96, AP Big Idea: LOR*

11. C  The Bill of Rights was ratified and added to the Constitution in 1789.
*Page reference: 88-89, AP Big Ideas: LOR, PMI*

12. D  The *Gitlow* case incorporated the speech provision of the First Amendment in 1925.
*Page reference: 88, AP Big Ideas: LOR, PMI*

13. B    *New York Times v. The United States* ruled that the "no prior restraint" rule prohibited prosecution before the papers were published.
*Page reference: 101, AP Big Ideas: LOR, PMI*

14. B    Although the *Roe* decision made abortion legal, it did not significantly change attitudes toward abortion.
*Page reference: 122, AP Big Ideas: LOR, PMI*

15. B    The Eighth Amendment prohibits cruel and unusual punishment and excessive bail and fine.
*Page reference: 118-119, AP Big Idea: LOR*

16. B    The *Miller* case stated that obscenity must be defined by "contemporary community standards."
*Page reference: 99, AP Big Ideas: LOR, PMI*

17. A    Even though civil liberties are personal freedoms that cannot be abridged by the government, they are subject to boundaries.
*Page reference: 87, AP Big Idea: LOR*

18. B    Libel is speech that defames a person's character and reputation which is put in writing and is not protected by the Constitution.
*Page reference: 100-101, AP Big Idea: LOR*

19. D    The "right to privacy" is not specifically mentioned in the Constitution but was established through judicial interpretation of the Constitution.
*Page reference: 121-122, AP Big Ideas: LOR, PMI*

20. D    The freedom of expression, which includes press and speech, was considered by the founders to be absolutely necessary for the establishment of a democracy.
*Page reference: 95-105, AP Big Idea: LOR*

# Free-Response Questions

*This rubric provides examples of many, but not all of the possible correct responses to the free-response questions.*

1. Use the table to answer the questions below:

   a. Define the incorporation of the Bill of Rights.

      - The incorporation doctrine is the legal concept under which the Supreme Court has nationalized the Bill of Rights by making most of its provisions applicable to the states through the Fourteenth Amendment.

   b. Describe the importance of *Gitlow v. New York* to the incorporation doctrine.

      - In 1925, the Supreme Court decision holding that freedoms of press and speech are "fundamental personal rights and liberties protected by the due process clause of the Fourteenth Amendment from impairment by the states" as well as by the federal government was handed down in the *Gitlow* case.

   c. There are four unincorporated sections of the Bill of Rights. Explain why these might not have been incorporated.

      - The four unincorporated sections of the Bill of Rights relate to the housing of soldiers, right to grand jury indictment, right to jury trial in civil cases, and freedom from excessive bail and fines. These have not been incorporated due to the fact the Supreme Court has not ruled on any cases relating to any of these topics.

2. Under the Constitution, the Supreme Court has the right of judicial review.

   a. Define judicial review.

      - Judicial review was established in the Supreme Court case of *Marbury v. Madison* early in our nation's history. In that case, the Court ruled that the Supreme Court should have the power to make sure that laws and executive actions conformed to the Constitution.

   b. Describe the application of judicial review to the decisions in two of the following cases:

      - *Brown v. Board of Education* (1954)
      - *Engel v. Vitale* (1962)
      - *Texas v. Johnson* (1989)
      - *Roe v. Wade* (1973)

- In the case of *Engel v. Vitale*, the state of New York had written a law that required school children to recite a prayer at the beginning of each school day. The Supreme Court used the Engel decision to declare that law unconstitutional, as a violation of the establishment clause of the First Amendment.

- In *Texas v. Johnson*, the court ruled that as an act of political speech, burning an American flag is an allowable form of symbolic speech. This overturned a Texas state law prohibiting flag burning, making it an example of judicial review.

c. Explain how each selected decision could be seen as an "activist" decision.

- These decisions were seen as activist decisions because the Court didn't just stick to the words of the Bill of Rights. It found that there was a right that was not mentioned in so many words. This was seen as an activist decision.

# 5

# Civil Rights and Public Policy

## Chapter Overview

**Civil rights** are policies designed to protect people against arbitrary or discriminatory treatment by government officials or individuals. In this chapter, we explore the development of civil rights in the United States. We begin by considering the uneven development of civil rights in the nineteenth century, focusing in particular on the initial expansion of civil rights under the Civil War Amendments, and their gradual erosion in practice through discriminatory state laws and Supreme Court decisions. We then examine developments in the twentieth century that led to an expansion of civil rights protections afforded to a diverse array of groups in the United States. We conclude by considering the ways in which civil rights policy affects democracy and increases the scope of government. By the end of the chapter, students should have a solid understanding of the historical development and current status of civil rights as a public policy issue in the United States.

# Study Outline

**Learning Objective 5.1: Differentiate the Supreme Court's three standards of review for classifying people under the equal protection clause. (p. 131)**

## *Conceptions of Equality*

- American society does not emphasize equal results or equal rewards.

- A belief in equal rights has led to a belief in equality of opportunity; in other words, everyone should have the same chance to succeed.

## *The Constitution and Inequality*

- The original Constitution did not mention equality, and under most state constitutions only white males were allowed privileges such as voting rights. The **Fourteenth Amendment** first clarified the concept of equality by ensuring that all citizens must receive "**equal protection of the laws.**"

- The Supreme Court's modern interpretation of equality has brought civil rights to the forefront of the political agenda.

- The courts have identified three **standards of review** for determining whether an inequality in public policy is impermissible.

- Race and ethnic classifications are inherently suspect and therefore subject to "strict scrutiny": They are presumed unconstitutional unless they serve a compelling public interest and are the least restrictive means of accomplishing that interest.

- Gender classifications are subject to "intermediate scrutiny," meaning that they must bear a substantial relationship to an important governmental purpose.

- In all other cases, a classification must simply bear a rational relationship to some legitimate governmental purpose (called the "reasonableness" or "rational basis" standard) and are presumed constitutional until proven otherwise.

# Learning Objective 5.2: Trace the evolution of protections of the rights of African Americans and explain the application of nondiscrimination principles of issues of race. (p. 133)

## *African Americans' Civil Rights*

### *Slavery*

- ***Dred Scott v. Sanford*** (1857) upheld the constitutionality of slavery and forbade Congress from banning it in new states.
- The **Thirteenth Amendment** (1865) outlawed slavery after the Civil War.

### *Reconstruction and Segregation*

- In the 1876 election, a deadlock in the Electoral College led to a deal that allowed the Republican candidate, Rutherford B. Hayes, to be selected by a commission created by the House of Representatives, in exchange for the promise to withdraw federal troops from the southern states.
- Civil rights advances came to a halt and Jim Crow laws took effect segregating blacks from whites in the South, and preventing blacks from voting and running for public office.
- The Supreme Court officially recognized a policy of "separate but equal" facilities, thereby allowing the practice of segregation, in ***Plessy v. Ferguson*** (1896).

### *Equal Education*

- ***Brown v. Board of Education*** (1954) overturned the *Plessy* decision—asserting that segregation is unconstitutional—and ordered the desegregation of public schools.
- Brown was the beginning of a string of Supreme Court decisions holding various forms of discrimination unconstitutional.
- Brown and these other cases gave the civil rights movement momentum that would grow in the years that followed.
- ***Swann v. Charlotte-Mecklenberg County Schools*** (1971): The Supreme Court allowed busing to be used as a means to balance racial percentages in schools, which became a matter of great national controversy.

### The Civil Rights Movement and Public Policy

- Congress also passed the **Civil Rights Act** (1964) which
    - outlawed racial discrimination in public places,
    - prohibited discrimination in employment,
    - withheld government funding from any school or institution that practiced discrimination,
    - established the Equal Employment Opportunity Commission to monitor job discrimination,
    - granted the Justice Department power to enforce civil rights laws by suing institutions still practicing segregation.

### Voting Rights

- The **Fifteenth Amendment** (1870) formally granted African Americans **suffrage—** the right to vote—but had little effect in practice.
- Southern states circumvented the law by instituting **literacy tests** that most former slaves could not pass.
- **Poll taxes** were implemented and most former slaves could not afford to pay.
- **Grandfather clauses** were implemented to exempt from literacy tests illiterate whites whose grandfathers had been allowed to vote before 1860.
- **White primaries** were implemented that restricted voting in Democratic Party elections (the only ones that mattered given Democratic dominance in the South) to whites.
- Most of these policies were struck down in the early 20th century.
- Grandfather clauses were found unconstitutional in *Guinn v. United States* (1915).
- The Supreme Court outlawed the use of **white primaries** to exclude African Americans from the election process in *Smith v. Allwright* (1944).
- The **Twenty-Fourth Amendment** (1964) outlawed the use of poll taxes.
- Congress passed the **Voting Rights Act** in 1965 to prevent states from using any methods to disenfranchise voters.
- The law provided for enforcement by allowing federal registrars to oversee elections and voter registration; therefore only with the Voting Rights Act did the Fifteenth

Amendment's guarantee of suffrage without regard to race become meaningful in practice.

<table>
<tr><td>5.3</td><td></td></tr>
</table>

# Learning Objective 5.3: Relate civil rights principles to progress made by other ethnic groups in the United States. (p. 140)

## *The Rights of Other Minority Groups*

- Other minority groups, including Native Americans, Hispanic Americans, and Asian Americans, have all suffered discrimination and benefited from advances made in the civil rights movement. The Civil Rights Act applies to all races and has encouraged many minority groups to speak out for their rights.

- **Native Americans** were isolated on "reservations" until the **Dawes Act of 1887** and they were given the right to vote only in 1924.
  - □ Beginning in 1970, they have used courts to pursue equal rights, largely through the Native Americans Rights Fund (NARF).

- **Hispanic Americans** (or "Latinos" as some prefer to be called) are now the largest minority group, with heritage from many Caribbean, Central American, and South American nations. *Hernandez v. Texas* extended protection against discrimination to Hispanics.
  - □ They have pursued equal rights in court through the **Mexican American Legal Defense Fund (MALDEF)**, as well as through labor organizations such as the **United Farm Workers**, led by César Chavez from the 1960s through the 1980s.

- **Asian Americans** are the most rapidly growing group, and while often hailed as the most successful, they have suffered significant discrimination, most notably the internment of Japanese Americans in isolated camps during World War II, which the Supreme Court upheld in *Korematsu v. U.S* (1944).
  - □ Though smaller in numbers than most minority groups, the **Arab and Islamic** population has faced significant challenges since the 9/11 attacks.

**Learning Objective 5.4: Trace the evolution of women's rights and explain how civil rights principles apply to gender issues. (p. 145)**

## *The Rights of Women*

- Women were also excluded from the rights of equality implied in the Constitution.

- The women's rights movement grew out of abolitionism in the 1840s, when female activists encountered discrimination among male activists.

- The efforts of the first generation of feminists culminated in the **Nineteenth Amendment** (1920), which granted women the right to vote.

- Progress bogged down after the Nineteenth Amendment was ratified and the **Equal Rights Amendment** (**ERA**, 1923) was intended to enforce full equality for women, who still were discriminated against in such areas as employment.

- It was passed by Congress in 1972 but was never ratified by the necessary three-fourths of state legislatures.

- The Second Wave of feminists relied heavily on the courts for progress. In ***Reed v. Reed*** (1971), the Supreme Court for the first time found a law unconstitutional based on arbitrary gender bias, and in 1976, ***Craig v. Boren*** established an "intermediate scrutiny" standard for determining gender discrimination.

- Since then, it has struck down laws that discriminate against both women and men.

- Recent efforts to promote gender equality have focused on the workplace.

- Civil rights legislation barring discrimination in the workplace applies to women as well as to other minority groups, and it includes employment opportunities, equal pay, and pregnancy leave.

- In 1986, the Supreme Court established a woman's right to sue employers for sexual harassment under the Civil Rights Act.

- The Supreme Court has not yet ruled on the issue of **comparable worth**, which insists that women be paid the same as men for jobs that require the same skills.

- Title IX of the Education Act of 1972 has helped to end employment discrimination because it forbids gender discrimination in federally subsidized education programs (which include almost all colleges and universities), including athletics.

- The Supreme Court extended this to prohibiting all-male schools in 1996 in a case involving the Virginia Military Academy.

- Women are allowed to serve in all branches of the military but cannot serve in ground combat units of the Army and Marine Corps.

- Despite increased equality, issues remain in combating sexual harassment.

## 5.5 Learning Objective 5.5: Show how civil rights principles have been applied to seniors, people with disabilities, and gays and lesbians. (p. 151)

### *Other Groups Active under the Civil Rights Umbrella*

- Discrimination laws prevent employers and universities from rejecting applicants because of their age.

- Congress also revoked the policy of mandatory retirement, unless a compelling reason can be provided based on age.

- The **Americans with Disabilities Act of 1990** protects disabled Americans against job discrimination and requires employers to provide "reasonable accommodations," but controversy has arisen over who is considered disabled.

- **LGBT rights** are protected by some laws but are frequently challenged by courts, legislatures, and voters.

- The **"don't ask, don't tell"** military policy introduced by President Clinton in 1993 bypasses restrictions on homosexuality by preventing labeling; even this restriction was struck down by a federal court in 2010 as the President and the Secretary of Defense asked Congress to repeal the law barring service by homosexuals.

- The right to privacy also factors into debates over gay rights; *Lawrence v. Texas* (2003) overturned state antisodomy laws as well as the Court's own decision in *Bowers v. Hardwick* (1986).

- Massachusetts, Hawaii, and Vermont have each legalized some form of **civil union** between same-sex couples, but the Defense of Marriage Act (1996) allowed other states to disregard these unions.

- In 2015 the Supreme Court resolved the marriage issue when it held in *Obergefell v. Hodges* that the Fourteenth Amendment requires states to license a marriage between two people of the same sex and to recognize a marriage between two people of the same sex when their marriage was lawfully licensed and performed out-of-state.

## 5.6 Learning Objective 5.6: Trace the evolution of affirmative action policy and assess the arguments for and against it. (p. 154)

### Affirmative Action

- **Affirmative action** is a policy that attempts to go beyond preventing discrimination by providing members of groups who have suffered discrimination some compensatory treatment.

- While originally tolerant of affirmative action programs, courts have become less so in the past decade.

- The Supreme Court ruled against set-aside government contracts for minority-owned businesses in *Adarand Constructors v. Pena* (1995), stating that even if the intent is to advance the opportunities of minorities, it still classifies people by race and is therefore unconstitutional unless it meets the strict scrutiny test: it must be narrowly tailored to achieve a compelling state interest.

- Courts have permitted affirmative action in education, but with tight restrictions.

- In *Regents of the University of California v. Bakke* (1978), the Court ruled that race could be used as one factor in choosing between applicants, but that enrollment quotas were unconstitutional.

- In *Grutter v. Bollinger* (2003), the court ruled that there was a compelling state interest in promoting diversity on campuses, and allowed a narrowly tailored program to continue.

- In *Gratz v. Bollinger* (2006), however, the court ruled that a blanket bonus system was, in effect, a quota and was therefore unconstitutional.

- In *Parents Involved in Community Schools v. Seattle School District No. 1* (2007), the court ruled that racial balancing (rather than remedying past discrimination) was not in itself a compelling state interest.

**Learning Objective 5.7: Establish how civil rights policy advances democracy and increases the scope of government. (p. 158)**

## *Understanding Civil Rights and Public Policy*

### *Civil Rights and Democracy*

- Civil rights policies advance democracy because equality is a basic principle of democratic government. When majority rule and minority rights are in conflict, minority rights must prevail.

### *Civil Rights and the Scope of Government*

- Civil rights policies limit government discrimination but also require an active government effort to protect the rights of minorities.

## For Additional Review

Use the following system to take notes on your reading:

1.  Use a notetaking column to record the information from the sections of the chapter.
2.  Read your notes and create a column and formulate questions on the specific topics. This sets up a perfect stage for exam-studying later.
3.  Cover the notetaking column with a sheet of paper and look at the questions you have written and recite your answers.
4.  Reflect on the material: What is the significance of these facts? What principles are the facts based on?
5.  Review the material in preparation of the unit test.

Debate continues over the policy of affirmative action. Make a chart listing arguments on each side of the issue and use this chart when reviewing and studying for the unit test.

# Review Questions

## Multiple-Choice Questions

1.  Affirmative action laws are designed to remedy which kind of discrimination?
    a.  de facto
    b.  ex post facto
    c.  de solis
    d.  habeas corpus

2.  The landmark case of *Brown v. Board of Education* ruled that segregated schools were not acceptable because of the
    a.  constitutional provision against Bills of Attainder.
    b.  due process of law clause of the Fifth Amendment.
    c.  "involuntary servitude" clause of the Thirteenth Amendment.
    d.  "equal protection" clause of the Fourteenth Amendment.

**Questions 3-4 refer to following table.**

Standards of Review for Classifications

| Basis of Classification | Standard of Review | Applying the Test |
| --- | --- | --- |
| Race and ethnicity | Inherently suspect — *difficult to meet* | Is the classification necessary to accomplish a compelling governmental goal? Is it the least restrictive way to achieve that goal? |
| Gender | Intermediate scrutiny — *moderately difficult to meet* | Does the classification bear a substantial relationship to an important governmental goal? |
| Other (age, wealth, etc.) | Reasonableness — *easy to meet* | Does the classification have a rational relationship to a legitimate governmental goal? |

3.  Which of the following statements is reflected in the table?
    a.  The privileges or immunities protected by the 14th Amendment.
    b.  The due process clause of the 14th Amendment.
    c.  The equal protection clause of the 14th Amendment.
    d.  The voting rights clause of the 14th Amendment.

4.  The Standards of Review for Classifications under the Equal Protection Clause include all of the following EXCEPT
    a.  gender.
    b.  age and wealth.
    c.  race and ethnicity.
    d.  state of residence.

5. In the case of *California v. Bakke*, the Supreme Court ruled that
   a. Japanese Americans could be placed in camps during World War II.
   b. migrant workers were entitled to compensation in case of injury through unemployment insurance.
   c. affirmative action admissions to a medical school could cause "reverse discrimination."
   d. women were entitled to equal pay for equal work.

6. Racial discrimination in public accommodations such as restaurants and hotels was banned in
   a. the Civil Rights Act of 1964.
   b. the Open Housing Act of 1968.
   c. the Twenty-Fourth Amendment.
   d. the Equal Rights Amendment.

7. Affirmative action refers to
   a. the U.S. Senate approving a presidential appointment to the cabinet under its "advice and consent" function.
   b. the president "faithfully executing" the appropriations of money under laws created by Congress.
   c. the Supreme Court upholding a lower court decision.
   d. a policy giving special consideration to groups that have been disadvantaged historically.

8. The Equal Rights Amendment (ERA) was proposed by Congress but fell three states short of the 38 needed for ratification. If adopted, the ERA would have banned discrimination based upon
   a. race.
   b. religious faith.
   c. gender.
   d. sexual orientation.

9. The biggest difference between civil rights and civil liberties is that
   a. civil liberties protect the majority while civil rights protect minorities.
   b. civil liberties have to do with individual protections while civil rights are protections on the basis of group attributes.
   c. civil liberties have to do with the freedoms of expression and religion while civil rights have to do with rights of people accused of crimes.
   d. civil liberties allow groups to organize into interest groups and make demands on government while civil rights allow for groups to seek redress of grievances through mass protests.

10. Which Supreme Court case upheld the placing of Japanese citizens in internment camps during World War II?
    a. *Craig v. Boren*
    b. *Smith v. Allwright*
    c. *Korematsu v. United States*
    d. *Santa Clara Pueblo v. Martinez*

11. Which of the following bars educational institutions that receive federal funds from discriminating against female students?
    a. Title IX of the Education Amendments of 1972
    b. The Equal Rights Amendment
    c. The Civil Rights Act of 1964
    d. Jim Crow Laws

12. One area in which African Americans have made substantial progress since the 1960s is
    a. elective office.
    b. federalism.
    c. in the penal system.
    d. in the penal and judicial systems.

13. All of the following statements are true EXCEPT
    a. women are more supportive than men of government programs for children.
    b. women are more supportive than men of government programs for the poor.
    c. women and men differ in their opinions and their votes.
    d. women tend to have a greater tendency to vote for Republican candidates than men.

14. The strict scrutiny test applies to
    a. race and ethnicity.
    b. age.
    c. gender.
    d. ethnicity.

15. What happened when federal troops withdrew from the South in 1877?
    a. Jim Crow laws were passed which segregated the races and, through the *Plessy v. Ferguson* decision, the Supreme Court established the separate but equal doctrine.
    b. Laws were enacted that integrated the races.
    c. In *Plessy v. Ferguson*, the Supreme Court justices ended separate and unequal treatment of African Americans.
    d. Laws were enacted that desegregated the races.

16. The Supreme Court overturned the constitutionality of separate but equal facilities in
    a. *Reed v. Reed.*
    b. *Plessy v. Ferguson.*
    c. *Craig v. Boren.*
    d. *Brown v. Board of Education.*

17. The Equal Rights Amendment states "Equality of rights under the law shall not be denied or abridged by the United States or any state on account of sex." Which of the following is true about the Equal Rights Amendment (ERA)?
    a. Congress never approved the ERA.
    b. The ERA fell three states short of the three-fourths majority it needed to be ratified.
    c. Congress required special ratifying conventions in the states.
    d. The ERA was not ratified by a single state.

18. At the end of the Civil War, as a result of the northern victory, which Amendments became part of the Constitution?
    a. Ninth, Tenth, and Eleventh
    b. Thirteenth and Fourteenth
    c. Thirteenth, Fourteenth, and Fifteenth
    d. Tenth and Eleventh

19. A clause of the Fourteenth Amendment guarantees all citizens receive "equal protection under the law." The restraints of equal protection apply to
    a. private individuals.
    b. actions of governments, not private individuals.
    c. commercial activities of large corporations.
    d. actions of the federal government only.

20. Rational basis is a
    a. test applied by the court when a classification is based on race requiring the government to show that there is a compelling reason for the law and no other less restrictive way to meet the interest.
    b. clause in the Fifth Amendment prohibiting state governments from depriving any person of life, liberty, or property without due process of law.
    c. clause in the Fourteenth Amendment that forbids any state to deny to any person within its jurisdiction the equal protection of the laws.
    d. standard developed by the courts to test the constitutionality of a law; when applied, a law is constitutional as long as it meets a reasonable government interest.

# Free-Response Questions

1. One of the key issues in civil rights had to do with gaining the right to vote for groups of citizens. African Americans and women fought for and eventually earned the right to vote through constitutional amendments, Supreme Court decisions, and congressional laws. Among the issues related to voting rights are:

   - the poll tax
   - the white primary
   - the grandfather clause
   - literacy tests
   - state laws prohibiting women OR blacks OR those younger than 21 from voting
   - discriminatory governmental practices that made it difficult to register and vote

   a. Identify and describe one Supreme Court case that declared one of these practices unconstitutional.

   b. Identify and describe one law passed by Congress that made one of these practices illegal.

   c. Identify and describe one constitutional amendment that addressed one of these practices.

2. Women have been participants in and beneficiaries of a civil rights movement during the past 50 years.

   a. Describe the impact of the battle for the Equal Rights Amendment on the debate over women's equality.

   b. Define "comparable worth" and explain the impact it has had on the debate over workplace equality.

   c. Describe the current policy regarding women serving in the military, and identify one argument in favor of the policy and one against it.

# Answers and Explanations

## Multiple-Choice Questions

1.  A   Preventing discrimination by law (de jure) can accomplish only so much; therefore, in order to remedy patterns of discrimination that have developed over time in fact (de facto), affirmative action is needed.
    *Page reference: 154-157, AP Big Ideas: LOR, PMI*

2.  D   *Brown v. Board of Education* decided that the equal protection clause required desegregation of schools because "separate educational facilities are inherently unequal."
    *Page reference: 135, AP Big Ideas: LOR, PMI*

3.  C   The table reflects the equal protection clause of the 14th Amendment.
    *Page reference: 132, AP Big Ideas: LOR, PMI*

4.  D   An individual's state of residence is not a classification for the standards of review for the 14th Amendment.
    *Page reference: 132, AP Big Ideas: LOR, PMI*

5.  C   In the case of *Regents of the University of California v. Bakke*, the Supreme Court found the university's quotas for enrolling minorities unconstitutional, therefore, Allan Bakke was denied enrollment in favor of a minority applicant to fulfill the university's quota, an unconstitutional "reverse discrimination."
    *Page reference: 155, AP Big Ideas: LOR, PMI*

6.  A   The 1964 Civil Rights Act was a broad sweeping law that had many characteristics; among its provisions was one banning discrimination in public accommodations.
    *Page reference: 137, AP Big Ideas: LOR, PMI*

7.  D   The purpose of affirmative action is to correct for past discrimination.
    *Page reference: 154-157, AP Big Ideas: LOR, PMI*

8.  C   All of the options have to do with different aspects of "equality," but only the rights of women were addressed in the ERA.
    *Page reference: 146-147, AP Big Ideas: LOR, PMI*

9.  B   This question asks students to differentiate between two basic issues, and while the answers all provide contrasts, only answer (b) is correct—civil liberties are individual rights, while civil rights ban discrimination against groups.
    *Page reference: 130-131, AP Big Idea: LOR*

10. C   The Japanese internment camps were upheld in the *Korematsu* decision.
    *Page reference: 144, AP Big Ideas: LOR, PMI*

11. B   Title IX is the only legislation that specifically barred educational institutions receiving federal funds from discriminating against female students.
*Page reference: 149, AP Big Ideas: LOR, PMI*

12. A   African Americans have gained significant ground in getting elected to office at all levels of government.
*Page reference: 138-140, AP Big Ideas: LOR, PMI*

13. D   Women do not tend to vote for Republican candidates more than men, making this the only incorrect choice.
*Page reference: 145-151, AP Big Ideas: LOR, CIV*

14. A   The strict scrutiny test is applied by the court when a classification is based on race or ethnicity, requiring the government to show that there is a compelling reason for the law.
*Page reference: 131-131, AP Big Ideas: LOR, PMI*

15. A   When Reconstruction ended in 1877, the states attempted to return former slaves to as close to the condition of slavery as possible by passing Jim Crow laws which, in *Plessy*, the Court upheld by asserting the separate but equal doctrine.
*Page reference: 133-135, AP Big Ideas: LOR, PMI*

16. D   The Supreme Court, in the *Brown v. Board of Education* decision, struck down the "separate but equal" doctrine that had justified segregated schools, but school districts responded slowly.
*Page reference: 135-136, AP Big Ideas: LOR, PMI*

17. B   The ERA was approved by Congress in the 1970s, but it fell short of the three-fourths majority it needed for ratification.
*Page reference: 146-147, AP Big Idea: LOR*

18. C   The "Civil War Amendments" which were added to the Constitution after the northern victory in the Civil War are the Thirteenth, Fourteenth, and Fifteenth Amendments.
*Page reference: 131-138, AP Big Ideas: LOR, PMI*

19. B   The 14th Amendment, adopted after the Civil War, contains an equal protection clause which restricts the actions of governments but not those of private individuals.
*Page reference: 131, AP Big Ideas: LOR, PMI*

20. D   The rational basis test is a standard developed by the courts to test the constitutionality of a law, and when it is applied, a law is considered constitutional as long as it meets a reasonable government interest.
*Page reference: 131-132, AP Big Ideas: LOR, PMI*

# Free-Response Questions

*This rubric provides examples of many, but not all of the possible correct responses to the free-response questions.*

1.     One of the key issues in civil rights had to do with gaining the right to vote for groups of citizens. African Americans and women fought for and eventually earned the right to vote through constitutional amendments, Supreme Court decisions, and congressional laws. Among the issues related to voting rights are:

   - the poll tax

   - the white primary

   - the grandfather clause

   - literacy tests

   - state laws prohibiting women OR blacks OR those younger than 21 from voting

   - discriminatory governmental practices that made it difficult to register and vote

   - A basic right of American citizens is the right to vote. In civil rights, the first step toward making progress regarding equality is the right to participate in the elections of members of congress and other representatives. Until all groups attain the right to vote, they can never truly be equal with other groups. To attain the right to vote, a number of barriers had to be overcome, including the poll tax, the white primary, the grandfather clause, and the literacy test. Both constitutional guarantees and laws addressing governmental practices had to be written. In short, it took concerted action of all areas of government to attain the right to vote.

   a.   Identify and describe one Supreme Court case that declared one of these practices unconstitutional.

   - One Supreme Court case that addressed this issue was the one that banned the white primary. In *Smith v. Allwright*, the court ruled that primary elections were a basic part of the election process, so people couldn't be kept from voting in primaries because of their race.

## 6.2 Learning Objective 6.2: Outline how various forms of socialization shape political opinions. (p. 170)

### *How Americans Learn About Politics: Political Socialization*

- People learn about politics and form their political beliefs through the process of **political socialization**.

- There are several different means through which people informally acquire political information.

- **The family:** Families have a significant degree of influence, especially over younger members. Most people identify with the same party that their parents do.

- **The mass media:** Most Americans, especially children and teenagers, watch a significant amount of **television**.

- Political information is often disseminated through TV.

- Younger people are much less likely to watch the news than are adults, however, and as a result, young people's political knowledge is significantly lower today than that of young people a few decades ago.

- **School:** Schools educate children in American values such as democracy and capitalism, both through academics and through practices such as reciting the Pledge of Allegiance.

- A good education also tends to produce more politically active and aware citizens.

- In addition to the influence of the educational system, young people are also influenced by members of their peer group when formulating their political attitudes and beliefs.

- **Religious** groups and associations also influence political attitudes. Ideology is now determined more by religiosity—the degree to which religion is important in one's life—than by religious denomination.

- Socialization is a dynamic process, with learning taking place over one's entire lifetime. Socialization is part of the very important nurturing process.

**6.3** **Learning Objective 6.3: Explain how polls are conducted and what can be learned from them about American public opinion. (p. 171)**

### *Measuring Public Opinion and Political Information*

- **Polls** are the most common means of assessing public opinion.

- A **sample** is a relatively small proportion of people who are chosen in a survey so as to be representative of the whole.

- **Random sampling** is the key technique employed by survey researchers, which operates on the principle that everyone should have an equal probability of being selected for the sample.

- Commonly, modern polls rely on **random digit dialing** to draw telephone samples.

- A famous nonrandom sample, *The Literary Digest* poll of 1936, wrongly predicted that Republican Alf Landon would defeat Franklin Roosevelt in that year's election.

- The wording of a question is critical, and ambiguously worded questions can affect the accuracy of a poll.

- The size of the sample can also affect the accuracy of a poll and thus the level of confidence in the poll (**sampling error**).

- **Exit polls** are conducted by media as voters leave the voting booth in order to predict the outcomes of elections.

- Some critics argue that polls allow politicians to be influenced easily by shifts in public opinion and that polls receive more media attention than do candidates' political platforms during elections.

- Others assert that, by advancing the public's political agenda to poll-sensitive politicians, polls advance the principles of democracy.

- Recent polls indicate that Americans have little political knowledge and little faith that the government is acting on their behalf.

- Public opinion polls have shown a trend indicating that Americans trust government less than they used to.

**6.4** **Learning Objective 6.4: Compare and contrast the principles of conservatism and liberalism.** (p. 180)

## What Americans Value: Political Ideologies

- **Political ideology** is a coherent set of beliefs about politics, public policy, and public purpose, which helps give meaning to political events.

- In recent years, more Americans have considered themselves conservative than moderate or liberal.

- **Conservatism** favors limited government and freedom of the private sector, is more likely to support military spending, free markets, prayer in school, and reduced taxes, and opposes abortion, affirmative action, and government spending on social programs.

- **Liberalism** favors an active central government with social and economic responsibilities, a more equal distribution of wealth, more government regulation of big business, more government spending on social programs, and abortion, and opposes increases in defense spending and military actions, prayer in school, and tax breaks for the wealthy.

- Some groups are more likely to hold one ideology than the other.

- Women and minorities tend to be more liberal.

- The **gender gap** is the pattern that predicts that women are more likely to vote for a Democratic candidate; however, this was less prevalent in the 2004 elections.

- Traditionally, people of higher socioeconomic classes tend to be conservative; this trend is declining, however.

- Ideology is not an important concept to most Americans.

- Today only about 20 percent of Americans are ideologues—people who think consistently in ideological terms.

- Most people think in terms of how policies affect groups they like or dislike.

## Learning Objective 6.5: Assess the influence of political ideology on political attitudes and behaviors. (p. 182)

### *The Influence of Political Ideology on Political Behavior*

- 65 percent of the American public calls themselves either conservatives or liberals, but many of these individuals are not ideologically consistent.

- Often individuals are conservative in principle but liberal in practice.

## Learning Objective 6.6: Identify the ways that people may participate in politics. (p. 183)

### *How Americans Participate in Politics*

- **Political participation:** all the activities used by citizens to influence the selection of political leaders or the policies they pursue. The most common means of political participation is voting; other means include protest and civil disobedience.

- Americans express their political views and try to influence policy by voting, petitioning, participating in protests, or corresponding with their representatives.

- Patterns of conventional participation are changing.

- **Voter turnout** has been declining over the last few decades, though it is still the most common way people participate in politics.

- Young people are the group least likely to vote.

- **Campaign contributions** to candidates as a form of political participation are on the rise.

- **Protest** and **civil disobedience** have a long tradition in American history.

- Protests against globalization and war continue to be a means of political expression today.

- People of high socioeconomic status are much more likely to participate in politics, although African Americans and Hispanic Americans are becoming more active.

**6.7** **Learning Objective 6.7: Analyze how public opinion about the scope of government guides political behavior. (p. 188)**

## Understanding Public Opinion and Political Action

- Conservatives typically believe the scope of government has become too wide and look to Ronald Reagan's pledge to get the government "off the backs of the American people" as inspiration. Liberals, on the other hand, believe the scope of government should be further increased and support policies like the Obama administration's health care reform law.

## For Additional Review

Use the following questions to guide your note-taking on political socialization:

1. What is political socialization?
2. Why do we need to socialize?
3. What are agents of political socialization?
4. What is political participation?
5. What forms can political participation take?
6. What is the relationship between political socialization and participation?

Use these notes when studying and reviewing for the unit test and the AP Government and Politics exam.

Create a chart of the methods for conducting different types of public opinion polls. For each method listed, describe the method and list the advantages and disadvantages of the method. Use this chart when studying and reviewing for the unit test and the AP Government and Politics exam.

# Review Questions

## Multiple-Choice Questions

1.    The nurturing process through which people learn their knowledge, feelings, and evaluations about the political world is called
   a.   political socialization.
   b.   political efficacy.
   c.   propaganda acquisition.
   d.   political ideology.

2.    Sampling error refers to
   a.   the pollster making mistakes in selecting a sample.
   b.   the sample not being representative of the population.
   c.   coding mistakes that mean that responses are not accurately reported.
   d.   the level of confidence in the findings of a public opinion poll.

3.    Which type of poll is most likely to be used by the media to predict the outcome of an election?
   a.   a benchmark poll
   b.   an exit poll
   c.   a matchup poll
   d.   a focus group poll

4.    Liberals are likely to support all of the following EXCEPT
   a.   freedom of choice in abortions.
   b.   government regulation.
   c.   increased taxes on the rich.
   d.   prayer in schools.

5.    The "gender gap" refers to the idea that women
   a.   are denied equal protection of the law in economic matters in the United States.
   b.   cannot take combat roles in the military.
   c.   are more likely to vote for Democrats than are men.
   d.   are proportionally underrepresented among members of Congress.

6.    Which of the following would older Americans be more likely to support than younger Americans?
   a.   protection of Social Security
   b.   decreased military spending
   c.   gays serving in the military
   d.   increased spending on education

7. Which of the following is the most common form of political participation in the United States?
   a. expressing one's ideas in a public opinion poll
   b. participating in a mass demonstration
   c. voting in a presidential election
   d. contacting a public official regarding a public issue

8. Which of the following is a random sample?
   a. interviewing people in a nonsystematic fashion
   b. a selection mechanism that gives each person an equal chance of being selected
   c. going up to people on the street and asking for their opinions
   d. asking every student in the Introduction to Psychology course to fill out a survey

**Questions 9-10 refer to the following chart.**

How Political Knowledge Varies According to Demographic and Political Factors
In the American national Election study of 2012, twelve factual questions were asked of a representative sample of the American public.

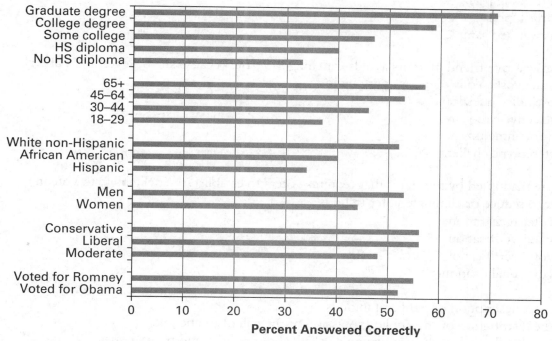

*Authors' analysis of the 2012 American National Election Study.*

9. Which of the following is reflected in the data in the chart?
   a. Differences in political knowledge are more accurately predicted by demographic rather than political factors.
   b. Differences in political knowledge are more accurately predicted by political rather than demographic factors.
   c. Differences in political knowledge cannot be predicted by either political or demographic factors.
   d. Differences in political knowledge can only be predicted by religious affiliation.

10. Political knowledge is important for all of the following reasons EXCEPT
    a. political knowledge is important to maintaining a democracy.
    b. individuals with higher levels of political knowledge are more likely to vote.
    c. individuals with higher levels of political knowledge are more likely to donate to political campaigns.
    d. individuals with higher levels of political knowledge are more likely to have stable opinions on policy issues.

11. Which of the following is a major weakness of public opinion polls?
    a. Polls can only measure the opinions of political elites.
    b. It is difficult to measure the intensity of feelings about issues.
    c. Polls are so fraught with error that their results are nearly meaningless.
    d. All of the above.

12. Which of the following polls is most likely to help a candidate evaluate the short-term effect of a certain campaign event?
    a. an exit poll
    b. a tracking poll
    c. a push poll
    d. a stratified sample

13. A conservative friend of yours avoids watching MSNBC because she believes it is a liberal news network. Your friend is engaging in
    a. prejudice questioning.
    b. selective exposure.
    c. infotainment.
    d. stereotype challenging.

14. A system adopted by the states that requires voters to establish their eligibility to vote in order to reduce or eliminate voter fraud is
    a. voter registration.
    b. voter verification.
    c. voter certification.
    d. voter qualification.

15. The best description of public opinion is
    a. the distribution of the public expression of the will of the people.
    b. the distribution of the population's beliefs about politics and policy issues.
    c. the distribution of media reflection of public attitudes.
    d. the distribution of the public expression of voter attitudes.

16. In general, public opinion
    a. has no relation to government action at all.
    b. has an impact on government action only during elections.
    c. constrains only the actions of incumbents in government.
    d. constrains the actions of government.

17. Political participation in the government is an essential component of
    a. freedom.
    b. independence.
    c. free enterprise
    d. self-government.

18. Voters who characterize themselves as Independents can best be characterized by which of the following descriptions?
    a. They typically have greater party loyalty to the Independent Party than Democrats and Republicans have to their parties.
    b. They will never cast a vote for a Democrat or a Republican.
    c. They typically have lower voter turnout than Democrats and Republicans.
    d. They typically have higher voter turnout than Democrats and Republicans.

19. The degree to which the sample estimates might differ from what the population actually thinks is called the
    a. standard deviation error.
    b. questioning error.
    c. probability error.
    d. sampling error.

20. Most political scientists and political observers assess public opinion primarily through
    a. polls.
    b. social media blogs.
    c. letters to the editor.
    d. voter registration rolls.

# Free-Response Questions

1.  In the United States, people can participate in politics in many different ways. Use the information from the chart below and your knowledge of political participation to answer the following questions:

Political Participation other than Voting, 1967-2014

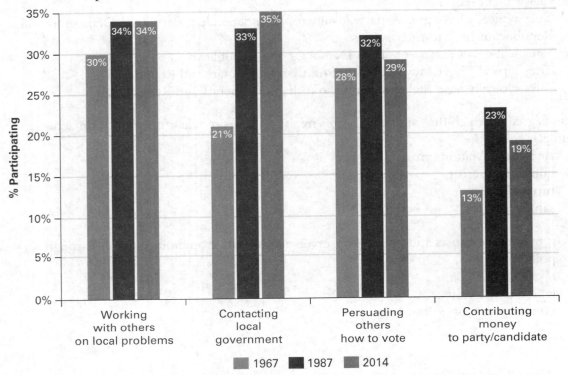

*Authors' analysis of the 2014 and 1987 General Social Surveys and the 1967 Political Participation in America Study*

   a.  Describe how each of the following conventional forms of political participation might impact public policy in the United States.

   ■ Voting in a presidential election

   ■ Joining an interest group

   ■ Running for political office

   b.  Describe how participating in a mass demonstration of protest might impact public policy in the United States.

   c.  Describe the relationship between social class and participation in the United States.

   d.  Explain how the relationship between social class and participation impacts Americans' perceptions regarding equality.

2.    One of the most consistent ways that Americans learn about public opinion is through polling. Using the political cartoon below and your knowledge of political polls, answer the following questions:

*Nate Beeler/The Columbus Dispatch/Cagle Cartoons, Inc.*

  a.  Describe the advantage of a random sample for public opinion polling over a nonrandom sample.

  b.  Describe one advantage and one disadvantage of telephone surveys compared to person-to-person interviewing.

  c.  Describe what public opinion polls tell us about Americans' levels of political knowledge.

  d.  Describe what public opinion polls tell us about Americans' political attitudes.

# Answers and Explanations

## Multiple-Choice Questions

1. A    Political socialization is defined in the root of the question.
   *Page reference: 170, AP Big Idea: PRD*

2. B    In all sampling, there is a potential that the sample drawn is not perfectly reflective of the population as a whole.
   *Page reference: 173, AP Big Ideas: PRD, MPA*

3. B    Exit polls are used by media on election days to predict the outcome of an election.
   *Page reference: 175, AP Big Ideas: PRD, MPA*

4. D    Liberals would not favor prayer in government-sponsored schools.
   *Page reference: 180-181, AP Big Ideas: PRD, MPA*

5. C    The term "gender gap" refers to the fact that since 1980, women have tended to be more supportive of Democrats than have men, and this trend is especially strong among unmarried women.
   *Page reference: 181, AP Big Ideas: PRD, MPA*

6. A    Younger voters tend to be more supportive of expanded welfare and environmental programs while older voters tend to support more spending on defense issues and to protect their Social Security benefits.
   *Page reference: 169, AP Big Ideas: PRD, MPA*

7. C    Even though there are many ways of participating in politics, voting is the only way in which more than half of Americans participate in politics.
   *Page reference: 183-188, AP Big Ideas: PRD, MPA*

8. B    A random sample is one in which each person in the population being sampled has an equal chance of being selected.
   *Page reference: 173, AP Big Ideas: PRD, MPA*

9. A    Differences in political knowledge are more accurately predicted by demographic rather than political factors.
   *Page reference: 178, AP Big Ideas: PRD, MPA*

10. C    Individuals with higher levels of political knowledge are not necessarily more likely to donate to political campaigns.
    *Page reference: 178, AP Big Ideas: PRD, MPA*

11. B   While a respondent might answer affirmatively to any question, it is likely that his or her feelings about issues such as abortion, or the death penalty are much more intense than their feelings about the Electoral College or types of voting machines. However, polls rarely have mechanisms to differentiate degrees of passion on an issue.
*Page reference: 172-176, AP Big Ideas: PRD, MPA*

12. B   Tracking polls enable a campaign to chart its daily rise or fall in support.
*Page reference: 172-176 Big Ideas: PRD, MPA*

13. B   Selective exposure is the process by which people consciously choose to get the news from information sources that have viewpoints compatible with their own.
*Page reference: 180-181, AP Big Ideas: PRD, MPA*

14. A   Voter registration is a system designed to reduce voter fraud by limiting voting to those who have established eligibility to vote by submitting the proper documents, including proof of residency.
*Page reference: 183-185, AP Big Ideas: PRD, MPA*

15. B   Public opinion is the distribution of individual preferences for or evaluations of a given issue, candidate, or institution within a specific population.
*Page reference: 163, AP Big Idea: PRD*

16. D   It is the public's task in a democracy to decide who will lead; therefore, the voices will be heard, holding public officials accountable.
*Page reference: 163-170, AP Big Ideas: PRD, MPA*

17. D   Political participation—all the activities used by citizens to influence the selection of political leaders or the policies they pursue—is absolutely necessary to the existence of self-government.
*Page reference: 183-188, AP Big Ideas: PRD, MPA*

18. C   The genuine Independents do not vote consistently and appear to have very little interest in politics.
*Page reference: 180-183, AP Big Ideas: PRD, MPA*

19. D   A sampling error measures the degree to which the sample's opinions might differ from what the population actually thinks. This is the level of confidence in the findings of a public opinion poll and the more people interviewed, the more confident one can be in the results.
*Page reference: 173, AP Big Ideas: PRD, MPA*

20. A   Polls are surveys of public opinion and they are the tool most political scientists and political observers use to assess public opinion.
*Page reference: 171-180, AP Big Ideas: PRD, MPA*

# Free-Response Questions

*This rubric provides examples of many, but not all of the possible correct responses to the free-response questions.*

1.  In the United States, people can participate in politics in many different ways. Use the information from the chart and your knowledge of political participation to answer the following questions:

    a.  Describe how each of the following conventional forms of political participation might impact public policy in the United States.

        ■ Voting in a presidential election

        ■ Joining an interest group

        ■ Running for political office

        ■ Political participation is a fundamental indicator of the health of a democracy. Since in a democracy, the government should respond to the people, the people should participate at high rates. Yet, in the United States, only about half of the people vote. If voting were the only mechanism for participation, that would, perhaps, indicate a problem with democracy.

        ■ Voting in a presidential election is the most common form of political participation. People can vote very easily in the United States since there is no fee for registering to vote, since the racial and gender barriers to voting have been reduced in recent years, and since we now have a motor-voter law that allows people to register even when they renew their driver's licenses. Voting is fundamental in a democracy because it allows people to elect the person who best reflects their ideas about how government should operate. By electing officials, the people have representatives in government. That is the nature of a republican government, and it is therefore a way to influence public policy. In other words, elections are the way that people can staff government with people who will do the people's business.

        ■ There are many less common forms of participation. Many people join interest groups. By joining an interest group, people make their views known, and give interest groups resources that they can use to press for policy changes. Very few people actually run for office, but doing so allows them to change policy directly if they win, and to contribute to debates about policy even if they don't win.

b. Describe how participating in a mass demonstration of protest might impact public policy in the United States.

- Conventional participation, such as voting or joining interest groups, is not the only way that people can affect public policy. Through nonconventional methods such as engaging in nonviolent civil disobedience, people can also get their ideas to be noticed by government. Martin Luther King, Jr. led much of the civil rights movement by using civil disobedience. Although he and other African Americans could not win elections in the South at that time, he could use civil disobedience to gain attention for the civil rights struggle. Eventually, that attention led to national outrage and the civil rights laws were passed. So, as one can see, civil disobedience, though a nonconventional form of participation, can have influence just as a conventional method might.

c. Describe the relationship between social class and participation in the United States.

- Interestingly, the two forms of participation discussed above might be seen as being tactics of people with different social status. People in higher income categories are far more likely to vote than are poor people.

d. Explain how the relationship between social class and participation impacts Americans' perceptions regarding equality.

- The gap in voting between those in different income categories would seem to indicate that equality cannot be realized in U.S. society. However, even poor people can engage in civil disobedience. As a result, equality might be realized.

2. One of the most consistent ways that Americans learn about public opinion is through polling. Using the political cartoon and your knowledge of political polls, answer the following questions:

   a. Describe the advantage of a random sample for public opinion polling over a nonrandom sample.

      ■ A random sample is better than a nonrandom sample because a random sample gives everyone an equal chance of being selected and therefore is more likely to be representative of the population as a whole. With a nonrandom sample, we cannot estimate how likely the sample is to represent the people.

   b. Describe one advantage and one disadvantage of telephone surveys compared to person-to-person interviewing.

      ■ Telephone surveys are both great and bad. They are great because everyone with a phone can be surveyed, and most people have phones. They are bad because people without telephones cannot be surveyed (for example, people who only have cell phones), and because people are less likely to respond to a phone survey than an in-person survey.

   c. Describe what public opinion polls tell us about Americans' levels of political knowledge.

      ■ Surveys tell us that Americans don't know much about politics. They can't answer even simple questions well. Surveys show that Americans know very little about political issues and even less abut geography.

   d. Describe what public opinion polls tell us about Americans' political attitudes.

      ■ Public opinion polls show that Americans most often see themselves as moderates and are less supportive of liberalism than they used to be.

# 7

# The Mass Media and the Political Agenda

## Chapter Overview

Democracy depends upon an informed citizenry, and the citizenry depends on the mass media for its information. As with many areas of American life, the future of the mass media may lie with the internet. The power of the mass media has expanded dramatically since the beginning of the twentieth century. In this chapter, we examine how the mass media function as part of the American political process. We begin by examining the way in which political campaigns and political leaders use the media to communicate their messages. Then, we explore the historical evolution of the media in the United States. Next, we consider the major factors that influence media coverage and attention, and analyze how media coverage affects politics and public policy. Along the way, we also examine how policy entrepreneurs try to use the media to influence the public agenda. We conclude by assessing the effect of the media on the scope of government and democracy in America. By the end of the chapter, students should have a good understanding of how the media function as a political institution, and how they interact with other political actors and institutions to affect politics in the United States.

# Study Outline

**7.1** Learning Objective 7.1: Describe the structure and the functions of the media, past and present (p. 193)

## *The Mass Media Today*

- **Mass Media:** Television, radio, newspapers, magazines, the internet, and other means of popular communication.
- **High tech politics:** A politics in which the behavior of citizens and policymakers and the political agenda itself are increasingly shaped by technology.
- Political leaders have learned to use the media to set their agendas.
- A **media event** is an event that is staged by a political leader with the purpose of getting it covered in the media to shape an image or draw attention to a chosen issue.
- In addition, they can more deliberately use the media to run advertisements.
- Such advertisements are often 30 seconds in length and make up the majority of spending on political campaigns.
- Presidents also use the media to make direct appeals to the public.
- Politics and the mass media go hand in hand.
- However, whereas they once worked together to communicate with the public, today they often oppose each other.
- The mass media came into existence in the 19th century with the birth of the daily newspaper, and blossomed with radio and the television in the middle of the 20th century.
- Franklin Roosevelt (FDR) built a close relationship between the office of the president and the press.
- **Press conferences**, now a common means by which presidents convey their goals and opinions to the public, began with FDR in the 1930s.
- He was also the first president to address the electorate directly through radio broadcasts.
- The Watergate scandal and the Vietnam War changed the government's relationship with the press, as the press became more suspicious about political motives.

- Today the media engage in **investigative journalism**, which often contributes to public cynicism and negativity about politics.

## The Print Media

- Only a few corporations own most of the newspapers in the United States, as well as radio and television stations.
- These major corporations have significant control over information conveyed in the media.
- Newspaper readers tend to be politically informed, active citizens, but newspaper circulation has been declining since the advent of television and the Internet.
- Most daily city newspapers are struggling financially.

## The Emergence of Radio and Television

- Now, most Americans, especially young people, get their information from the **broadcast media**. **Electronic media** includes radio, television, and the Internet.
- Television shifts the public's focus from a politician's achievements and political views to his or her **appearance** and performance in front of the cameras.
- Cable television encourages **narrowcasting**, which allows viewers to select what information they do and do not want to see.
- Critics fear that this will lead to an even less informed electorate that can selectively avoid politics, which is known as **selective exposure**.
- Media in America is free and independent because it is privately owned, but that also means it is totally dependent upon advertising.
- Over four-fifths of the newspapers in America are owned by large corporations (**chains**), as is much of the broadcast media, as well.
- The Federal Communications Commission (FCC) is a regulatory agency that monitors the use of the airwaves.
- While it is independent, the FCC is subject to many political pressures.
- Congress controls the funding of the agency and presidential appointments to the agency are made with political considerations in mind.

- The FCC prevents monopolies, conducts periodic examinations of stations as part of its licensing authority, and issues fair treatment rules concerning access to the airwaves for political candidates and officeholders.
- If a person is attacked on the air, they have the right to respond on the same station; however, the fairness doctrine that was once in place (which required equal time to differing views) was abolished.

### From Broadcasting to Narrowcasting: The Rise of Cable and Cable News

- The first major news networks were described as "broadcasting" because messages were sent to a broad audience.
- With the development of cable TV, narrowcasting (media programming on cable TV or Internet that is focused on one topic and aimed at a narrow audience) is a more appropriate term.
- While there is now a wide variety of news programs available, the quality of content has not necessarily improved. The profit motive is still the driving force behind most news programs.
- **Selective Exposure:** The process through which people consciously choose to get the news from information sources that have viewpoints compatible with their own.

### The Impact of the Internet

- The Internet has made political information easily accessible.
- Citizens can use it to easily retrieve voting records and text of legislation, for example.
- However, researchers have discovered that few Americans are taking advantage of the technology to be better-informed citizens.
- The Internet has also changed reporting.
- The rise of blogs and Twitter has made it more difficult for traditional reporters— faced with competition from everyone who has an opinion on a topic—to file well-researched, objective, and in-depth stories.
- The most popular blogs, though, are written by people who are well-informed and educated, with strong analytical and writing skills.

## Private Control of the Media

- In the United States, control of virtually all media outlets is in private hands. Media in America today tend to be part of large conglomerates, such as Disney or General Electric.

- In the newspaper business, chains control newspapers that together represent over 80 percent of the nation's daily circulation.

- Because of private ownership of the media and the First Amendment right to free speech, American journalists have long had an unfettered capacity to criticize government leaders and policies.

- But the American media are totally dependent on advertising revenues to keep their businesses going, which means that getting the biggest possible audience is the primary objective.

- **Chains:** Groups of newspapers published by media conglomerates and today accounting for over four-fifths of the nation's daily newspaper circulation.

## 7.2 Learning Objective 7.2: List the major criteria that determine which news stories receive the most media attention. (p. 205)

### Reporting the News

- Newscasting is a business geared toward achieving high ratings.

- This can have detrimental consequences for both the political agenda addressed in the news and for the political knowledge of Americans.

- Profits largely determine what is considered news, and sensational, unusual, or negative events usually receive more attention than more positive or everyday policymaking does.

- This leads the public to believe that most of politics is scandalous and to distrust political leaders.

- Journalists usually have regular **beats**, such as the White House, the Senate, or the Pentagon.

- Most of their information comes directly from press secretaries at these institutions.

- This has significant advantages for politicians, who can control how much information is reported to the public, including intentional leaks (**trial balloons**), which can gauge political reaction.

- News reporting, especially through the broadcast media, has very little depth of content.

- Information is reported in **sound bites**, which gloss over the complexity of issues and focus the public's attention on politicians rather than on their policies.

- Sound bites allow politicians to craft political personas without having to directly address an issue.

- They do not have to say much since a typical sound bite is only seven seconds long, and this contributes further to Americans' lack of political knowledge.

- **Bias** is not apparent so much in the way news is presented, but it is a factor in determining what news is reported and what news is not. Television is particularly biased toward stories that generate good pictures instead of using a **talking head**, which is a shot of a person's head talking directly to the camera.

- There is little evidence of bias toward an ideological position or political party, but dramatic or sensational stories are more likely to draw an audience, so they are more likely to be featured in the news.

## 7.3 Learning Objective 7.3: Analyze the impact of the media public opinion and political behavior. (p. 210)

### *The News and Public Opinion*

- The mass media have an enormous influence over the **policy agenda** (the issues that attract the serious attention of public officials and other people actively involved in politics at the time).

- **Policy entrepreneurs:** People who invest their political "capital" in an issue.

- When they select what issues to focus on, news organizations define which are the most pressing political topics and thereby determine the political priorities of the public.

- Policy entrepreneurs seek to influence the policy agenda by getting the media to pay attention to the issues that they are particularly concerned with.

- They employ a variety of strategies to obtain media coverage, including press releases, press conferences, and letter writing.

- Sometimes they will resort to staging dramatic events that are so interesting and unusual that reporters can hardly resist covering them.

- By selectively assigning importance to certain issues, the media essentially tell Americans what to think about.

- The media have shifted attention to individual politicians and away from government as a whole.

- The biggest consequence of this is the increasing amount of attention paid to the president, which as a result enhances his power.

- The media perform a watchdog function by forcing the government to be answerable to the public.

- However, they strongly discourage Americans from thinking critically about politics.

- At the same time, because the news is based on ratings, its content reflects what citizens want to see and read—and they seem to express little interest in politics.

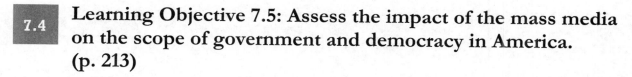 **Learning Objective 7.5: Assess the impact of the mass media on the scope of government and democracy in America. (p. 213)**

## Understanding the Mass Media

- The media acts as a key linkage institution between the people and government.

- The media's watchdog function also helps to restrict politicians and the scope of government

- The watchdog orientation of the press can be characterized as liberal or conservative.

## For Additional Review

As you are reading, take notes on how the media and its role in American society have changed over the last century. Your notes should indicate a "change over time" not only in the types of media, but in the financing, ownership, control, and influence of the media. Use these notes to prepare for the unit test and for the AP Government and Politics exam.

Create a chart in order to compare and contrast the impact of the media on public opinion. List the sources of information along the side of the chart (internet, television, blogs, radio, etc.) and across the top of your chart, create two columns where you will discuss the "pros" and "cons" of each type of media as a source of information. Be sure to address narrowcasting and selective exposure when rating the use of the media. Use this chart when studying for the unit test and when preparing for the AP Government and Politics exam.

# Review Questions

## Multiple-Choice Questions

1.   Which of the following is most likely to effectively use the national media to set the policy agenda?
     a.   the Supreme Court
     b.   Congress
     c.   the president
     d.   state legislators

2.   Which of the following is the best example of a media event?
     a.   the State of the Union Address
     b.   a news report of a presidential candidate reading to elementary school students
     c.   an assassination attempt
     d.   the signing of bipartisan legislation

3.   The Federal Communications Commission (FCC) is which of the following?
     a.   an arm of the U.S. Congress devoted to communications issues
     b.   a special interest group
     c.   the federal judiciary
     d.   an independent regulatory agency

4.   Which of the following is the best example of a trial balloon?
     a.   A presidential nominee leaks the name of one of his choices for vice president to gauge public opinion.
     b.   A president interviews a nominee for a federal judicial appointment.
     c.   Special interest groups testify in order to block a confirmation.
     d.   A citizen launches a fake story on a website to criticize a politician.

5.   All of the following can be accurately stated about sound bites EXCEPT
     a.   presidential candidates use them to state a theme of their campaign.
     b.   they are 15 seconds or shorter.
     c.   they are the way many citizens learn about their candidates.
     d.   they provide detailed policy information.

6. What is the main focus of the media during a presidential campaign?
   a. issues that the candidates support
   b. background and qualification of the candidates
   c. personality of candidates
   d. platform of the party

7. Which of the following best describes the impact of the Internet on politics?
   a. citizens are more informed
   b. citizens have more access to information
   c. citizens are more likely to be liberal
   d. citizens have more trust in government

8. Which of the following have been decreasing over the years?
   a. news outlets
   b. press conferences
   c. State of the Union Addresses
   d. media events

9. Which newspaper broke the Watergate scandal?
   a. *Washington Post*
   b. *USA Today*
   c. *New York Times*
   d. *Chicago Tribune*

10. Which of the following best describes the correlation between the media and trust in government?
    a. As the availability of news has increased, trust in government has decreased.
    b. There is no relationship between the two.
    c. News stories are supportive of political leaders and lead to increased trust.
    d. The media has caused trust in government to rise.

**Questions 11-12 refer to the following graph.**

How the Audiences of Cable News Channels are Polarized by Political Ideology

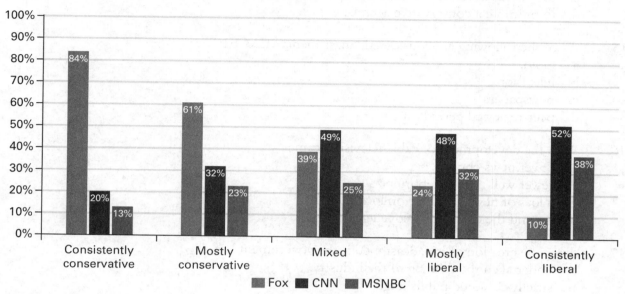

*2014 Pew Research Center Survey Data*

11. Which of the following is demonstrated by the graph?
    a. the tendency of the media to frame political events using well-established stereotypes
    b. the tendency of the media to focus on domestic events rather than international events
    c. the increasing reliance of the media on political pundits
    d. targeting media programs at specific segments of the population, known as narrowcasting

12. The chart indicates media typically have little influence on public opinion because
    a. the media are required to present both sides of a story, leaving little room to influence public opinion.
    b. the media are owned by the same corporations that conduct public opinion polls.
    c. people tend to ignore all political information from the media due to its well-known biases.
    d. typically, people only pay attention to media coverage that is consistent with their own political preferences.

13. What is agenda setting?
    a. the ability of the media to influence public opinion about which issues the government should address
    b. the tendency to remember only those news stories that are consistent with one's predispositions
    c. the ability of the media to influence the public's opinions on issues
    d. the media's focus on scandal and corruption

14. The deepest bias among political journalists is
    a. the desire to produce content that will gain the highest ratings or readership.
    b. to promote a liberal agenda.
    c. to provide accurate—even if boring—information to the public.
    d. to promote a conservative agenda.

15. All of the following are considered "mass media" EXCEPT
    a. radio.
    b. television.
    c. newspapers.
    d. peer-reviewed periodical.

16. With the development of cable television came
    a. fewer news choices.
    b. fewer well-trained reporters.
    c. a loss of news coverage on local stations.
    d. around the clock news coverage.

17. Since the creation of broadcast media, the government has
    a. undertaken the funding of the industry.
    b. strictly censored publishing.
    c. taken a "hands off" approach to the industry.
    d. engaged in regulation of the industry.

18. Which of the following media has grown into an unprecedented source of public information for the world?
    a. CNN
    b. MSNBC
    c. PBS
    d. the Internet

19. The relatively high cost of advertising using this medium accounts, in part, for the high cost of political campaigns.
    a. newspapers
    b. the Internet
    c. television
    d. radio

20. The mass media targets
    a. the wealthy.
    b. the largest audience possible.
    c. elected officials.
    d. registered voters.

## Free-Response Questions

1.     Use the information from the photo below and your knowledge of the mass media's impact on the scope of government and democracy in America to answer the following questions:

*Brett Carlson/Getty Images News/Getty Images*

    a. Describe the watchdog role of the media.

    b. Describe how media crusades against injustices in American society.

    c. Explain how the crisis in Flint, Michigan over contaminated drinking water relates to both a. and b.

2.     The mass media greatly impacts the course of a president's administration. Defend this statement by doing all of the following:

    a. Define three of the terms below.

- press conferences
- fireside chat
- sound bites
- media event

    b. For each term you defined, explain its impact on the course of a presidential administration.

# Answers and Explanations

## Multiple-Choice Questions

1. C   Most modern presidents have successfully used television to make direct appeals to the public. President Reagan, for example, used prime time television to make direct appeals to citizens to take grassroots action on a political issue. Other organizations such as Congress are more decentralized and therefore have a more difficult time collectively using the media.
   *Page reference: 194-196, AP Big Ideas: PRD, PMI*

2. B   Media events are deliberately staged events by political figures to get attention. While the State of the Union gets broad media coverage, it is an event required by the U.S. Constitution and therefore is not the best example of a media event. Events that are not in a politician's control would not be good examples of media events, nor would events that do not get much media attention.
   *Page reference: 194, AP Big Ideas: PRD, PMI*

3. D   The Federal Communications Commission is an independent regulatory agency.
   *Page reference: 198, AP Big Idea: PRD*

4. A   A trial balloon occurs when a political figure leaks information to the public to try to decide what the public would think if an event were to occur. For example, Al Gore leaked his choice of Joe Lieberman as a running mate in order to see if the public approved of his choice.
   *Page reference: 206, AP Big Idea: PRD*

5. D   Sound bites do not provide much information to citizens about candidates.
   *Page reference: 208, AP Big Idea: PRD*

6. C   Political races today are called candidate-centered because of the focus on candidate personality, rather than issues, background or qualifications.
   *Page reference: 193-198, AP Big Ideas: PRD, PMI*

7. B   The Internet has not made citizens more informed or changed their opinion, but has made information more widely available.
   *Page reference: 201-204, AP Big Ideas: PRD, PMI*

8. B   Presidents are holding fewer regularly scheduled press conferences.
   *Page reference: 195, AP Big Ideas: PRD, PMI*

9. A   The *Washington Post* broke the Watergate Scandal.
   *Page reference: 195; 207, AP Big Ideas: PRD, PMI*

10. A   Trust in government has declined as the availability of information about government has increased.
    *Page reference: 210-212, AP Big Idea: PRD*

11. D   Narrowcasting is media programming on cable TV or the Internet that is focused on a particular interest and aimed at a particular audience, in contrast to broadcasting.
*Page reference: 199, AP Big Idea: PRD*

12. D   Studies show that people tend to ignore media information that is inconsistent with their existing beliefs or personal experiences.
*Page reference: 201, AP Big Idea: PRD*

13. A   Agenda setting is the process of forming the list of issues to be addressed by the government.
*Page reference: 212-213, AP Big Idea: PRD*

14. A   The media depend on an audience for success, and even survival. This compels them to seek out stories that will attract viewers or readers. While the dynamics of narrowcasting sometimes results in slanting a story ideologically to capture higher ratings, the primary driver is the audience.
*Page reference: 209-210, AP Big Idea: PRD*

15. D   A peer-reviewed journal is an academic journal specific to a particular discipline and does not receive mass circulation.
*Page reference: 193-194, AP Big Idea: PRD*

16. D   The advent of cable television provided the opportunity for 24-hour-a-day news channels and programs.
*Page reference: 199-201, AP Big Idea: PRD*

17. D   Since its inception, the government has regulated broadcast media using the Federal Communications Commission.
*Page reference: 198, AP Big Ideas: PRD, PMI*

18. D   The Internet, since its creation, has become a massive source of public information around the world.
*Page reference: 201-204, AP Big Idea: PRD*

19. C   Television advertising is an important part of political campaigns, and due to the expense of television advertising, the use of this medium has contributed to the high cost of campaigning.
*Page reference: 203-204, AP Big Ideas: PRD, PMI*

20. B   The mass media, driven by ratings, selects programming in order to reach the largest audience possible.
*Page reference: 194204, AP Big Ideas: PRD, PMI*

# Free-Response Questions

*This rubric provides examples of many, but not all of the possible correct responses to the free-response questions.*

1.  Use the information from the photo and your knowledge of the mass media's impact on the scope of government and democracy in America to answer the following questions:

    a.  Describe the watchdog role of the media.

        - The media's watchdog function helps keep politicians in check. This is one of the aspects of the media's job performance that American's consistently evaluate positively. Research has consistently demonstrated that a clear majority of the public has said that press criticism of political leaders does more good than harm. The majority of the public believes it keeps leaders from doing things that should not be done (but others believes it keeps political leaders from doing their jobs.)

    b.  Describe how media crusades against injustices in American society.

        - Reporters often see their jobs as crusading against foul play and unfairness in government and society. This focus on injustice inevitably encourages enlarging the scope of government.

    c.  Explain how the crisis in Flint, Michigan over contaminated drinking water relates to both a. and b.

        - The crisis in Flint, Michigan, drew much media attention. Reporters called for the government to address the need for a clean and reliable supply of drinking water to the citizens of Flint. The coverage of this problem is a demonstration of the watchdog function of the media because it pointed to governmental issues that caused the problem and called for officeholders to use their positions to solve the problem. The media crusaded for the resolution of the problem and advocated for local, state, and national solutions to the problem.

2.    The mass media greatly impacts the course of a president's administration. Defend this statement by doing all of the following:

a.   Define three of the terms below.

- press conferences
- fireside chat
- sound bites
- media event

b.   For each term you defined, explain its impact on the course of a presidential administration.

- The First Amendment to the Constitution gives freedom to the press and allows media outlets to publish critical stories about the president of the United States. This freedom has an important impact on the president because information both flattering and unflattering about the president is widely available in the United States. Presidents have access to the media and can use this power to improve their image. At the same time, the independent media is likely to publish stories that are negative in tone.

- Press conferences are meetings held by the president with members of the press. They can have a negative impact on presidential approval. These meetings are not required by law or the Constitution, therefore presidents have some control over how many press conferences are held. Presidents can also ask their press secretary to hold the meetings for them. Press conferences are frequently confrontational in nature and can lead to discussions about scandals that have been published. For example, during Bill Clinton's presidency, he was directly asked about the Monica Lewinsky scandal in a press conference in spite of the fact that he had tried to turn the conversation to other topics. Because of the possibility of being questioned about scandals and unflattering events, modern presidents have tended not to hold press conferences.

- The fireside chat began with FDR's presidency. These take place when presidents use the radio to communicate directly with citizens. They tend to have a positive impact on the president's term because there are no or few combative questions directed at the president. The president can set the tone of the talks and provide the information that he wants. Such "chats" are frequently used to attempt to change public opinion. FDR used fireside chats to change public opinion to favor the country's entry into World War II.

- Sound bites are short video clips of approximately 10 seconds, and are frequently all that are shown of a president's speech on the news. These can have a positive or negative impact on the president, depending on how the statements are portrayed in the media. A president may choose a particular sound bite and repeat it in order to generate a high likelihood that it is on the news, but also the media may choose a sound bite that the president is unhappy about.

# 8

# Political Parties

## Chapter Overview

America's Founding Fathers were more concerned with their fear that political parties could be forums for corruption and national divisiveness than they were with the role that parties could play in making politics user-friendly for ordinary voters. In his farewell address, President George Washington warned against the growing influence of political parties.

Today, most observers would agree that political parties have contributed greatly to American democracy. The strength of the parties has an impact not only on how we are governed but also on what government does. Major expansions and contractions of the scope of government have generally been accomplished through the implementation of one party's platform. Currently, the Democrats and Republicans differ greatly on the issue of the scope of government. Which party controls the presidency and whether the same party also controls the Congress make a big difference.

In this chapter, we analyze the role of political parties in American politics. We begin by outlining the functions that parties perform in American democracy. Then we explore the significance of party identification. We describe how parties are organized in the United States, and evaluate how well parties generally implement their platforms. Next, we examine the historical evolution of political parties in the United States. We conclude by evaluating the role of third parties in the American political system, and determine why the two-party system has persisted. By the end of the chapter, students should have a good understanding of the role of political parties in American politics.

# Study Outline

**Learning Objective 8.1: Identify the functions of political parties. (p. 219)**

### The Meaning of Party

- A **political party** is a team of men and women seeking to control the governing apparatus by gaining office in an election.
- Political parties carry out several tasks, including choosing candidates, running campaigns, giving cues to voters, articulating policies, and coordinating policymaking.
- Political parties serve as **linkage institutions**, which are channels through which concerns become political issues on the government's policy agenda.
- **Rational choice theory** explains the actions of voters, politicians, and parties.
- It assumes that individuals act in their best interest and weigh the costs and benefits of possible alternatives.
- In order to win office, candidates select policies that are widely favored.
- The majority of voters are in the middle ideologically, so centrist parties win elections.
- This has led to criticism of the two major parties for being too similar.

**Learning Objective 8.2: Determine the significance of party identification in America today. (p. 223)**

### The Party in the Electorate

- Many voters cast their ballots on the basis of **party identification**.
- For instance, people who consider themselves Democrats usually vote for Democratic candidates.
- Party identification is declining, however; as of 2000, the more voters considered themselves Independent than either Democratic or Republican.
- **Party image** is the voter's perception of what the Republicans and Democrats stand for, such as conservatism and liberalism.

- **Ticket splitting**, or voting for members of different parties for different offices in an election, is also on the rise.
- This practice leads to a divided party government—the president may be of a different party from the majority party in Congress, for example.

| 8.3 | **Learning Objective 8.3: Describe the structure of political parties at the national, state, and local level. (p. 225)** |
|---|---|

## *The Party Organizations: From the Grass Roots to Washington*

- Unlike the more formal parties of other countries, American political parties are fairly decentralized, with city, state, and national administrative bodies.
- State parties are becoming more formally organized, but most presidential campaigning is still conducted through the candidate's personal campaign organization.
- Holding elections is one important task performed by the states, each of which has its own unique party organization.
- Each state's parties go about the election process differently, such as by choosing which type of primary to hold. There are three main types of primaries: closed, open, and blanket.
- Until the 1930s, local parties had tremendous influence over city governments.
- These often-corrupt **party machines** maintained their power by using the **patronage system** to reward loyal members with important positions in the government.
- Today local parties have declined, while county-level organizations have increased their election activities.
- **Closed Primaries:** Elections to select party nominees in which only people who have registered in advance with the party can vote for that party's candidates, thus encouraging greater party loyalty.
- **Open Primaries:** Elections to select party nominees in which voters can decide on Election Day whether they want to participate in the Democratic or Republican contests.

- The national party organization, or **national committee**, writes the official party platform and holds the **national convention** through which a presidential and vice presidential candidate are nominated.
- **National Chairperson:** The person responsible for running the ongoing activities of the national party organization.
- The national committee maintains the party organization during nonelection years.

## 8.4 Learning Objective 8.4: Evaluate how well political parties generally do in carrying out their promises. (p. 229)

### The Party in Government: Promises and Policy

- Parties help members of Congress form **coalitions** that support a particular policy objective; however, presidents do not need to rely on party support as much as they used to because they can gain the favor of the public directly through television.

## 8.5 Learning Objective 8.5: Trace the Evolution of political parties in America. (p. 229)

### Party Eras in American History

- Most democratic nations have multiparty systems that allow many interests to be represented.
- The United States, however, has always had a two-party system. Political scientists divide American history into **party eras** in which one party dominated politics for a significant period of time.
- Party eras change when a **critical election** reveals new issues and a failure of the traditional coalitions. This usually causes **party realignment**, when the party redefines itself and attracts a new coalition of voters.
- The **First Party System** (1796–1824) started with Alexander Hamilton's short-lived Federalist Party, the first American political party.
- For most of the period, though, Thomas Jefferson's Democratic-Republicans maintained control of the White House.

- During the period of the **Democrats and the Whigs** (1828–1856), Andrew Jackson appealed to the masses rather than to the elite.

- He formed a new coalition and, ultimately, the Democratic Party.

- The opposition party was the Whig Party, though it had little political success.

- The **Two Republican Eras** (1860–1928) were dominated by the Republican Party, but these eras saw a major realignment of party coalitions under the same name.

- The Republican Party formed out of a coalition of antislavery groups and nominated Abraham Lincoln as its first presidential candidate.

- The election of 1896 began another strongly Republican era during which industrialization and capitalism were advanced.

- The **New Deal Coalition** (1932–1964) formed when Franklin Roosevelt brought the Democratic Party back into favor by starting scores of federal programs to combat the Great Depression.

- The new Democratic coalition brought together the poor, Southerners, African Americans, city dwellers, Catholics, and Jews. Kennedy's New Frontier and Johnson's Great Society and War on Poverty continued the Democratic New Deal tradition.

- Since 1968, we have seen **Southern realignment** and **divided party government**.

- The states in the South have realigned and are now strongholds of the Republican Party.

- President Nixon was able to capture the South, which had previously been solidly Democratic.

- When Nixon became president, there was divided government for the first time in the 20th century, with one party controlling Congress and another controlling the White House.

- This became a frequent election pattern for most presidents that followed him.

- The trend in divided government has led many political scientists to believe that the party system has dealigned rather than realigned.

- **Party dealignment** means that people are gradually moving away from both parties.

## 8.6 Learning Objective 8.6: Evaluate the role of minor parties in the U.S. electoral system. (p. 236)

### Third Parties: Their Impact on American Politics

- **Third parties** occasionally arise to challenge the two major parties, but they rarely gain enough support to put a candidate in office.

- Some parties form around a specific cause; some are splinter parties, formed from smaller factions of the two major parties, and some form around a specific individual.

- Though they rarely win, third-party candidates do force particular issues onto the political agenda and allow Americans to express their discontent with the two major parties.

- They may also shift the votes of the electorate; for example, many political scientists think George W. Bush won the 2000 election because Green Party candidate Ralph Nader took votes away from Democrat Al Gore. The American **winner-take-all system** is an electoral system in which legislative seats are awarded to candidates who come in first.

- In presidential elections, the candidate who comes in first gets all of the state's electoral votes. This makes only two parties likely.

- **Proportional representation** is an electoral system in which seats in a legislative branch are awarded in proportion to the percentage of the vote received, making it likely that many parties will win seats.

- This often makes a **coalition government** necessary, in which two or more parties join together to form a majority in a national legislature.

## 8.7 Learning Objective 8.7: Evaluate the advantages and disadvantages of responsible party government. (p. 237)

## Understanding Political Parties

### Democracy and Responsible Party Government

- Political parties today are considered to be essential to a democratic system and the prevention of totalitarian rule, although the framers of the Constitution were wary of political parties.

- Critics of the two-party system allege that there is little choice for voters because the two parties keep to the middle of the road, that there is less opportunity for political change, and that the party system is so decentralized that it fails to translate campaign promises into policy because politicians do not have to vote with the party line.

- Critics of the two-party system have proposed the **responsible party model**, which describes how parties should offer choices to voters, follow through with campaign promises, and accept responsibility as a party for the performance of the government.

- American officeholders do not always follow the platform planks of their party; for example, the Texas Democrats do not always want to vote in line with New York Democrats.

### American Political Parties and the Scope of Government

- American political parties do not require party discipline the way many European party systems do.

- The weak party structure of the United States makes it harder to pass legislation.

- Political parties have declined in strength.

- The political party is no longer the major source of information for citizens.

## For Additional Review

Design a pyramid diagram depicting the top-down leadership structure within a political party (national level, state level, local level). Place the various party members on the pyramid along with a description of the role played by each. Use this pyramid diagram when reviewing and studying for the unit test and the AP Government and Politics exam.

Create a timeline depicting the evolution of political parties in the United States. Place the major eras of political party development on the timeline along with a description of each era, including the political parties, their platforms, and accomplishments. Use this timeline when reviewing and studying for the unit test and the AP Government and Politics exam.

# Review Questions

## Multiple-Choice Questions

1. All of the following are functions of political parties EXCEPT
   a. dictating policies.
   b. choosing candidates.
   c. running campaigns.
   d. giving cues to voters.

2. Which of the following is true of the Southern states?
   a. They have always leaned Republican.
   b. They have always leaned Democratic.
   c. They have no political leaning.
   d. They were once loyal to the Democratic Party but now are loyal to the Republican Party.

3. All of the following are true of the party machine EXCEPT
   a. they were successful in creating party loyalists.
   b. they provided jobs and favors for voters.
   c. they were corrupt.
   d. legislation has largely dismantled them.

4. Which of the following is true of an open primary?
   a. They allow crossover voting.
   b. They receive high turnout.
   c. They are the only system used to select a presidential candidate.
   d. They require that voters be registered with the party.

5. Which of the following is the best definition of "realignment"?
   a. the abandonment of citizens from the two major parties to be independent
   b. the requirement that members of a party vote together
   c. the party that controls the White House loses control in Congress
   d. a major ideological and demographic shift within a party

6. Which of the following was least likely to join the New Deal coalition?
   a. minority voters
   b. blue-collar voters
   c. voters without a college education
   d. wealthy voters

7. Obstacles to third parties' success include all of the following EXCEPT
   a. the winner-take-all rule.
   b. lack of funding from interest groups.
   c. inability to participate in the debate.
   d. inability to get media attention.

8. A two-party system differs from a multiparty system in that it
   a. encourages moderation in policymaking and discourages change.
   b. offers voters no choice among ideologies.
   c. usually includes a liberal and a conservative party.
   d. relies on popular elections to change the party in power.

9. Which of the following has led to ticket splitting in recent elections?
   a. partisan dealignment
   b. open primaries
   c. party realignment
   d. patronage system

10. The event in which the parties formally nominate their candidate for the presidency is called
   a. a critical election.
   b. a national convention.
   c. an open primary.
   d. a closed primary.

11. The U.S. has a "single member, plurality" system, often referred to as
   a. direct representation.
   b. proportional representation.
   c. winner-take-all.
   d. winner-take-most.

**Questions 12-13 refer to the following graph.**

Party Identification in the United States, 1952-2016

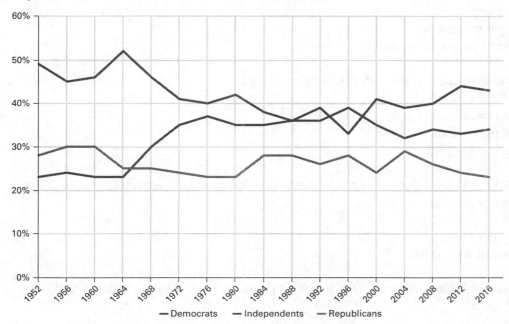

Note: A small percentage of people who identify with a minor party or who cannot answer the question are excluded.
*American National Election Studies, 1952–2012; an average of eight ABC News/Washington Post polls conducted between January and October of 2016.*

12. Which of the following statements is reflected in the data of the graph?
    a. In 1952-1980, Republicans greatly outnumbered Democrats.
    b. In 2016, there were 10% more Republicans than Democrats.
    c. In 2016, 42% of the population called themselves Independents.
    d. In 1964, there were more than twice as many Republicans than Democrats.

13. A citizen's personal affinity for a political party, which results in the citizen voting for candidates of that political party, is known as party
    a. identification.
    b. registration.
    c. alignment.
    d. coalition.

14. Which of the following statements about political parties is accurate?
    a. The U.S. has never had a third party.
    b. The Democratic and Republican parties have been on the presidential ballot for every election since the presidency of George Washington.
    c. Third parties are prohibited by the Constitution.
    d. While the Democrats and Republicans have dominated American politics, they have also seen competition from a wide variety of third parties.

15.　　Many Americans do not associate with either major political party and instead claim to "vote for the ____ and not the ____."
a. party; person
b. person; party
c. challenger; incumbent
d. free-rider; policy entrepreneur

16.　　The top official of each of the two major parties is the
a. national convention chair.
b. national committee chair.
c. national party chair.
d. national party leader.

17.　　Even though the United States has many minor political parties, it remains
a. a multiparty system.
b. a two-party system.
c. a third party system.
d. a parliamentary system.

18.　　The political condition in which different political parties control the presidency and the Congress is called
a. gridlock.
b. dual federalism.
c. cooperative federalism.
d. divided government.

19.　　Political party platforms can best be described as which of the following?
a. They are strictly followed by elected officials.
b. They are written by the president.
c. They are intentionally vague.
d. They are different from state-to-state.

20.　　The gradual disengagement of people from the political parties in order to become Independents is known as
a. realignment.
b. misalignment.
c. party patronage.
d. dealignment.

# Free-Response Questions

1. The power of the political party has declined over the past fifty years. Using your knowledge of party eras in American History, complete the tasks below.

   a. Define each of the terms below:

   - Dealignment
   - Political machine
   - National party conventions

   b. Choose two of the terms above and explain how they have contributed to the decline of political parties since 1960

2. The Democratic and Republican parties have gone through several realignments. Using the graph below and your knowledge of political party realignment, answer the following questions:

Realignment in the South

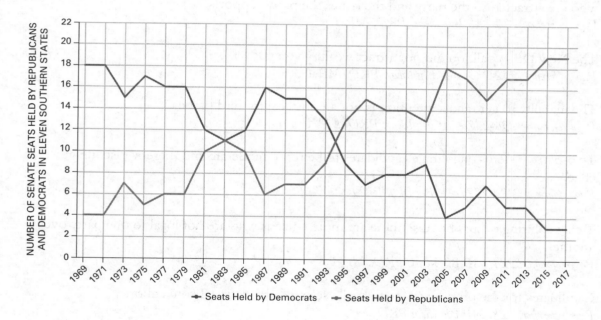

Seats Held by Democrats    Seats Held by Republicans

   a. Define realignment.

   b. Identify one realignment for the Democratic Party and one for the Republican Party.

   c. Explain the significance of realignments for American politics.

# Answers and Explanations

## Multiple-Choice Questions

1. A   American political parties may articulate policy preferences, but they are unable to dictate policy.
   *Page reference: 219-221, AP Big Idea: PRD*

2. D   The South was once "solidly Democratic" but now leans Republican.
   *Page reference: 233-235, AP Big Ideas: PRD, MPA*

3. D   The party machines relied on the patronage system.
   *Page reference: 225, AP Big Idea: PRD*

4. A   Open primaries allow citizens of either party to participate in the primary and this allows crossover voting, or a person of one party voting in another party's primary.
   *Page reference: 227, AP Big Idea: PRD*

5. D   Realignments are major changes within a party. Change occurs both in the type of voters who are attracted to the party and the issues the party supports.
   *Page reference: 230, AP Big Ideas: PRD, MPA*

6. D   The New Deal coalition did not attract wealthy voters.
   *Page reference: 232-233, AP Big Ideas: PRD, MPA*

7. D   The inability to get media attention is not an obstacle to third parties.
   *Page reference: 236-237, AP Big Ideas: PRD, MPA*

8. A   Two-party systems encourage candidates to be more moderate and thereby discourage change.
   *Page reference: 229-237, AP Big Idea: PRD*

9. A   Ticket splitting occurs because there are more citizens who are not loyal to one party over another.
   *Page reference: 224, AP Big Ideas: PRD, MPA*

10. B   Candidates for the presidency are formally selected at a national convention.
    *Page reference: 228, AP Big Idea: PRD*

11. C   National level elections in the U.S. use a system in which the party that receives at least one more vote than any other party wins the seat in question, which is known as winner-take-all.
    *Page reference: 236, AP Big Idea: PRD*

12. C   In 2016, 42% of the population called themselves Independents.
    *Page reference: 223-225, AP Big Ideas: PRD, MPA*

13. A   A citizen's personal affinity for a political party, usually expressed by a tendency to vote for the candidates of that party, is called the citizen's party identification.
*Page reference: 224, AP Big Ideas: PRD, MPA*

14. D   Although third-party candidates rarely win elections, several have appeared on the ballot over the years and have had some effect on the political debate, and possibly the outcome of elections.
*Page reference: 236-237, AP Big Idea: PRD*

15. B   With the decline in party identification, the plurality of voters considered themselves Independent rather than Democratic or Republican, and many Americans insist that they vote for "the person, not the party."
*Page reference: 223-225, AP Big Ideas: PRD, MPA*

16. B   The top official of each of the two major political parties is the national committee chair.
*Page reference: 228, AP Big Idea: PRD*

17. B   The United States still remains predominately a two-party system despite the existence of minor parties.
*Page reference: 236-237, AP Big Idea: PRD*

18. D   Divided government is governance divided between the parties, as when one holds the presidency and the other controls one or both houses of Congress.
*Page reference: 229 AP Big Idea: PMI*

19. C   Party platforms are often written in vague terms to avoid controversy.
*Page reference: 233-236, AP Big Ideas: PRD, PMI*

20. D   The gradual disengagement of people from parties, as seen in part by shrinking party identification, is party dealignment.
*Page reference: 236, AP Big Ideas: PRD, MPA*

# Free-Response Questions

*This rubric provides examples of many, but not all of the possible correct responses to the free-response questions.*

1.  The power of the political party has declined over the past fifty years. Using your knowledge of party eras in American History, complete the tasks below.

    a.  Define each of the terms below:

        ■ Dealignment

        ■ Political machine

        ■ National party conventions

    b.  Choose two of the terms above and explain how they have contributed to the decline of political parties since 1960.

        ■ The power of the party has declined over the past one hundred years. This is due to a dealignment movement. Dealignment refers to the abandonment of citizen's affiliations with the two major political parties to become "independent" voters. Such independent or swing voters have hurt the power of the party because the members of the party must now battle for the ideological center rather than loyalists in order to win an election. The party can no longer depend on large numbers of citizens to vote a straight ticket, and thus the election results become a little more unpredictable. Also, presidents are less likely to staff government with all party loyalists and are more likely to turn to independents.

        ■ The decline of the political (party) machine has also hurt the power of the party. The party machine can be described as a party organization with lots of power in large cities. Such a machine once guaranteed social services and jobs to new immigrants, ran conventions, and staffed city government. This created a group of party loyalists that lasted for generations. Some of these activities became illegal, causing the party to lose strength as the generations of party loyalists diminished.

        ■ Finally, the national party convention was once a source of party strength, but this strength has diminished greatly. The national party used to determine the nominee for the presidency, with no voter involvement at all. The progressive reforms stripped this power from the party at the state level and eventually all states began holding primaries and caucuses to determine the nominee, taking the power away from the party.

2. The Democratic and Republican parties have gone through several realignments. Using the graph and your knowledge of political party realignment, answer the following questions:

   a. Define realignment.

      - A realignment usually occurs after a critical election. A realignment marks a major change in the nature of the political party. The change occurs in both the demographic groups that once supported the party as well as the agenda of the party. In a realignment, the party that was once the majority usually becomes the minority. The change is national as well as local, and the change is not simply marked by one election but has some permanence.

   b. Identify one realignment for the Democratic Party and one for the Republican Party.

      - Most political scientists argue that there have been four major realigning periods. Perhaps the most remembered realignment for the Republican Party took place after the election of 1860—sometimes referred to as the "birth of the Republican Party." The new president, Abraham Lincoln, had captured a new group of voters and his party dominated politics (the party realigned several times after that). Perhaps the most remembered realignment for the Democratic Party came after the election of 1932. Franklin D. Roosevelt began a "New Deal" coalition, which would unify the Democratic Party for years to come.

   c. Explain the significance of realignments for American politics.

      - Realignments are significant to American politics because they mark major changes in the nature of the party, and the party emerges as a completely different organization. Understanding realignments helps to explain how parties have changed. For example, it is surprising to some that Thomas Jefferson was a Democrat because he was a states' rights advocate, and the Democratic Party today has advocated federal power in most domestic policy areas. The explanation for this is that the Democratic Party has realigned since Thomas Jefferson was a member of the party.

# 9

# Campaigns and Voting Behavior

## Chapter Overview

In the United States, the current style of long and arduous campaigns reflects many reformers' belief that the cure for the problems of democracy is more democracy. Whether this approach is helpful or harmful to democracy is a question that provokes much debate, specifically with respect to American political campaigns. Some scholars believe it is important that presidential candidates go through a long and difficult trial by fire. Others, however, worry that the system makes it difficult for politicians with other responsibilities—such as incumbent governors and senior senators—to take a run at the White House. This chapter will give you a better understanding of the pros and cons of having a nomination and campaign process that is so open and democratic. As you read this chapter, consider whether today's nomination and campaign process provides *too much* opportunity for interaction between the public and candidates for office, and consider whether the entire process takes too much time and costs too much money. These are very important topics of debate in American politics.

# Study Outline

## 9.1 Learning Objective 9.1: Evaluate the fairness of the presidential primary and caucus system. (p. 245)

### *The Nomination Game*

- A nomination is a party's official endorsement of a candidate for office.
- Politicians begin their bid for a presidential nomination more than a year in advance of the election. In most other countries, campaigns are limited to only a few months.
- Most candidates have previously held a government post, such as representative, senator, governor, or military general.
- The master game plan candidates lay out to guide their electoral campaign is the **campaign strategy**.

### *Competing for Delegates*

- Each state selects delegates to send to the Democratic and the Republican **national conventions**, which have the supreme power to select the presidential nominee for the party.
- **McGovern-Fraser Commission:** A commission formed at the 1968 Democratic convention in response to demands for reform by minority groups and others who sought better representation at the convention.
- Some convention seats are reserved for **superdelegates**, party leaders and politicians who automatically earn a vote at the convention.
- The Democratic Party makes greater use of superdelegates than the Republican Party.
- A few states still use traditional **caucuses** to choose delegates, which are closed meetings of party regulars who participate in party building activities and select nominees.
- Most states now use **primaries** where voters can nominate a presidential candidate directly, or else they can choose delegates who have pledged to vote for that candidate.

- State parties may have open primaries, where any registered voter can fill out a party nomination ballot, or closed primaries, where advanced party registration is required.
- **Invisible primary:** The period before any votes are cast when candidates compete to win early support from the elite of the party and to create a positive first impression of their leadership skills.
- **Frontloading:** The recent tendency of states to hold primaries early in the calendar in order to capitalize on media attention.
- The political parties in each state decide how to divide its delegates' votes.
- Delegates are apportioned to each candidate based on their proportion of the vote in each state congressional district.
- The Republican Party gives all votes to the candidate with the majority vote in each district.
- The Democratic Party divides delegates proportionally by district and statewide. The rise of primaries has allowed the electorate to take control of the election process away from political parties.
- The primary system has raised numerous criticisms:
  - The early caucuses and primaries receive far too much media attention, which can distort campaigns and candidates who do not score early victories are likely to be dismissed by the media and the public and to be unable to raise funds to continue campaigning.
  - The lengthy campaign and rigors of the primary season discourage some capable politicians from running.
  - It requires and encourages an exorbitant amount of spending in campaigns.
  - Primaries are unrepresentative of the electorate because few people vote in them, and those who do are more likely to be older and wealthier than the majority of Americans.
  - It allows the media, which focuses on winners and dismisses losers early in the running, tremendous influence in shaping campaigns.
- One proposal by critics of the current system is a **national primary**, which would replace the extended primary calendar with a nationwide primary held on one day.
- Another proposal calls for regional primaries, which would allow regions to have primaries, with rotation of the order of regional primaries every four years.

## The Convention Send-Off

- The delegates selected in each state's primary attend the **national convention**, where they cast their votes for their presidential candidate.

- The parties, especially the Democrats, have made efforts to reform delegate selection to ensure representation of youth, minorities, women, and organized labor at the convention.

- Some convention seats are reserved for **superdelegates**, party leaders and politicians who automatically earn a vote at the convention.

- The Democratic Party makes greater use of superdelegates than the Republican Party.

- The outcome of conventions today is usually predetermined by previous primary results, so conventions today are media events.

- At a national convention, delegates support their candidate, the party presents its official **party platform** for the next four years, the winning candidate formally accepts the party's nomination, and the party's vice-presidential nominee is chosen, usually based on the presidential nominee's preference for a running mate.

## 9.2 Learning Objective 9.2: Describe campaigning methods and strategies. (p. 253)

### The Campaign Game

- The two presidential candidates then embark on a **national campaign** to win the votes of different groups in different regions of the country.

- Modern campaign techniques include television advertising, televised public appearances, **direct mail** campaigns, and an official website to advance the candidate's platform and collect campaign contributions.

- The media closely follow campaigns and coverage focuses on the candidates' daily activities, campaign strategies, and poll results.

- Studies show that voters learn more about the candidates' positions on important issues from their advertisements than from the news.

- Critics fear that campaigns have become centered on candidates' images rather than their political beliefs.
- To coordinate a campaign, a candidate must hire a campaign team that serves to organize his or her daily activities and conducts the allocation of scarce resources of time, money and energy to achieve the goal of winning elections for political office. This adds significantly to the enormous cost of a campaign.

## Learning Objective 9.3: Identify how the financing of federal campaigns is regulated and evaluate the influence of money in elections. (p. 257)

### *Money and Campaigning*

- Candidates rely on television to communicate directly with the electorate, and airtime often translates into votes, and therefore, the necessity of television has made American campaigns extremely expensive.
- **Campaign contributions:** Donations that are made directly to a candidate or a party and that must be reported to the FEC. As of 2016, individuals were allowed to donate up to $2,700 per election to a candidate and up to $33,400 to a political party.
- **Independent Expenditures:** Expenses on behalf of a political message that are made by groups that are uncoordinated with any candidate's campaign.
- Politicians spend as much time fundraising as doing their jobs.
- In 1974, Congress passed the **Federal Election Campaign Act (FECA)** to attempt to control campaign costs and donations, which established the **Federal Election Commission** to enforce campaign laws, and initiated public financing of elections.
- Taxpayers can choose to donate $3 to a federal campaign fund that is divided among all candidates by checking a box on their income tax form (**Presidential Election Campaign Fund**).
- FECA also set limits for spending in each election by those who accept public funds.
- Under FECA, candidates are required to **report all campaign contributions and how the money was spent**. Individual campaign contributions were limited to $2,000 in the original legislation, but increased to $2,700 in 2016.

- **Soft money** is one loophole through which businesses and wealthy individuals can make unlimited contributions.
- Soft money is intended for a party's general use; since it is therefore not a donation to a specific candidate, it can be channeled into presidential campaigns.
- The **Bipartisan Campaign Reform Act (BCRA or McCain–Feingold)** attempted to ban soft money, as the candidate often rewards contributors once he or she is in office.
- The Supreme Court upheld the act against a constitutional challenge in 2003.
- A loophole in the BCRA allowed 527 organizations to form and raise unlimited amounts of money to spend on advertising and voter mobilization efforts.
- **Political action committees (PACs)**, established in 1974 by the FECA, are another method through which interest groups try to influence policy through campaign contributions.
- To contribute to a campaign, an interest group must channel money through a PAC, which must be registered with the FEC so that it can be monitored.
- There is **no limit** to the amount PACs can spend. **Super PACs** may accept donations of any size and can endorse candidates.
- PACs can act independently of the candidate and his or her campaign team by running an advertisement without the candidate's approval.
- Created to provide unions and other groups the opportunity to contribute, PACs have been organized and used by businesses to affect elections.
- Candidates rely on PACs to help finance costly campaigns.
- PACs play a greater role in congressional elections than in presidential elections, which are partially funded by the public.
- **527 groups:** Independent political groups that are not subject to contribution restrictions because they do not directly see the election of particular candidates. Section 527 of the tax code specifies that contributions to such groups must be reported to the IRS.
- *Citizens United v. Federal Election Commission:* A 2010 landmark Supreme Court case that ruled individuals, corporations, and unions could donate unlimited amounts of money to groups that make independent political expenditures.

- **501(c) groups:** Groups that are exempt from reporting their contributions and can receive unlimited contributions. Section 501(c) of the tax code specifies that such groups cannot spend more than half their funds on political activities.
- Despite the massive amount of money spent on campaigns and the media's constant focus on them, campaigns rarely convert voters away from their predisposed party identification.

## Learning Objective 9.4: Determine why campaigns have an important yet limited impact on election outcomes. (p. 262)

### *The Impact of Campaigns*

- In general, politicians tend to overestimate the impact of campaigns; political scientists have found that campaigning primarily reinforces citizens' views rather than changing views.
- Factors such as **selective perception**, party identification, and the incumbency advantage tend to weaken the ability of campaigns to influence voters' decisions.

## Learning Objective 9.5: Identify the factors that influence whether people vote. (p. 263)

### *Whether to Vote: A Citizen's First Choice*

- **Suffrage** has been expanded several times throughout American history and, although the Constitution left the issue up to the states, generally only white, male property owners had the right to vote.
- Today, almost **all Americans over the age of 18** can vote in elections.
  - The Fifteenth Amendment granted suffrage to African Americans.
  - The Nineteenth Amendment extended voting privileges to women.
  - The Twenty-Sixth Amendment set the minimum voting age at 18.
- Although more people are able to vote, fewer people are exercising this right.
  - Some people do not vote because they believe that one vote in more than 100 million makes little difference.

- Some people do not vote because they are unable to take time off of work to vote on a Tuesday; reformers have suggested moving Election Day to a Saturday.
- Some people do not vote because **voter registration** is difficult or inconvenient in most states.
- Procedures have been made easier, especially with the **Motor Voter Act**, but turnout has still decreased.
- Some people do not vote because there is little ideological difference between the two parties' candidates.
- Some people are more likely to vote because they perceive a significant ideological difference between the two parties' candidates.
- Some people are more likely to vote because they have a sense of **political efficacy**—they believe their vote will make a difference.
- Some people are more likely to vote because they want to perform their **civic duty** in a democracy.

## Who Votes?

- People with a college education are more likely to vote.
- Older people, especially senior citizens, are more likely to vote.
- Hispanic Americans and African Americans are less likely to vote, but those with higher levels of education vote in greater percentages than educated Caucasians.
- More women than men have voted in recent elections.
- Union members are more likely to vote.
- People who are married are more likely to vote.
- Politicians who rely on these voters to be elected are more likely to address their concerns in the policy arena.
- Studies show that if turnout increased among groups with low turnout rates, Democrats would probably receive more votes.
- Reforms are unlikely because Republicans do not want to lose this advantage.

## 9.6 Learning Objective 9.6: Analyze why people vote as they do. (p. 269)

### *How Americans Vote: Explaining Citizens' Decisions*

- The idea that the winning candidate has a mandate from the people to carry out his or her platforms and politics is the **mandate theory of elections**.
- Some people vote according to their **party identification**.
- A candidate of their chosen party probably shares their political beliefs and they do not have to decide on or become informed about every issue.
- This trend is declining as parties have lost some significance in the political process.
- Some voters evaluate what they know and see of the **candidates' personalities** to make a decision.
- A candidate's appearance may play an unconscious role in voter decision making.
- People tend to value integrity, competence, and reliability in a candidate.
- Voters with a college education are actually more likely to base their decision on a candidate's personality, using it to make assumptions about the candidate's performance.
- Some people vote for candidates who share their **policy preferences (policy voting)**; this assumes that voters have firm policy convictions, they are familiar with each candidate's policy preferences, and that they are able to discern differences among candidates' stands on issues.
- A person may also **vote retrospectively** by choosing a candidate who vows to continue policies helpful to him or her, or by choosing the opposing candidate who promises to change the policy.
- Candidates may avoid taking a clear stand on a controversial issue, making **policy voting** difficult. This method requires a lot of effort on the part of voters.

**9.7** **Learning Objective 9.7: Evaluate the fairness of the Electoral College system for choosing the president. (p. 275)**

## The Last Battle: The Electoral College

- In the United States, the president is not chosen directly by the people in a popular election; the **Electoral College** casts the final vote.

- The writers of the Constitution created this institution to keep the presidency at a distance from the masses; it was intended to allow only the elite to choose the president.

- Each state's number of electors is equal to its total number of representatives and senators. Electors are chosen by the state party organizations.

- Almost all states are **winner-take-all**: The candidate who receives the highest popular vote in the state gets all of that state's electoral votes.

- The key states that the presidential campaigns focus on because they are most likely to decide the outcome of the Electoral College are known as **battleground states**.

- Electors convene in December and deliver their votes to the president of the Senate (the vice president), who officially announces the majority winner at the opening of the congressional session in January.

- If no candidate receives a majority of the electoral votes (at least 270), the members of the House of Representatives vote, with each state delegation having one vote.

- This system has received an enormous amount of criticism.
    - It gives an unfair advantage to states with larger populations, because they have a greater number of electoral votes at stake; large states and their policy concerns receive more attention from presidential candidates.
    - A candidate may need to win in only a few large states to win the election.
    - This neglects the less populous states (although George W. Bush used a small-state strategy to win the presidency in 2000 and 2004).
    - Because most large states also have large cities, the system is biased in favor of urban voters.
    - It is possible to win the popular vote but lose the election because of the electoral votes. This happened to Al Gore, who won the popular vote in 2000.

**9.8** **Learning Objective 9.8: Assess the advantages and disadvantages of the U.S. system of campaigns and elections. (p. 277)**

- American election campaigns are easily the most open and democratic in the world.

- They are extraordinarily long, perhaps excessively burdening politicians and leading politicians to make many promises that increase the scope of government.

- Long campaigns do give little-known candidates a chance to emerge and provide a strenuous test for all the candidates.

## For Additional Review

Create a "Campaign Finance" graphic organizer (chart, etc.) to identify key legislation and Supreme Court decisions impacting the campaign finance process. Use this graphic organizer when reviewing and studying for the unit test and the AP Government and Politics exam.

Use the graphic organizer to create a timeline in order to examine the historical and current rules for campaign funding and finance. Place the rules, practices, etc. on the timeline and connect each change to the key legislation and Supreme Court decisions cited in the graphic organizer. Relate the timeline to the arguments for and against campaign finance reform. Use this information when reviewing and studying for the unit test and the AP Government and Politics exam.

# Review Questions

## Multiple-Choice Questions

1. A caucus is
   a. held at the national level to select a nominee.
   b. a closed-door meeting of party regulars.
   c. open to all who want to participate.
   d. a meeting of members of Congress.

2. A primary is
   a. held at the national level to select a nominee.
   b. a closed-door meeting of party regulars.
   c. either open or closed.
   d. a meeting of members of Congress.

3. When the Democrats select delegates to their national convention, they
   a. require all delegates to vote based on a vote held at the state level.
   b. use a winner-take-all system to allocate delegates.
   c. mix use of proportional representation to select delegates with delegates who are not pledged.
   d. hold a series of closed primaries.

4. Superdelegates are
   a. used more often by Republicans than by Democrats.
   b. used by Democrats to ensure a voice for party officials and for particular constituencies.
   c. not able to vote at the conventions.
   d. staff of the national parties.

5. The main loophole to the McCain-Feingold legislation is
   a. 527s.
   b. soft money.
   c. hard money.
   d. bundling.

6. The goal of the Federal Election Campaign Act was to
   a. make delegate selection easier.
   b. make campaigns more fair and transparent.
   c. enforce party discipline.
   d. cause a realignment.

7. PAC money gives the greatest advantage to
   a. the president's party.
   b. incumbents.
   c. Supreme Court justices.
   d. cabinet nominees.

8. Federal matching funds are available to
   a. governors.
   b. members of the House.
   c. senators.
   d. presidential candidates.

9. Where is the first caucus held?
   a. Iowa
   b. New Hampshire
   c. Washington, D.C.
   d. Florida

10. All of the following are criticisms raised against the primary system EXCEPT
    a. this process of selecting delegates is unfair because it prevents representation of minority groups at the national conventions.
    b. too much weight is placed on the early primaries, especially because states like Iowa are not representative of the American electorate.
    c. it has extended the length of the campaign process to an impractical and unmanageable degree.
    d. it prevents many qualified politicians from running, because fundraising for and participating in primaries distracts them from their current office.

11. For a candidate to gain office in a winner-take-all election, the candidate must
    a. receive a 2/3 majority of the votes.
    b. receive at least one vote more than any other competitor.
    c. receive a majority of the total votes cast.
    d. receive at least 10% more of the vote than his/her nearest competitor.

**Questions 12-13 refer to the passage below.**

The executive Power shall be vested in a President of the United States of America. He shall hold his Office during the Term of four Years, and, together with the Vice-President chosen for the same Term, be elected, as follows:

Each State shall appoint, in such Manner as the Legislature thereof may direct, a Number of Electors, equal to the whole Number of Senators and Representatives to which the State may be entitled in the Congress: but no Senator or Representative, or Person holding an Office of Trust or Profit under the United States, shall be appointed an Elector.

*--U.S. Constitution*

12. The Electoral College was created by the framers of the Constitution because they
    a. were skeptical of the influence of state governments in the election of the president.
    b. wanted to increase the states' influence in the election of the president.
    c. wanted to increase the influence of small states in the election of the president.
    d. were skeptical of the direct influence of the people in the election of the president.

13. The number of electoral votes a state has is determined by
    a. the number of male registered voters.
    b. the number of registered voters.
    c. the number of senators and representatives a state has.
    d. a formula devised by the first Congress.

14. Political contributions raised in unlimited amounts by political parties for party-building purposes is
    a. hard money.
    b. independent expenditures.
    c. illegal.
    d. soft money.

15. A political party's statement of its goals, policies, and beliefs for the next four years is known as the party's
    a. platform.
    b. caucus.
    c. political culture.
    d. realignment.

16. Spending for campaign activity that is not coordinated with a candidate's campaign is known as
    a. illegal.
    b. independent expenditures.
    c. hard money.
    d. loans.

17. This federal law banned soft money as a part of the election reform movement.
    a. Soft Money Reform Act
    b. Hard Money Reform Act
    c. Campaign Contributions Act
    d. Bipartisan Campaign Reform Act

18. Candidates need money to do all of the following EXCEPT
    a. conduct political polls.
    b. ask their party for support.
    c. purchase television advertising.
    d. hire campaign managers.

19. Contributions given to candidates and party committees that are limited and committed to candidate-specific electoral activity are known as
    a. independent expenditures.
    b. soft money.
    c. salaries.
    d. hard money.

20. This system was created to reduce voter fraud and voting abuses.
    a. Internet voting
    b. mail-in-voting
    c. the 15th Amendment
    d. registration

# Free-Response Questions

1. Nominating a presidential candidate occurs through an indirect process. Using the political cartoon below, and your knowledge of the nomination process, answer the following questions:

*John Cole/Cagle Cartoons, Inc.*

    a. Describe the role of delegates in the nomination process.

    b. Define winner-take-all and proportional representation and identify where each system is used in the nomination process.

    c. Explain a campaign strategy that results from the indirect election process.

    d. Is the disproportionate share of media attention paid to Iowa and New Hampshire a serious problem, why or why not?

2. Despite the Supreme Court's decisions to uphold much of the Federal Election Campaign Act (FECA) and the Bipartisan Campaign Reform Act (BCRA), the fight to reverse this reform has continued.

    a. Define each of the following:

        ■ Issue advocacy

        ■ Independent expenditures

        ■ Super PACs

    b. Explain how each of these is being used to attempt to reverse the reforms established in FECA and BCRA.

# Answers and Explanations

## Multiple-Choice Questions

1. B   In a caucus, only members who are registered with the party can participate.
*Page reference: 248, AP Big Idea: PRD*

2. C   Primaries can be open to any citizen or they can be restricted to members who are registered with the party.
*Page reference: 248-251, AP Big Idea: PRD*

3. C   In most states, Democrats use proportional representation to select delegates. However, a large percentage of delegates to the national convention for the Democratic Party are unpledged delegates.
*Page reference: 246-248, AP Big Idea: PRD*

4. B   Superdelegates were instituted as part of a compromise between party regulars and those who wanted primaries to be the determinant of the nomination.
*Page reference: 247, AP Big Idea: PRD*

5. A   527 groups are able to advertise for an issue and thus enable some to thwart the goal of the McCain-Feingold legislation.
*Page reference: 260, AP Big Ideas: PRD, PMI*

6. B   The goal of the Federal Election Campaign Act was to make campaigns more fair and transparent.
*Page reference: 257, AP Big Ideas: PRD, PMI*

7. B   PAC money benefits incumbents.
*Page reference: 258, AP Big Ideas: PRD, PMI*

8. D   Federal matching funds are available for presidential candidates who meet certain rules.
*Page reference: 258-259, AP Big Ideas: PRD, PMI*

9. A   The first caucus is held in Iowa.
*Page reference: 248-250, AP Big Ideas: PRD, PMI*

10. A   Democrats mandate minority participation at the national convention and Republicans have made efforts to include minorities.
*Page reference: 250-252, AP Big Ideas: PRD, PMI*

11. B   A winner-take-all system is an electoral system in which the party that receives at least one more vote than any other party wins the election.
*Page reference: 275-276, AP Big Ideas: PRD, PMI*

12. D  The Founders wanted the president to be elected by the nation's elite, not directly by the people; therefore, they established the Electoral College.
*Page reference: 275-276, AP Big Ideas: CON, PMI, PRD*

13. C  Each state, according to the Constitution, has as many electoral votes as it has U.S. senators and representatives.
*Page reference: 275-276, AP Big Ideas: CON, PMI, PRD*

14. D  Soft money involves unlimited political contributions earmarked for party-building expenses at the grassroots level or for generic party advertising.
*Page reference: 259, AP Big Ideas: PRD, PMI*

15. A  A party platform is a political party's statement of its goals and policies for the next four years. The platform is drafted prior to the party convention by a committee whose members are chosen in rough proportion to each candidate's strength.
*Page reference: 253, AP Big Idea: PRD*

16. B  Independent expenditures are expenses on behalf of a political message that are made by groups that are uncoordinated with any candidate's campaign.
*Page reference: 257, AP Big Ideas: PRD, PMI*

17. D  The Bipartisan Campaign Reform Act, also known as the McCain-Feingold Act, largely banned soft money, restored a long-standing prohibition on corporations and labor unions for using general treasury funds for electoral purposes, and narrowed the definition of issue advocacy.
*Page reference: 259-260, AP Big Ideas: PRD, PMI*

18. B  Candidates do not need funds in order to ask for support from their political party.
*Page reference: 257-262, AP Big Ideas: PRD, PMI*

19. D  Hard money refers to political contributions given to a party, candidate, or interest group that are limited in amount and fully disclosed. Raising such funds is harder than raising unlimited soft money, hence the term hard money.
*Page reference: 257-262, AP Big Ideas: PRD, PMI*

20. D  Registration is a system adopted by the states that requires voters to register prior to voting. Some states require citizens to register as much as 30 days in advance, whereas others permit Election Day registration.
*Page reference: 266-267, AP Big Idea: PRD*

# Free-Response Questions

*This rubric provides examples of many, but not all of the possible correct responses to the free-response questions.*

1. Nominating a presidential candidate occurs through an indirect process. Using the political cartoon, and your knowledge of the nomination process, answer the following questions:

   a. Describe the role of delegates in the nomination process.

      - The selection of candidates for the presidency occurs through an indirect election. Voters are allowed to participate in primaries or caucuses at the state level. Their votes, however, translate into delegates that attend a national convention and cast an official vote for the nominee.

   b. Define winner-take-all and proportional representation and identify where each system is used in the nomination process.

      - For the Democratic Party, most states allocate their delegates in proportion to voters' choices, which is proportional representation. The Republican Party mostly allocates their delegates on a winner-take-all basis, meaning that the candidate who wins the most votes in a state gets all of that state's delegates to the national convention.

   c. Explain a campaign strategy that results from the indirect election process.

      - There are several campaign strategies that result from the rules of this contest. One is known as frontloading, in which the candidates will put all their time, money, and resources into states with earlier primaries and caucuses in an effort to gain momentum. Another strategy is to concentrate on states that award more delegates for the effort, such as Texas, which holds a lot of delegates in both conventions. Candidates may not campaign at all in states with nonbinding primaries.

   d. Is the disproportionate share of media attention paid to Iowa and New Hampshire a serious problem, why or why not?

      - Articulate a defensible claim and support it with evidence.

2. Despite the Supreme Court's decisions to uphold much of the Federal Election Campaign Act (FECA) and the Bipartisan Campaign Reform Act (BCRA), the fight to reverse this reform has continued.

a. Define each of the following:

- Issue advocacy
- Independent expenditures
- Super PACs

- **Issue advocacy** is promoting a particular position or an issue paid for by interest groups or individuals but not candidates.
- **Independent expenditures** refer to money spent by individuals or groups not associated with candidates to elect or defeat candidates for office.
- A **Super PAC** is an independent expenditure only first allowed in 2010 after court decisions allowing unlimited contributions to such PACs.

b. Explain how each of these is being used to attempt to reverse the reforms established in FECA and BCRA.

- Issue advocacy attempts to challenge the restrictions on campaign finance by running ads for or against candidates without specifically expressing advocacy of election or defeat. Issue advocacy is able to circumvent the controls of FECA and BCRA by not using the words "vote for," "elect," "cast your vote for," "vote against," "defeat" or any other such words. Ads that do not use these words are considered to be ads that deal with issues and not candidates, therefore, they do not violate FECA or BCRA.
- The Supreme Court ruled, in 1996, that FECA did not limit individual or group spending for or against candidates. BCRA also does not constrain independent expenditures as long as those expenditures are independent of the candidate and fully disclosed by the FCC. This allows individuals or groups to attempt to influence elections independently instead of going through a political party.
- In 2010, the Supreme Court rejected the ban on unions and corporations using their general funds on ads about the election or the defeat of a candidate. This allows Super PACs to receive unlimited funds from individuals, unions, and corporations.

# 10

# Interest Groups

## Chapter Overview

Interest groups have long been central to American politics. During the debate over ratification, James Madison discussed the role of "factions" in a democratic polis. His writings, particularly in *The Federalist No. 10*, outlined a vision of a political system that checked the power of factions. Today, we generally refer to these "factions" as "interest groups," the topic of this chapter. We begin our analysis of interest groups by describing the role of interest groups in American politics and contrasting the three leading theories of interest group politics: pluralism, elitism, and hyperpluralism. Then, we analyze the factors that make some interest groups more successful than others in the political arena and assess the four basic strategies that interest groups use to try to shape policy. Next, we contrast the various types of interest groups. We conclude by evaluating ideas to limit the reach and influence of interest groups. By the end of the chapter, students should have a good understanding of the nature and role of interest groups in the United States.

# Study Outline

**Learning Objective 10.1: Explain the origins of interest groups in America and the theories of their role in our democracy. (p. 284)**

## *The Role Interest Groups*

- **Interest group:** An organization of people with a shared policy goal, or goals, who enter the policy process at one or more points, in one or more policy arenas, to try to achieve their goals.

- Interest groups may pursue any kind of policy, in all levels and branches of government.

- They differ from political parties in several ways.

- They pursue their agenda through the political process, whereas parties advance their agendas through elections.

- Interest groups specialize in one or two policy areas, whereas parties focus on general policies to win a majority.

## *Theories of Interest Group Politics*

- **Pluralist theory:** Interest groups are important to democracy because they allow people to organize themselves to change policies.

- Because hundreds of interest groups must compete for influence, no one group will dominate the others.

- Groups put up a fair fight; they do not engage in illegal activities to surpass other groups. Groups are equal in power because they have different resources at their disposal.

- **Elite theory:** There may be hundreds of interest groups, but only a select few have any real power.

  - The interests of only a handful of elites, usually business people, are almost always favored over other interests.

  - The policy battles that smaller interests do win are usually minor.

  - Power rests mostly with large multinational corporations.

- The system of elite control is maintained by a well-established structure of interlocking policy players.
- **Hyperpluralist theory** or **interest group liberalism**: **Subgovernments**, or **iron triangles**, form around specific policy areas.
- These are composed of an **interest group**, a **federal agency**, and any **legislative committees** or **subcommittees** that handle the policy area.
- By avoiding having to choose between policy initiatives, the government creates conflicting policies that waste time and money.
- Groups have too much political influence because they usually get what they want.
- Competing subgovernments only add to the confusion.

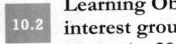 **Learning Objective 10.2: Analyze the factors that make some interest groups more successful than others in the political arena. (p. 289)**

## *What Makes an Interest Group Successful?*

- **Potential group:** All the people who might be interest group members because they share some common interest.
- **Actual group:** The people in the potential group who actually join.
- Smaller groups are more effective than large groups because they can organize more easily.
- A member of a small group is more likely to experience the group's success and, therefore, is more likely to work harder than a member of a large group.
- However, groups do experience the **free rider problem**, where individuals can benefit from the work of the group without actually joining the group.
- **Selective benefits:** Goods that a group can restrict to those who actually join. This helps overcome the free rider problem.
- According to Olson's law of large groups, this problem is greater with larger groups.
- Intensity is another important factor.
- **Single-issue groups** form around a specific policy and tend to pursue it uncompromisingly.

- Single-issue groups often deal with moral issues that people feel strongly about and members of single-issue groups often vote according to a candidate's stand on the group's issue.

- Politicians are most likely to serve the needs of people or groups with money.

- Money allows groups to mobilize, conduct research, and maintain an administration.

## 10.3 Learning Objective 10.3: Analyze the methods and activities that interest groups use to influence political outcomes. (p. 292)

### *How Groups Try to Shape Policy*

- **Lobbying:** Professional lobbyists attempt to persuade lawmakers to act on behalf of their group.

- The more helpful a lobbyist is, the more power he or she has with a politician.

- Lobbyists serve as policy experts in their interest area, act as consultants who advise legislators on how to approach policy issues and debates, mobilize support for politicians during reelection, and suggest innovative policy ideas.

- **Electioneering:** Interest groups endorse a candidate who supports their interests and work to get that candidate elected.

- The groups encourage people to vote for the candidate and help finance the candidate's campaign through **PACs**.

- Congressional candidates have become largely dependent on PAC money, and most PAC money goes to incumbents rather than challengers.

- **Litigation:** Interest groups use lawsuits to change policies that have already gone through the legislative process.

- Even the threat of a lawsuit may be enough to influence policymaking.

- Groups can file *amicus curiae* briefs to state their side in a court case and to assess the consequences of the decisions the court might make.

- Groups can also file class action lawsuits—suits on behalf of a larger group in the electorate.

- Mobilizing public opinion: Interest groups try to influence the public because they know that politicians' careers depend on public opinion.

- Groups cultivate a positive image of themselves in the eyes of the public and they encourage public participation to advance interests from the point of view of the constituency.

## 10.4 Learning Objective 10.4: Identify the various types of interest groups and their policy concerns. (p. 299)

### *Types of Interest Groups*

- **Economic interests** such as business, labor, and farmers are often against regulations and tax increases, and want tax advantages, subsidies, and contracts for work.
- Organized labor is the second largest group (e.g., the AFL-CIO, the National Education Association).
- **Union shop:** A provision found in some collective bargaining agreements requiring that all employees of a unionized business join the union within a short period of being hired, usually 30 days, and remain members as a condition of employment.
- **Right to work laws:** State laws that forbid the creation of union shops. These laws were specifically authorized by the Taft-Hartley Act of 1947.
- The interest group with the largest membership is the American Association for the Advancement of Retired Persons (**AARP**), which represents the interests of older Americans.
- Businesses are the most widely represented interests in Washington.
- **Environmental interests** are the fastest-growing type of interest group, favoring wilderness protection, pollution control, and energy alternatives, while opposing policies that damage the environment; examples include the Sierra Club and the Nature Conservancy.
- **Equality interests** such as civil rights, women's rights, and social welfare groups' concerns center on fair treatment in jobs, housing, and education.
  - Examples include the American Civil Liberties Union (ACLU) and the Southern Poverty Law Center.
- **Consumers' interests** and **public interests (public interest lobbies)** address issues in which the whole public benefits from certain policy actions, such as product

safety, which was introduced by Ralph Nader, and also represent groups that cannot assert their interests themselves: children, the mentally ill, or animals, for example.

- Some groups advocate for fair and open government or government reform. Examples include Consumer Alert and the Children's Defense Fund.

 **Learning Objective 10.5: Evaluate how well Madison's ideas for controlling the influence of interest groups have worked in practice. (p. 304)**

## *Understanding Interest Groups*

- The issue of controlling interest groups remains as crucial to democracy today as it was in James Madison's time. Some scholars believe that the growth of interest groups has helped to divide political influence, while others see the PAC system as the new way in which special interests corrupt American democracy.

## For Additional Review

Create a graphic organizer, in chart form, for interest groups. At the top of the graph, put the definition of interest groups and describe the entities through which interest groups work. Next, create 3 columns for the chart: Classification, Purpose, and Example. In the Classification column, list the TYPES of interest groups; in the Purpose column, describe the PURPOSE of that type of interest group; and in the third column, list EXAMPLES of the type of interest group identified in the first column. Use this organizer when studying for the unit test and the AP Exam.

Create a second graphic organizer, this time in diagram form, explaining how interest groups influence. In the center circle, place the main topic of the diagram. In smaller circles, write the methods by which interest groups exercise influence, including an explanation of each method identified. Use this organizer when studying for the unit test and the AP Exam.

# Review Questions

## Multiple-Choice Questions

1.  Which of the following is the best definition of pluralism?
    a.  A multitude of groups compete for and share power at any given time.
    b.  A multitude of interest groups have the ability to form and survive.
    c.  Several small, single-issue groups tend to hold power.
    d.  The number of groups continues to increase as society becomes more complicated.

2.  Elite theorists believe that the power of interest groups
    a.  is derived from their equal access to the government.
    b.  comes mostly from public support.
    c.  is evenly distributed among them.
    d.  is held by only a few wealthy groups.

3.  The hyperpluralist theory holds that
    a.  interest group intensity places pressure on members of Congress.
    b.  the large number of groups slows down the policymaking process.
    c.  it is common for one group to rapidly split up into other groups.
    d.  many groups compete for and share power.

4.  Lawmakers often rely on lobbyists for all of the following reasons EXCEPT
    a.  to come up with new policy ideas that they can introduce in Congress.
    b.  for advice on strategies to advance or prevent a piece of legislation.
    c.  for money that would allow them to travel to their constituencies.
    d.  to encourage group members to vote for them during reelection.

5.  Iron triangles are composed of
    a.  a cabinet department, a legislative committee, and a federal judge.
    b.  a corporate board, an interest group, and the Speaker of the House.
    c.  a PAC, an interest group, and a congressional candidate.
    d.  an interest group, a legislative committee, and a federal agency.

6.  Proponents of the pluralist theory argue that, for the most part, power is evenly distributed among interest groups because
    a.  the public participates equally in different types of interest groups.
    b.  all interest groups receive the same amount of federal funds.
    c.  each policy area is assigned a limited number of related interest groups.
    d.  competition prevents any one group from becoming more influential.

7. All of the following statements accurately describes methods interest groups employ to influence policymaking EXCEPT
   a. Class action lawsuits allow interest groups to sue in the name of a larger section of the public.
   b. Interest groups meet with judges about cases that affect their policy area.
   c. Interest groups make almost all of their PAC contributions to incumbents rather than challengers.
   d. Lobbyists use their policy expertise to make themselves indispensable to politicians.

8. Interest groups do all of the following EXCEPT
   a. link the public to the political process.
   b. nominate candidates for elective office.
   c. try to shape specific policy goals.
   d. play a part in political campaigns.

9. Which of the following interest groups is known to be the largest in membership size?
   a. National Rifle Association (NRA)
   b. League of Conservation Voters
   c. Christian Coalition
   d. American Association of Retired Persons (AARP)

10. Which of the following groups has primarily used litigation to advance its issues?
    a. National Rifle Association (NRA)
    b. League of Conservation Voters
    c. Christian Coalition
    d. National Association for the Advancement of Colored People (NAACP)

**Questions 11-12 refer to the passage below.**

**Madison** defines a **faction** as "a number of citizens, whether amounting to a minority or majority of the whole, who are united and actuated by some common impulse of passion, or of interest, adverse to the rights of other citizens, or to the permanent and aggregate interests of the community."

*--The Federalist No.10*

11. The groups that, according to James Madison, arose from the unequal distribution of property or wealth and had the potential to cause instability in government are known as
    a. politiques.
    b. factions.
    c. cliques.
    d. parties.

12. Interest groups are sometimes negatively referred to as
    a. radicals.
    b. elitists.
    c. cliques.
    d. special interests.

13. When interest groups find the popular political channels closed to them, they may turn to
    a. celebrities.
    b. the president.
    c. litigation.
    d. governors.

14. Interest groups often create political action committees (PACs) to
    a. get the support of the national and state courts.
    b. create a new political party.
    c. nominate a candidate for political office.
    d. contribute money to candidates and political parties.

15. The U.S. government attempts to regulate interest groups by
    a. regulating membership requirements.
    b. banning some specific groups considered too extreme.
    c. regulating media access to the groups.
    d. regulating the practice of lobbying.

16. The activities of a group or organization that seek to persuade political leaders to support the group's position are known as
    a. pluralism.
    b. free-riding.
    c. hyperpluralism.
    d. lobbying.

17. All of the following are appropriate lobbying strategies EXCEPT
    a. litigation.
    b. threatening members of Congress.
    c. electioneering.
    d. helping formulate campaign strategy.

18. This is considered to be the most important resource interest groups and PACs can provide to candidates.
    a. strategies
    b. volunteers
    c. campaign workers
    d. money

19. Labor unions and trade associations are examples of what type of interest group?
    a. grassroots
    b. single-issue
    c. public
    d. economic

20. Most political action committees represent
    a. government groups.
    b. labor unions.
    c. citizens' groups.
    d. business groups.

# Free-Response Questions

1. Interest groups use a variety of techniques to pursue their goals. For each of the interest groups below, identify a technique that has been important to the group's success in the policy process and explain why the group used this technique.

    a. NAACP

    b. AARP

    c. NRA

2. Interest groups are often criticized for hurting the political process by making PAC contributions. Using the graph below, and your knowledge of interest groups, answer the following questions:

Should PACs be Eliminated?

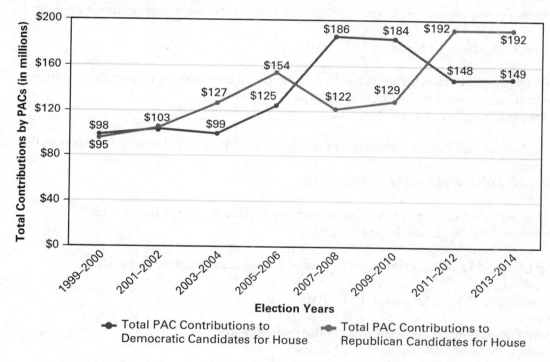

*Harold Stanley and Richard Niemi, Vital Statistics on American Politics, 2015–2016 (Los Angeles: CQ Press, 2015), 102–104*

    a. Identify one argument against allowing PACs to make contributions.

    b. Identify one argument in favor of allowing PACs to make contributions.

    c. Identify one law that regulates PACs and explain why it has or has not been effective.

    d. Articulate a defensible thesis concerning the elimination of PACs. Support your position with relevant evidence.

# Answers and Explanations

## Multiple-Choice Questions

1. A    Pluralists argue that political power is shared among many groups.
*Page reference: 286-287, AP Big Ideas: PRD, PMI*

2. D    Elitists argue that political power is primarily held by the wealthy.
*Page reference: 287, AP Big Ideas: PRD, PMI*

3. B    Hyperpluralists argue that the number of interest groups can slow down our system as members of Congress are bombarded with competing information.
*Page reference: 287-289, AP Big Ideas: PRD, PMI*

4. D    Lawmakers do not depend on interest groups for votes since votes must come from their district.
*Page reference: 292-294, AP Big Ideas: PRD, PMI*

5. D    Iron triangles are the relationship between congressional committees, government agencies, and interest groups who work together on policies.
*Page reference: 288, AP Big Ideas: PRD, PMI*

6. D    Pluralists believe that power is shared and that interest groups will check one another in the policy arena.
*Page reference: 286-289, AP Big Ideas: PRD, PMI*

7. B    Interest groups do not meet with judges about cases that affect their policy area.
*Page reference: 292-299, AP Big Ideas: PRD, PMI*

8. B    Interest groups do not run candidates for office but, instead, attempt to influence policymakers.
*Page reference: 292-299, AP Big Ideas: PRD, PMI*

9. D    The AARP is the largest interest group in the United States.
*Page reference: 299-304, AP Big Ideas: PRD, MPA*

10. D    The NAACP has used litigation in cases such as *Brown v. Board of Education* when other techniques were not useful.
*Page reference: 297-298, AP Big Ideas: PRD, PMI*

11. B    James Madison, in *The Federalist No. 10*, described factions as working adverse to the interests of the nation as a whole and he tried to design the constitutional system to prevent such groups from having too much power.
*Page reference: 304-306, AP Big Ideas: CON, PRD*

12. D  An interest group is an organization of people with shared policy goals entering the policy process at several points to try to achieve those goals. Because these groups share a specific agenda they are also known as special interest groups.
*Page reference: 285-286, AP Big Ideas: PRD, MPA*

13. C  If an interest group fails in Congress or gets only a vague piece of legislation, the next step is to go to court in the hope of getting specific rulings in its favor. Using the courts to achieve its goal is referred to as litigation.
*Page reference: 292-299, AP Big Ideas: PRD, PMI*

14. D  Political action committees are groups that raise money from individuals and then distribute it in the form of contributions to candidates that the group supports.
*Page reference: 292-297 AP Big Ideas: PRD, PMI*

15. D  The U.S. government has passed legislation to regulate lobbying in order to regulate interest groups.
*Page reference: 292-297, AP Big Ideas: PRD, PMI*

16. D  Lobbying, according to Lester Milbrath, is a communication by someone other than a citizen acting on his or her own behalf, directed to a governmental decision maker with the hope of influencing his or her decision.
*Page reference: 292-297, AP Big Ideas: PRD, PMI*

17. B  Threatening a member of Congress is an illegal activity and therefore would not be an appropriate lobbying strategy.
*Page reference: 292-297, AP Big Ideas: PRD, PMI*

18. D  Even though interest groups and PACs can provide many important resources to candidates, due to the increasing expense associated with running for office, money is considered to be the most important resource that can be provided.
*Page reference: 292-297, AP Big Ideas: PRD, PMI*

19. D  The primary purpose of an economic interest group is to promote the financial interests of its members. Labor unions work for the interest of their workers, while trade associations work to advance the economic good for the firms in their industry; hence, both would be examples of economic interest groups.
*Page reference: 300-302, AP Big Ideas: PRD, PMI*

20. D  PACs can be categorized according to the type of interest they represent, and the greatest growth has been seen in the PACs representing corporations and trade organizations.
*Page reference: 294-297, AP Big Ideas: PRD, PMI*

# Free-Response Questions

*This rubric provides examples of many, but not all of the possible correct responses to the free-response questions.*

1. Interest groups use a variety of techniques to pursue their goals. For each of the interest groups below, identify a technique that has been important to the group's success in the policy process and explain why the group used this technique.

   a. NAACP

      - The NAACP is best known for using litigation to pursue its goals. In particular, the NAACP made history when its attorneys took on a class action lawsuit that reached the Supreme Court, *Brown v. Board of Education*, in 1954. Litigation is advantageous to groups like the NAACP, after attempts to use more traditional lobbying techniques are unsuccessful. Federal judges hold their positions for life, and are therefore not swayed by public opinion. Supreme Court case rulings are the final legal authority in the U.S., unless overturned by a constitutional amendment.

   b. AARP

      - The AARP is best known for its extraordinary large membership base. The members are also very active in grassroots lobbying: calling members of Congress, e-mailing, and making other similar types of contact with lawmakers. The AARP is powerful because elected officials depend on their votes to win, so their large membership base gains the attention of politicians.

   c. NRA

      - The NRA is known for making large campaign contributions. Campaign contributions are useful because elected officials rely on such contributions to run effective campaigns, and try to give as much as they can to their contributors to keep the contributions flowing.

2. Interest groups are often criticized for hurting the political process by making PAC contributions. Using the graph, and your knowledge of interest groups, answer the following questions:

   a. Identify one argument against allowing PACs to make contributions.

      - One argument against allowing PACs to make contributions is that it can lead to corruption. Those who subscribe to this view would argue that PACs essentially buy legislation by making contributions.

   b. Identify one argument in favor of allowing PACs to make contributions.

      - One argument in favor of allowing PACs to make contributions is that making a contribution is a type of expression, which is protected by the First Amendment of the Constitution.

   c. Identify one law that regulates PACs and explain why it has or has not been effective.

      - There are several laws that regulate PACs. The most recent law is called the Bipartisan Campaign Reform Act, also referred to as the McCain-Feingold Act. This law was designed to stop PACs from making unlimited contributions to the political party and thus banned so-called soft money. This law has been somewhat effective; however, one of the loopholes in this law is citizens' ability to make unlimited contributions to 527 groups. These groups support issues, not specific parties, and are identified by their status in the federal tax code. By making unlimited contributions to these groups, PACs have gotten around the McCain-Feingold law because the groups run similar ads to support candidates that the parties once did.

   d. Articulate a defensible thesis concerning the elimination of PACs. Support your position with relevant evidence.

      - Use reasoning to explain why your evidence supports your thesis.

# 11

# Congress

## Chapter Overview

The Framers of the Constitution conceived of the legislature as the center of policymaking in America. Their plan was for the great disputes over public policy to be resolved in Congress, not in the White House or the Supreme Court. Although the prominence of Congress has ebbed and flowed over the course of American history, as often as not, Congress has been the true center of power in Washington.  In this chapter, we examine the role of Congress in U.S. politics. We begin by considering the electoral politics of Congress, exploring how representative members of Congress are of the U.S. population in general, and identifying the factors that influence congressional elections. Then we examine the committee structures, leadership positions, and support staff that shape Congress's business. We consider in particular the role of the Congress in lawmaking, appropriations, and oversight. By the end of the chapter, students should understand the complex role and functions of Congress in the context of American government.

# Study Outline

**11.1** **Learning Objective 11.1: Characterize the backgrounds of members of Congress and assess their impact on the ability of members of Congress to represent average Americans. (p. 310)**

## *The Representatives and Senators*

- Congress is composed of 435 representatives and 100 senators, for a total of 535 members.
- Congress is not a very diverse place.
- Most members are lawyers or businesspeople.
- The members of both houses have always been largely Caucasian.
- The House is more diverse than the Senate, which is almost exclusively white.
- The ratio of men to women in both the House and the Senate is about five to one.
- Most election years leave both houses about evenly divided between Democrats and Republicans, with one or two independents in each.

**11.2** **Learning Objective 11.2: Identify the principal factors influencing the outcomes in congressional elections. (p. 313)**

## *Congressional Elections*

- Congressional elections are held every two years in November.
- The most important factor that determines which candidate wins an election is incumbency.
- **Incumbents** are elected officials who already hold office and are running for reelection. Incumbents win reelection more than 90 percent of the time.
- Incumbency allows senators and representatives to gain valuable experience and bring some stability to Congress; however, this may also work to insulate members of Congress from change, making it more difficult for constituents to effect change.
- Senatorial races are usually intense because incumbents, who tend to have higher profiles, are more likely to be held accountable for public policy successes or failures.

- Their challengers are also more likely to be known already in the political arena because senatorial races often draw former representatives or governors.
- Still, incumbents usually win, though by a narrower margin. In fact, turnover in Congress usually occurs only when members retire.

## The Advantages of Incumbents

- Incumbents engage in three activities that increase the probability of being elected:
  - **Advertising:** Advertising makes a candidate visible to many constituents and name recognition is an important advantage for incumbents.
    - The number of votes a candidate receives is fairly proportional to his or her airtime on television and the frequency of his or her public appearances.
    - Advertising requires a great deal of campaign funds, particularly for senators, which explains in part why Congress is composed mostly of wealthy men.
  - **Credit claiming:** Incumbents have the benefit of being able to present their **congressional record** to their constituents to demonstrate their hard work in service of the district or state.
    - They may have helped specific people or groups sidestep bureaucratic red tape (**casework**), or they may have helped with federal programs and institutions (**pork barrel**).
    - From this record of service to the constituency, incumbents can build a more clearly defined public image, whereas challengers new to politics are less likely to be able to convey their position on issues to the public.
  - Position taking: Incumbents' public image is strengthened because they have already taken a stand on issues relevant to their constituency; and at election time, this can work in their favor to identify them in the minds of the public.

## The Role of Party Identification

- **Party identification:** Voters for the most part cast their ballots along **party lines**; therefore, a predominantly Democratic district, for example, is most likely to elect and then reelect a Democratic candidate.

### Defeating Incumbents

- While defeating an incumbent is very difficult, it does happen occasionally.

- Sometimes redistricting can occur, forcing incumbents to attempt to win over an unfamiliar constituency, or even making them compete against another incumbent.

- Sometimes incumbents are involved in scandals that are visible in the media, which tarnishes their name.

- Occasionally, the unpopularity of a president of the same party as the incumbent can have a negative impact on the incumbent's chances of success.

### Open Seats/Stability and Change

- When an incumbent leaves a seat open, there is more likely to be competition; however, the competition usually occurs within the primary, as most seats are safe for one party or the other.

- Because real competition for seats is unusual, Congress does not change very much or very often.

 **Learning Objective 11.3: Assess the roles of leaders, political parties, and committees in Congress. (p. 319)**

## How Congress Is Organized to Make Policy

- A **bicameral legislature** is divided into two houses.
- Legislation must pass both houses of Congress to become law.
- The Senate is designed to represent states and the House is designed to represent the population.

### The House

- A state's population determines how many representatives it has.
- A state is divided into congressional districts, each with an equal population.
- Every ten years, district lines must be redrawn according to the population data supplied by the national census.
- The political party in power in each state will try and draw district lines to their advantage, a process called gerrymandering.

- States therefore can lose or gain a seat in the House, but total membership remains at 435.
- Other characteristics of the House:
  - Members tend to vote along party lines.
  - Power is usually hierarchical.
  - Special responsibilities include introducing revenue bills and articles of impeachment.
- Key to agenda setting in the House is the House Rules Committee.
- The House Rules Committee gives each bill a rule for debate, schedules the bill on a calendar, allows time for debate, and may specify what types of amendments can be offered.
- The Speaker of the House chairs the Rules Committee.

### The Senate

- Power is more evenly distributed among senators.
- Senators act more independently of their parties.
- Special responsibilities include approving presidential nominations, ratifying treaties, and the trial of impeached federal officials.
- Senators can **filibuster** and this power of unlimited debate means that they can talk so long that they delay or even prevent voting on a piece of legislation.
- Senators can stop a filibuster by voting for **cloture**, which halts debate.
- This rarely happens because it requires 60 votes; the majority party usually holds fewer than 60 seats, making cloture nearly impossible.

## Congressional Leadership

- There are several elected positions in the House of Representatives. At the beginning of each congressional term, the parties will meet in caucus to elect these leaders.
- The leader of the House is the **Speaker of the House**, who is chosen by the majority party, and who presides over each session and is largely responsible for assigning representatives to committees or party positions.
- The vice president of the United States is president of the Senate, however, this role is more formal than active because most authority rests with party leaders in the Senate.
- In the House, the **majority leader** assists the Speaker of the House in assigning majority party members to committees and scheduling legislation.
- The **minority leader** leads the minority party in opposing the agenda of the majority, and in choosing minority party members for committees.
- The **majority leader** in the Senate is usually the most active or seasoned member of the majority party.
- The majority leader manages the schedule of debate and rallies party votes for party legislation or against proposals of the minority party.
- The **minority leader** rallies the support of the minority party around legislation and acts as its spokesperson.
- The majority and minority **whips** are responsible for "counting votes" for proposed legislation, working with members of their party to get enough votes to pass or defeat a piece of legislation.

## The Committees and Subcommittees

- Committees are the nuts and bolts of Congress.
- Most members serve on at least five committees and subcommittees; senators usually serve on more committees than representatives do.
- There are four basic types of committees.
  - **Standing committees** handle a **specific policy area**, such as agriculture, finance, energy, and commerce; both the House and Senate have standing committees and each committee is often divided into **subcommittees**.

- Joint committees are composed of both senators and representatives and are responsible for legislation that overlaps policy areas.
- Select committees are appointed to handle a specific issue, such as an investigation or impeachment trial.
- **Conference committees** are composed of members of both houses and they iron out the differences between the House and Senate version of a bill.

- Committees are responsible for researching, assessing, and revising the thousands of bills that are introduced by members of Congress each year.
- Committees also conduct legislative oversight, which is the monitoring of federal agencies and their execution of the law.
- Oversight usually takes the form of investigation—often committees hold hearings to question agency officials about the activities of their departments.
- As the federal bureaucracy has grown over the last few decades, so has the process of legislative oversight.
- One key to a new member of Congress's success is getting on a high-profile committee.
- Members seek committees that will help them to assist their constituency, or provide publicity to help them get reelected.
- Committee placement is decided by the chamber leadership.
  - **Committee chairs** influence the agenda of the committee.
  - The chair is always a member of the majority party, and usually is the most senior member of the majority party on the committee.
  - The minority party member of the committee with the longest tenure is called the ranking member.
  - The **seniority system** was a formal rule used to select chairs, but is no longer a requirement.

### Caucuses: The Informal Organization of Congress

- A **caucus** is a group of members of Congress who share a similar interest.
- Each party has a caucus, and there are hundreds of caucuses, some more active than others.

- The Congressional Black Caucus and the Congressional Caucus for Women's Issues are two examples.
- Caucuses may hold hearings and put pressure on committees to try to influence legislation.

## Congressional Staff (Personal Staff, Committee Staff, Staff Agencies)

- Senators and members of the House of Representatives each have a number of staff who assist them in serving their constituencies, researching legislation, and communicating with those who contact the office.
- The Committees also employ staff to organize hearings, draft reports, and perform other duties.
- Finally, Congress has staff agencies such as the *Congressional Research Service (CRS)* to track the progress of bills and perform research for members of Congress.

**Learning Objective 11.4: Describe the process of lawmaking in Congress. (p. 325)**

## *The Lawmaking Process*

- Policymaking is a slow and laborious process, and often a final bill has changed significantly from the original.

- The authors of the Constitution intentionally devised a complicated legislative system as a means to prevent hasty decisions and to encourage compromise in policymaking. The following diagram shows how proposed legislation usually follows a path through Congress.

1. A single member of Congress or a small group in either the House or Senate formally introduces a bill.

2. The bill goes to a subcommittee of the appropriate standing committee.

3. The subcommittee conducts research and holds hearings on the proposal and rewrites it as necessary.

4. The approved bill then moves to the standing committee, which assesses the legislation in a formal report, rewrites the bill as necessary, and ultimately decides whether to pass it on for debate or to kill it.

5. The bill is introduced for debate on the floor of the chamber. Committee members usually serve as authorities on the proposal to whom their colleagues turn, and they often rally support for it. Amendments may be added to the bill.

6. If passed by both houses, the bill goes to the president for final approval as law. If different versions are passed in each house, the two bills go to a conference committee that resolves the differences between them. Then both houses vote on the final version of the bill and it is sent to the president.

- Some important committees to know:
  - The **House Rules Committee** reviews all bills submitted by committees before they go to the House floor, assigns them a slot on the calendar, allocates time for debate, and even decides whether the bill may be amended or not. This committee is unique to the House and has a significant degree of power.
  - The **House Ways and Means Committee** writes bills concerning tax and other public revenue, which are subject to the approval of both houses.
  - The **Senate Finance Committee** works in conjunction with the House Ways and Means Committee to write **tax and revenue bills**.
  - The **Appropriations Committee in each house** decides how government money will be **apportioned** to federal agencies. This is the largest committee on each side, and divides into many subcommittees that attach to each of the standing committees.
  - **Legislative Oversight:** Congress' monitoring of the executive branch bureaucracy and its administration of policy, performed mainly through committee hearings.

## 11.5   Learning Objective 11.5: Describe the factors that influence how members of Congress make decisions. (p. 331)

### Influences on Congressional Decision Making

*Party, Constituency, and Ideology*

- Members of Congress do not always vote with their party.
- Partisanship tends to be strongest on economic and welfare issues, however, on other issues, members of Congress may act more independently, especially to fulfill the needs of their constituents.
- When representatives or senators do act independently, what influences their vote?
  - If the issue is of significance to their constituency, or is likely to be highly publicized, members of Congress tend to vote as the constituency would want them to.

- On the many other issues about which the public is less informed, representatives and senators are more likely to vote according to their own personal views and convictions.

- Over the past three decades, Republicans in Congress have become consistently more conservative, Democrats have become consistently more liberal, and the distance from the center of each party has increased.

- As a result of these ideological differences between the parties in Congress, it has been more difficult to reach any compromises.

- Increasingly divergent electoral coalitions and districts, which are more one-sided, have played an important role in this.

## Lobbyists and Interest Groups

- With lobbyists dominating Washington, how effective is Congress in representing the people? You should be familiar with both sides of this debate.

## Congress Represents the Interests of the Electorate

- Interest groups are organized by groups of "the people" to make their views known so that policymakers will act on their behalf.

- As pluralists contend, the competition among groups for the support of members of Congress ensures that compromise will play a part in policymaking.

- The issues on which Congress focuses are as diverse as the interests pushing them to the forefront, thereby decentralizing the political agenda and power in each house.

## Congress Serves the Interest Groups, Not the Public

- Critics argue that those interest groups with enough money to buy influence dominate the policy agenda and distract policymakers from the needs of the public.

- So many competing interests prevent the formation of cohesive policy. In fact, different committees may handle the same policy issue in drastically different ways.

- Ultimately, the government wastes a significant amount of money by attempting to appease so many interests.

**Learning Objective 11.6: Assess Congress' role as a representative body and the impact of representation on the scope of government. (p. 336)**

## *Understanding Congress*

■ Although Congress is an elite institution, it is responsible to the people when they make their wishes clear. Congress is open to influence, but this openness may also reduce its ability to make good public policy. Members of Congress often support expanding government to help their constituents, but also fight to limit the scope of government.

## For Additional Review

As you read your textbook, keep a list of all the committees you come across. For each committee, jot down what kind of committee it is and its role or policy specialty. Not only will this information help you prepare for Section I of the AP Government and Politics: United States Exam, but also, it may contain good examples for use in your free-response answers.

Create a chart comparing and contrasting the qualifications, organization, and powers of the House and the Senate. Use this chart when studying and preparing for the unit test and for the AP United States Government and Politics exam.

# Review Questions

## Multiple-Choice Questions

1. Which demographic group is the most underrepresented in Congress?
   a. African Americans
   b. Latinos
   c. Asians
   d. women

2. Which of the following is most likely to determine a candidate's chance of getting elected to Congress?
   a. their personal wealth
   b. their connections to the media
   c. their incumbency status
   d. their campaign style

3. Riders are frequently unpopular with the general public because
   a. the public does not understand them.
   b. they funnel federal money into targeted areas.
   c. they are secret.
   d. lobbyists oppose them.

4. Which of the following would be an attractive committee for a member of Congress from Montana looking to serve his or her constituency?
   a. Ways and Means
   b. Rules
   c. Education
   d. Agriculture

5. Descriptive representation refers to
   a. representing the interests of groups.
   b. serving constituents through pork barrel projects.
   c. representing constituents by mirroring their personal, politically relevant characteristics.
   d. All of the above.

6.    A senator can effectively prevent the Senate from voting by
   a.   conducting oversight.
   b.   filibustering.
   c.   introducing another bill.
   d.   holding hearings.

7.    Which of the following ends debate in the Senate?
   a.   cloture
   b.   vote by the Rules Committee
   c.   conference committee
   d.   markup

8.    Most of the time, members of Congress vote with
   a.   the president.
   b.   their state.
   c.   celebrities.
   d.   their party.

**Questions 9-10 refer to the chart below.**

How a Bill Becomes Law

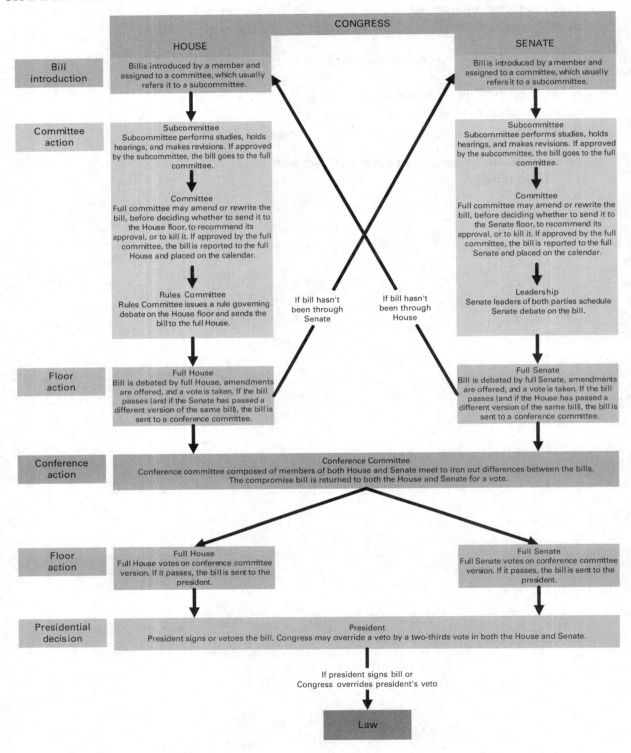

9. After a House committee reviews a bill and writes its report, the bill goes to the
   a. Senate.
   b. appropriate subcommittee.
   c. president.
   d. House Rules Committee.

10. Differences in House and Senate bills are resolved by
    a. the President.
    b. the Speaker of the House.
    c. the Senate Rules committee.
    d. conference committees.

11. Which of the following is the best example of legislative oversight?
    a. The vice president presides over the Senate.
    b. The Rules Committee amends a bill.
    c. Debate is limited.
    d. A hearing is held to investigate misuse of funds within a federal agency.

12. All of the following is true of Congress EXCEPT
    a. Most members of Congress today are professional politicians.
    b. The majority of incumbents get reelected.
    c. More than 50% of legislators are women.
    d. About 1/3 have studied law.

13. The second most powerful official in Washington, D.C., after the president, is the
    a. U.S. Senate *pro tempore*.
    b. chief justice of the Supreme Court.
    c. Speaker of the House of Representatives.
    d. vice president.

14. Most of the work in Congress is done
    a. on the floor of the House.
    b. in conjunction with the president.
    c. in meetings with lobbyists.
    d. in standing committees.

15. All of the following are true of congressional oversight EXCEPT
    a. members tend to spend more time on things other than oversight.
    b. oversight is administered through the committee system.
    c. members spend less time on oversight when there is a scandal.
    d. the biggest obstacle of oversight is the lack of electoral advantage.

16. The term for redrawing Congressional districts to favor a particular political party is
    a. apportionment paradox.
    b. gerrymandering.
    c. redistricting.
    d. redlining.

17. This office is involved in the preparation of Congress' budget.
    a. Office of Management and Budget
    b. General Accounting Office
    c. Congressional Accounting Office
    d. Congressional Budget Office

18. In the House of Representatives, the _____ controls the scheduling of bills for debate.
    a. House Ways and Means Committee
    b. Speaker of the House
    c. House Rules Committee
    d. Chief Administrative Officer

19. The power of impeachment belongs to
    a. the Senate.
    b. the House.
    c. a Federal Grand Jury.
    d. the Supreme Court.

20. The custom followed in Congress specifying that majority party members with the longest record of service will become committee chairs is
    a. senatorial courtesy.
    b. ageism.
    c. the seniority rule.
    d. elder custom.

# Free-Response Questions

1. Occasionally, one party will have control of Congress and the presidency. This will give the majority party advantages in Congress, yet passing legislation is still difficult.

   a. Describe the legislative advantages of the majority party in Congress with respect to both committee structure and leadership.

   b. Explain why, even with single-party control, passing legislation is difficult. Use two examples to support your explanation.

2. "...If angels were to govern men, neither external nor internal controls on government would be necessary. In framing a government which is to be administered by men over men, the great difficulty lies in this: you must first enable the government to control the governed; and in the next place oblige it to control itself."

   --*The Federalist No. 51*

   a. In addition to passing laws, Congress performs other functions. Describe each of the following functions Congress (or one of its chambers) may perform:
      - Oversight of the bureaucracy
      - Confirmation of presidential nominees
      - Impeachment and trial

   b. Explain why the Framers of the Constitution considered these to be important functions.

# Answers and Explanations

## Multiple-Choice Questions

1. D  Women make up a small percentage of both the House and the Senate that is far lower than the percentage of women in the general population.
   *Page reference: 310-313, AP Big Ideas: PMI, PRD*

2. C  Incumbency is the most important determinant in a candidate's chance of getting elected.
   *Page reference: 313, AP Big Idea: PMI*

3. B  Riders are unpopular with the general public when the targeted money does not benefit them.
   *Page reference: 325-331, AP Big Idea: PMI*

4. D  Being on the Agriculture Committee would enable a member of Congress to assist his or her constituents in farming and ranching.
   *Page reference: 322-325, AP Big Idea: PMI*

5. C  The idea behind descriptive representation is that citizens are best represented by people like themselves.
   *Page reference: 310-313, AP Big Ideas: PRD, PMI*

6. B  The filibuster stalls the debate process and therefore prevents the Senate from voting.
   *Page reference: 329, AP Big Idea: PMI*

7. A  Cloture (which requires 60 votes) ends a filibuster.
   *Page reference: 329, AP Big Idea: PMI*

8. D  While party discipline is not required, on most legislative issues members of Congress will vote with their party.
   *Page reference: 331-335, AP Big Idea: PMI*

9. D  After being discussed and marked up in committee, a bill goes to the Rules Committee, which will schedule it for debate on the floor of the House.
   *Page reference: 326, AP Big Idea: PMI*

10. D  Conference committees are formed when the Senate and the House pass different versions of the same bill.
   *Page reference: 326, AP Big Idea: PMI*

11. D  Oversight committees routinely hold hearings and ask questions of members of an agency to investigate claims of misuse of funds.
   *Page reference: 327-329, AP Big Idea: PMI*

12. C  Women make up significantly less than 50% in both houses of Congress, with only 78 women in the House and only 20 in the Senate.
*Page reference: 310-313, AP Big Ideas: PMI, PRD*

13. C  The Speaker of the House is a member of the majority party who has both formal and informal powers and is second in line in presidential succession. The Speaker is the most powerful member of Congress.
*Page reference: 320, AP Big Idea: PMI*

14. D  Standing committees are permanent, subject-matter committees that handle bills in different policy areas and through which all bills must pass in both houses.
*Page reference: 322-323, AP Big Idea: PMI*

15. C  Oversight is Congress's monitoring of the bureaucracy and its administration of policy, performed mainly through hearings, and occurs especially in times of scandal.
*Page reference: 327-328, AP Big Idea: PMI*

16. B  Gerrymandering is the drawing of congressional districts to produce a particular electoral outcome (usually in favor of a particular party) without regard to the shape of the district.
*Page reference: 319-320, AP Big Ideas: CON, PMI*

17. D  The Congressional Budget Office advises Congress on the probable consequences of its decisions, and forecasts revenues.
*Page reference: 325, AP Big Idea: PMI*

18. C  The House Rules Committee reviews most bills coming from a House committee before they go to the full House.
*Page reference: 322-323, AP Big Idea: PMI*

19. B  The power of impeachment, the political equivalent of indictment in criminal law, was given to the House of Representatives by the Constitution.
*Page reference: 319-322, 347-348, My PoliScilab/Constitution, AP Big Ideas: CON, PMI*

20. C  The seniority rule is a legislative practice that assigns the chair of a committee or subcommittee to the member of the majority party with the longest continuous service on the committee.
*Page reference: 323, AP Big Idea: PMI*

# Free-Response Questions

*This rubric provides examples of many, but not all of the possible correct responses to the free-response questions.*

1.  Occasionally, one party will have control of Congress and the presidency. This will give the majority party advantages in Congress, yet passing legislation is still difficult.

    a.  Describe the legislative advantages of the majority party in Congress with respect to both committee structure and leadership.

        ■  The majority party in Congress has numerous advantages in the legislative process. All committee chairs come from the majority party and there are more members of the majority party on committees. The chair of the committee can decide to hold a vote on moving a piece of legislation to the next stage, and is usually successful since he has more members from his party on the committee. The majority party also selects the Speaker of the House, who chairs the Rules Committee, schedules legislation, oversees the rules for the legislation, and oversees the debate on the legislation.

    b.  Explain why, even with single-party control, passing legislation is difficult. Use two examples to support your explanation.

        ■  Even when one party controls both the White House and Congress, passing legislation is still difficult. There are many things that can stop legislation from passing. First, there is no guarantee of party discipline. One defecting member of a political party has the potential to slow the legislation. Oftentimes members within a party will disagree significantly during the markup process. One committee chair can also essentially hold a piece of legislation hostage in committee. Finally, in the Senate, there are maneuvers that give the minority party power, such as filibustering. All a minority party senator has to do is declare their intent to filibuster, and then there is a requirement that 60 votes cut off the filibuster. If the majority party does not have 60 in the Senate, passing any legislation will be difficult.

2. "…If angels were to govern men, neither external nor internal controls on government would be necessary. In framing a government which is to be administered by men over men, the great difficulty lies in this: you must first enable the government to control the governed; and in the next place oblige it to control itself."

*--The Federalist No. 51*

   a. Congress has several nonlegislative functions. Describe the relevance of each of the following and provide an example.

oversight of the bureaucracy

- One nonlegislative function of Congress is oversight of the federal bureaucracy. This occurs when a committee investigates how a federal department or agency is doing its job. Normally, Congress does this by holding hearings and asking questions of federal employees. This information-gathering process results in reports, recommendations and, often, new legislation. This is done publicly, and video clips of these hearings are often shown on television. One example is the 9/11 Commission. This commission was created to try to figure out how our intelligence system could perform better and avoid another 9/11 catastrophe. Hearings were held and a major report was published, which resulted in the reorganization of U.S. intelligence services.

confirmation of political appointees

- Another nonlegislative function of Congress is confirming presidential appointees. Most often, the Senate Judiciary Committee performs this function. The committee holds a hearing and interviews the potential nominee. Former employers and those who know the nominee may also testify. The committee makes a recommendation about whether or not to approve the nominee and then the full Senate must vote by a simple majority in order for the nominee to be confirmed. One recent example is Michael Mukasey's nomination as U.S. attorney general.

impeachment

- Finally, impeachment is a nonlegislative function. If the president has committed a "high crime or misdemeanor," then the House may conduct an investigation of wrongdoing. The House then votes by simple majority and the Senate can conduct a trial to see if the allegations warrant removal of the president from office. The Senate is required to vote by a two-thirds majority in order to remove the president.

b. Explain why the Framers of the Constitution considered these to be important functions.

- The Framers of the Constitution considered these to be important functions because they work to strengthen the system of checks and balances, which allowed the Framers to minimize the threat of tyranny from any one branch.

# 12

# The Presidency

## Chapter Overview

In this chapter you will learn about the office of President of the United States, who serves both as the head of the government of the United States and the ceremonial representative of the country. We begin by considering how presidents are chosen. We then examine the formal and informal powers of the Office of the President, including the presidency itself, the vice president, the first lady, the cabinet, the Executive Office of the President, and the White House staff. Then we turn to consider how the president interacts with the Congress in the development of governmental policy. We conclude by exploring how presidential popularity and the president's relationship with the media influence the success of their term in office.

# Study Outline

 **Learning Objective 12.1:** Characterize the expectations for and the backgrounds of presidents and identify paths to the White House and how presidents may be removed. (p. 343)

## *The Presidents*

- **Presidents** can reach the Oval Office in different ways:
  - Most are former governors or members of Congress who, after being nominated by their party, campaigned and won the election.
  - Some presidents were vice presidents who took over after the death or removal of a president.
  - **Vice presidents** can also become president in the event the president resigns or is convicted in an impeachment trial.
  - **Twenty-Second Amendment:** Ratified in 1951, the amendment limits presidents to two terms of office.
  - The **Twenty-Fifth Amendment** establishes the procedures for filling vacancies in both the offices of president and vice president, and it also makes provisions for presidential disability.
- The Constitution sets forth the process of **impeachment** of a president who has abused his powers or committed a "high crime or misdemeanor" worthy of removal from office.
- The **House** may vote for the impeachment of the president by a simple majority.
- The **Senate** conducts the impeachment trial and the chief justice of the Supreme Court presides over the trial.
- It takes a two-thirds vote in the Senate to remove the president from office.
- **Watergate:** The events and scandal surrounding a break-in at the Democratic National Committee headquarters in 1972 and the subsequent cover-up of White House involvement, leading to the eventual resignation of President Nixon under threat of impeachment. Nixon is the only American president to resign from office.
- Only **two presidents** have been impeached, though neither was removed from office.

- Andrew Johnson was tried but not convicted in 1868, and Bill Clinton was acquitted by the Senate in 1999.

 **Learning Objective 12.2: Evaluate the president's constitutional powers and the expansion of presidential power. (p. 348)**

## Presidential Powers

- The Constitution grants the president fairly limited powers that were designed to prevent him or her from gaining too much authority, thus maintaining the balance of power among government institutions.
- The power to "take care that the laws be faithfully executed," as specified in the Constitution, is one of the more overlooked responsibilities of the president.
- As the bureaucracy has grown, it has become nearly impossible for the president alone to execute and enforce all laws; instead, the president now appoints numerous administrative officials, including cabinet members and department heads.
- Some have argued that during the 1950s and 1960s the presidency became "imperial" in nature, taking nearly full control over American politics.
- Since then, the power waned considerably but grew again with concerns about national security after the September 11 attacks.

**Learning Objective 12.3: Describe the roles of the vice president, cabinet, Executive Office of the President, White House staff, and First Lady. (p. 350)**

## Running the Government: The Chief Executive

- **Executive Orders:** Regulations originating with the executive branch and are one method presidents can use to control the bureaucracy.
- **Vice presidents** traditionally have few responsibilities and little political prominence.
- Vice presidents are second in line to assume the presidency if the president is unable to fulfill the duties of office.

- The vice president is the president (presiding officer) of the Senate and casts a vote whenever there is a tie.

- Today, vice presidents assume more responsibilities, depending on how the president they are serving entrusts functions to them.

- Vice presidents may serve as diplomats representing the president, take part in important policy meetings, or help raise funds for their party.

- The **cabinet** is a group of officials who act as advisors to the president.

- The cabinet is not mentioned in the Constitution, but it quickly became an institution that has accompanied every presidency.

- The modern cabinet is composed of the attorney general and the heads, or secretaries, of the 13 executive departments.

- The president has the power to appoint all of these officials, but each appointment must be confirmed by the Senate.

- Each cabinet member heads a department that deals with a different policy area.

- The departments, created by Congress, carry out all the administrative work necessary to enforce laws or assist the president in his executive duties.

- The Executive Office of the President (E.O.P) is a collection of administrative and advisory bodies that assist the president in overseeing policy.

- The EOP includes the **National Security Council**, the **Council of Economic Advisors**, and the **Office of Management and Budget**.

- The White House Staff includes important personal and political advisors to the president, such as the legal counsel to the president, the president's personal secretary, and the chief of staff.

- This office takes care of the president's political needs and manages the press.

- The first lady has no official government position, yet she is often at the center of national attention.

**12.4** **Learning Objective 12.4: Assess the impact of various sources of presidential influence on the president's ability to win congressional support. (p. 356)**

## *Presidential Leadership of Congress: The Politics of Shared Powers*

- Though not a member of the legislative branch, presidents do have a role to play in the legislative process.

### *Chief Legislator*

- The power to **veto** legislation can be an effective tool of intimidation.
- Because a veto rejects a bill in its entirety, the president can have a good deal of influence over the shaping of each specific provision.
- If the president does veto a bill, it goes back to Congress, which, by a two-thirds vote, can override the veto; however, this rarely happens.
- The president also has the power to reject any legislation submitted at the end of the congressional session without the possibility of his veto being overruled.
- If he does not sign a bill submitted by Congress within 10 days of its adjourning, the bill is automatically rejected, which is a **pocket veto**.

### *Party Leadership*

- To influence policy, presidents must work closely with Congress.
- Specifically, they rely on close ties with members of Congress who are members of their political party.
- Political parties help bridge the gap between the legislative and executive branches.
- A president and a representative of the same party were most likely elected by the same body of people, or by voters who have similar political views, so they probably share political priorities.
- Members of Congress who support the president's legislative agenda are likely to receive support for some of their projects and initiatives in return.
- A close relationship with a popular president can also be beneficial to members of Congress during reelection (presidential coattails).

- The president must rely on members of Congress to introduce legislation for him or her and to win support for it during the legislative process; therefore, the president must work closely with party leaders to convince representatives to vote the party line.
- Even if a president's party is the majority party in either or both houses, he may not necessarily have the full support of representatives, who might not vote with the party line.

## Public Support

- Public support for the president factors heavily in his congressional support.
- Representatives are much more likely to vote in favor of the initiatives of a president who is popular with the electorate, and presidents are well aware that public opinion is an incredibly powerful tool of persuasion.
- Public approval gives a president more leeway in pursuing policy goals, because representatives are more likely to support his objectives in the hope of being reelected by an electorate that has confidence in their president.
- Public support lends a president a greater degree of legitimacy. Congress is more likely to respond to the will of a president who was elected by a large margin, especially on legislation proposed early in his term.
- The policies of a president who is perceived as weak are more likely to be cast into doubt by Congress, making it harder for the president to garner legislative support.

## Legislative Skills

- Presidents may also exert their influence over the political agenda by employing specific strategies at key times in the legislative process.
- To strengthen a presidential coalition, presidents often bargain with representatives by offering support on one piece of legislation in exchange for receiving it on another.
- Members of Congress may also receive certain presidential favors, such as joint public appearances during campaigns.

- Presidents present many proposals to Congress soon after their election during what is called the "honeymoon period," when there is a fresh sense of community in Washington.

- Presidents work hard to focus the attention of Congress on their own specific agendas.

- By setting priorities, they are able to concentrate their resources to push through a few key policy objectives.

## 12.5 Learning Objective 12.5: Analyze the president's powers in making national security policy and the relationship between the president and Congress in this arena. (p. 365)

### *The President and National Security Policy*

- The president is both the commander in chief of the armed forces and the chief U.S. diplomat.

- The diplomatic powers of the president include establishing formal recognition of other governments, negotiating treaties, formulating **executive agreements** with other foreign leaders (which, unlike treaties, do not require congressional approval; most executive agreements are administrative in nature), and using U.S. influence to arbitrate conflicts between other nations.

- Military powers include the decision to use weapons of mass destruction, authorizing military actions during war, and sending troops into specific areas of conflict.

- The **War Powers Resolution**, passed in 1973, was intended to limit this power by requiring that these troops be withdrawn within 60 days unless Congress declares war or issues an extension.

- Many believe that it is unconstitutional, and all presidents have treated it as such.

- **Legislative veto:** A vote in Congress to override a presidential decision. Although the War Powers Resolution asserts this authority, there is no reason to believe that, if challenged, the Supreme Court would find the legislative veto in violation of the doctrine of separation of powers.

- **Crisis manager:** A crisis – a sudden, unpredictable, and potentially dangerous event would require the president to play the role of crisis manager.

# Learning Objective 12.6: Identify the factors that affect the president's ability to obtain public support. (p. 370)

## *Power from the People: The Public Presidency*

- Because presidents know that public approval works enormously in their favor, they work hard to sell their agenda to the public.
- A voter's approval of the president is determined by whether the voter identifies with the political party of the president.
- A voter's approval of the president is determined by how the president responds to economic shifts or handles other current issues.
- A voter's approval of the president is determined by how effective a public speaker the president is, and his appearance in front of the cameras.
- A voter's approval of the president is determined by whether the president appeals to the public directly, in which case the public usually responds positively.
- A voter's approval of the president is determined by how the media interprets the actions of the president.
- The efforts of the White House to influence public opinion are not always successful, however. The public tends to be fickle in its approval, and the media often mislead the public by oversimplifying political and economic issues.

# Learning Objective 12.7: Characterize the president's relations with the press and news coverage of the presidency. (p. 374)

## *The President and the Press*

- The press is the principal intermediary between the president and the public.
- Presidents and the press are frequently in conflict over the amount, nature, and tone of the coverage of the presidency.
- There has been an increase in the negativity of coverage and there are an increasing number of ideologically biased sources of news.

**Learning Objective 12.8: Assess the role of presidential power in the American democracy and the president's impact on the scope of government. (p. 377)**

## Understanding the American Presidency

- There is always a fear of a presidential power that is harmful to democracy, however, there are many checks on presidential power. Support of increasing the scope of government is not inherent in the presidency, and presidents have frequently been advocates of limiting government growth.

## For Additional Review

Take notes on the following areas of increased presidential power:

1. war powers
2. diplomacy by executive agreements
3. secrecy and executive privilege
4. government by veto

For each of the above areas of presidential power, explain how it has increased presidential power. Use these notes to help prepare for the unit test and the AP Government and Politics Exam.

Create a chart listing the roles of the president. Under each role, list the powers the president exercises when performing the duties for each role. Use this chart when reviewing and studying for the unit test and the AP Government and Politics Exam.

# Review Questions

## Multiple-Choice Questions

1. Congress can override a presidential veto of legislation
   a. by appealing to the U.S. Supreme Court.
   b. by negotiating a deal with the vice president.
   c. by getting approval of the bill in three-fourths of the state legislatures.
   d. with a two-thirds vote in both houses of Congress.

2. According to the Constitution, the vice president
   a. chairs all cabinet meetings.
   b. is ineligible to run for president after two terms as vice president.
   c. is the president of the Senate.
   d. must be of the same party as the president.

3. Which of the following presidential appointments requires Senate confirmation?
   a. press secretary
   b. chief of staff
   c. White House counsel
   d. secretary of state

4. All of the following are true statements about the impeachment process EXCEPT
   a. the chief justice of the United States presides over the trial.
   b. the Supreme Court decides guilt or innocence.
   c. the trial must be held in public.
   d. the Senate serves as the jury.

5. A president is most likely to gain public support for a public policy proposal by
   a. sending the vice president out to conduct high-profile town hall meetings.
   b. placing ads in respected newspapers with large circulations.
   c. vetoing a bill passed by Congress.
   d. appealing to the public directly via the broadcast media.

6. The Twenty-Fifth Amendment is significant because it
   a. clarifies the terms under which the vice president may become president if the president becomes disabled.
   b. defines the line of succession to the president.
   c. clarifies the formal roles, duties, and responsibilities of all parties involved in a presidential impeachment trial.
   d. defines the process to be used for creating new cabinet positions.

7.  One of the primary tools presidents use to control the bureaucracy is
    a.  the line-item veto.
    b.  congressional oversight committees.
    c.  campaign finance reform.
    d.  the presidential power to appoint and remove top-level administrators.

8.  Which of the following statements about the president as commander in chief is true?
    a.  The president has the authority to declare war for up to 60 days without consulting Congress.
    b.  The president decides if and when to use weapons of mass destruction in times of war.
    c.  Presidents with no prior military experience are not allowed to make major military decisions alone.
    d.  The president is required by law to consult with the Joint Chiefs of Staff before deploying the military.

**Questions 9–10 refer to the table below.**

Constitutional Powers of the President

| National Security Powers |
| --- |
| Serve as commander in chief of the armed forces |
| Make treaties with other nations, subject to the agreement of two-thirds of the Senate |
| Nominate ambassadors, with the agreement of a majority of the Senate |
| Receive ambassadors of other nations, thereby conferring diplomatic recognition on other governments |
| **Legislative Powers** |
| Present information on the state of the union to Congress |
| Recommend legislation to Congress |
| Convene both houses of Congress on extraordinary occasions |
| Adjourn Congress if the House and Senate cannot agree on adjournment |
| Veto legislation (Congress may overrule with two-thirds vote of each house) |
| **Administrative Powers** |
| Execute federal laws |
| Nominate officials as provided for by Congress and with the agreement of a majority of the Senate |
| Request written opinions of administrative officials |
| Fill administrative vacancies during congressional recesses |
| **Judicial Powers** |
| Grant reprieves and pardons for federal offenses (except impeachment) |
| Nominate federal judges, who are confirmed by a majority of the Senate |

9.  All of the following are powers of the president EXCEPT
    a.  conducting diplomatic relations
    b.  negotiating treaties
    c.  dismissing Supreme Court justices
    d.  appointing cabinet officers

10. All of the following are powers of the president EXCEPT
    a. the power to convene Congress
    b. the power to nominate federal judges
    c. the power to veto legislation
    d. the power to declare war

11. Which of the following is NOT in the line of presidential succession?
    a. chief justice of the Supreme Court
    b. secretary of state
    c. secretary of the interior
    d. attorney general

12. The vice president possesses only one real constitutional duty, which is
    a. to break tie votes in the Senate.
    b. to serve as an advisor to the Supreme Court.
    c. to break tie votes in the House of Representatives.
    d. to act as chief diplomat.

13. This is a formal agreement negotiated by the president of the United States and one or more nations, requiring approval of the Senate by a two-thirds vote.
    a. treaty
    b. executive order
    c. executive agreement
    d. executive memorandum

14. The President and Congress tend to agree
    a. during the first year of a president's first term.
    b. during the first year of a president's second term.
    c. when the president is a lame duck.
    d. when there is an unpopular president.

15. The body within the White House Staff of the President that advises the president on economic issues is
    a. the Treasury Office.
    b. the National Economic Council.
    c. the Office of Management and Budget.
    d. the Council of Economic Advisors.

16. All of the following are the formal constitutional qualifications for becoming president EXCEPT that the candidate
    a. must be a resident of the U.S. for at least 14 years.
    b. must be at least 35 years old.
    c. must be a white male.
    d. must be a natural born citizen.

17. All of the following are in the Executive Office of the President EXCEPT
    a. the Council of Economic Advisors
    b. the General Accounting Office
    c. the National Security Council
    d. the Office of the Vice President

18. The annual statement the president presents to Congress and the nation is called the
    a. State of the Country Address.
    b. State of the Budget Address.
    c. State of the Union Address.
    d. State of the State Address.

19. The director of which of the following departments is considered MOST central to the president's agencies?
    a. Energy
    b. Management and Budget
    c. Defense
    d. Homeland Security

20. This amendment to the Constitution established term limits for the president.
    a. Twelfth
    b. Twenty-second
    c. Twenty-fifth
    d. Twenty-first

## Free-Response Questions

1.  The president is the single most powerful individual in government. Some of the president's most important responsibilities and powers fall in the area of national security as stated in Article II of the Constitution:

    "The President shall be Commander in Chief of the Army and Navy of the United States, and of the Militia of the several States, when called into the actual Service of the United States...He shall have Power, by and with the Advice and Consent of the Senate, to make Treaties, provided two thirds of the Senators present concur; and he shall nominate, and by and with the Advice and Consent of the Senate, shall appoint Ambassadors, other public Ministers and Consuls..."

    *--The United States Constitution*

    a.  Identify and explain two national security powers or responsibilities granted to the president in the Constitution.

    b.  Identify and describe two constitutional limitations on presidential national security power.

2.  The president plays an important policymaking role in the federal system.

    a.  Identify and explain two ways the president influences policy.

    b.  Identify and describe two limitations on the president's policymaking power.

# Answers and Explanations

## Multiple-Choice Questions

1. **D**   While a presidential veto usually effectively kills proposed legislation, Congress can override the veto with a two-thirds majority vote in both houses, and has done so in about four percent of the vetoes. The Constitution gives the president the power to veto as a means to check Congress, and it gives Congress the power to override a veto as a means of checking the president.
   *Page reference: 357, AP Big Ideas: CON, PMI*

2. **C**   The Constitution assigns vice presidents the relatively minor tasks of presiding over the Senate and voting in case of a tie among the senators.
   *Page reference: 351, AP Big Idea: PMI*

3. **D**   The Secretary of State is a member of the president's cabinet, and nominees for Secretary of State must be confirmed by the Senate.
   *Page reference: 351-352, AP Big Idea: PMI*

4. **B**   The Supreme Court plays no role in the presidential impeachment process.
   *Page reference: 347-348, AP Big Ideas: CON, PMI*

5. **D**   Public support is one of president's most important resources for getting their policy agenda enacted. Presidents who have the backing of the public have an easier time influencing Congress. Using the mass media to directly appeal to the public is an effective tool for gaining public support.
   *Page reference: 360-362, AP Big Idea: PMI*

6. **A**   The Twenty-Fifth Amendment, passed in 1967, is significant because it clarifies the terms under which the vice president may become president in the event that the president becomes disabled. It also outlines how a recuperated president can reclaim the job.
   *Page reference: 346, AP Big Ideas: CON, PMI*

7. **D**   The power to appoint and remove top-level administrators gives the president significant influence over what the federal bureaucracy does or does not do.
   *Page reference: 348-350, AP Big Idea: PMI*

8. **B**   As commander in chief of military forces, the president decides if and when American armed forces use weapons of mass destruction in times of war.
   *Page reference: 366-368, AP Big Ideas: CON, PMI*

9. **C**   Dismissing Supreme Court justices is not a power of the president.
   *Page reference: 348, AP Big Ideas: CON, PMI*

10. **D**   The power to declare war is not a power of the president.
    *Page reference: 348, AP Big Ideas: CON, PMI*

11. A  The chief justice is not in the line of presidential succession. The Constitution authorizes the vice president to take over the office of the presidency if the president dies, resigns, is impeached, or is otherwise unable to perform his duties.
*Page reference: 346, AP Big Ideas: CON, PMI*

12. A  The Constitution assigns vice presidents the minor tasks of presiding over the Senate and voting in case of a tie among senators.
*Page reference: 351, AP Big Ideas: CON, PMI*

13. A  A treaty is a formal, public agreement between the United States and one or more nations that must be approved by two-thirds of the Senate.
*Page reference: 356-357; 362-365, AP Big Ideas: CON, PMI*

14. A  The "honeymoon" period occurs at the beginning of a new president's term and it is the period during which the president enjoys generally positive relations with the press and Congress, usually lasting about six months.
*Page reference: 356-362, AP Big Idea: PMI*

15. B  The National Economic Council is a division of the policy offices housed in the White House Staff and it advises the president on economic issues.
*354, AP Big Idea: PMI*

16. C  This is not a constitutional qualification for president.
*Page reference: MyPoliSciLab/Constitution, AP Big Ideas: CON, PMI*

17. B  The General Accounting Office is a congressional office and not part of the Executive Office of the president.
*Page reference: 352-354, AP Big Idea: PMI*

18. C  The State of the Union Address is the annual statement the president gives to Congress and to the nation.
*Page reference: 356-365, AP Big Ideas: CON, PMI*

19. B  The director of the Office of Management and Budget heads the department that prepares the president's budget and also advises presidents on proposals from departments and agencies and helps review their proposed regulations.
*Page reference: 353, AP Big Idea: PMI*

20. B  The Twenty-second Amendment limits the president to two terms, or ten years total.
*Page reference: 346, AP Big Ideas: CON, PMI*

# Free-Response Questions

*This rubric provides examples of many, but not all of the possible correct responses to the free-response questions.*

1.  The president is the single most powerful individual in government. Some of the president's most important responsibilities and powers fall in the area of national security as stated in Article II of the Constitution:

    "The President shall be Commander in Chief of the Army and Navy of the United States, and of the Militia of the several States, when called into the actual Service of the United States...He shall have Power, by and with the Advice and Consent of the Senate, to make Treaties, provided two thirds of the Senators present concur; and he shall nominate, and by and with the Advice and Consent of the Senate, shall appoint Ambassadors, other public Ministers and Consuls..."

    *--The United States Constitution*

    a.  Identify and explain two national security powers or responsibilities granted to the president in the Constitution.

        - **Commander in chief.** Because the framers wanted civilian control of the military, they made the president commander in chief of the armed forces. As commander in chief, the president controls where and how the military is deployed. The president also commands the vast arsenal of weapons of mass destruction. While only Congress can declare war, the president can interject U.S. troops into armed conflict on a limited basis.

        - **Diplomatic powers.** The president alone extends diplomatic recognition to foreign governments. The president can also terminate relations with other countries.

        - **Power to make treaties with other nations.** The president has the sole power to negotiate treaties with other countries, although the Constitution requires the Senate to approve them by a two-thirds vote.

    b.  Identify and describe two constitutional limitations on presidential national security power.

        - Although the president has power to deploy U.S. troops, only Congress has the constitutional power to declare war.

        - Treaties that presidents negotiate with foreign countries must be approved by a two-thirds vote in the Senate.

- Congress has the power of the purse. A president's national security agenda requires a willingness on the part of Congress to appropriate the necessary funds to support it.

2. The president plays an important policymaking role in the federal system.

   a. Identify and explain two ways the president influences policy.

      - **Executive orders.** The president can issue executive orders that have the effect of law. These can be powerful tools for the president to change the course of policy. For example, President Harry Truman used an executive order to desegregate the armed forces.

      - **Setting the legislative agenda.** Many presidents play major roles in setting the agenda of Congress. They not only make policy proposals but also use lobbyists to steward proposals through the policymaking process.

   b. Identify and describe two limitations on the president's policymaking power.

      - **Congress has the power of the purse.** Although the president can make policy proposals, only Congress can appropriate funds.

      - **The Supreme Court has judicial review.** The Supreme Court can review the constitutionality of executive orders or regulations promulgated by the bureaucracy.

# 13

# The Budget: The Politics of Taxing and Spending

## Chapter Overview

Every year the President and Congress must appropriate funds. If they fail to do so, the government will come to a virtual standstill. Obtaining funds and spending them is the essence of budgeting, and budgeting is central to policymaking. A **budget** is a policy document allocating burdens (taxes), which are the **revenues,** and benefits (**expenditures**). In this chapter we examine the politics of the budget. We start by describing the sources of funding for the federal government and assess the consequences of tax expenditures and borrowing. Then we analyze federal expenditures and the growth of the budget, outline the budgetary process, and explain the role that politics plays. We conclude by assessing the impact of democratic politics on budgetary growth and of the budget on the scope of government. By the end of the chapter, students should have a good understanding of the basic dynamics and controversies surrounding the federal budget.

# Study Outline

**Learning Objective 13.1: Describe the sources of funding for the federal government and assess the consequences of tax expenditure and borrowing. (p. 363)**

## Federal Revenue and Borrowing

- **Income taxes:** A percentage of what a person earns goes directly to the government.
    - The **Sixteenth Amendment** (1913) officially authorized Congress to collect income taxes.
    - The Internal Revenue Service (IRS) collects income taxes, monitors people's payments through audits, and investigates and prosecutes cases of tax evasion.
    - The income tax is progressive—people with higher incomes pay a greater percentage in taxes.
    - Opponents suggest a flat tax in which everyone pays an equal rate; such a tax is considered proportional.
    - Others propose a sales tax to replace the income tax; because poorer people pay a higher percentage of their income in sales tax—they spend much more of their income than they save or invest—such a tax is called regressive.
    - Corporations also pay taxes on their income, but most tax money comes from individual income taxes.
- **Social insurance taxes:** Social Security taxes are paid by both businesses and their employees.
    - Money collected from this tax is used specifically to pay current monthly benefits to senior citizens.
    - These taxes have grown significantly and now account for about one-third of the federal revenue.
    - As the population ages, more people will be expecting payments from the government. Economists are concerned that the baby boom generation may drain the system.

- **Borrowing:** The federal government has borrowed a huge amount of money over the years.
  - It borrows from foreign investors, foreign governments, and the American people by selling government bonds.
  - The government gets the money, but must pay it back to the bondholder with interest.
  - The money the government owes is the **national debt**.
  - An excess of federal expenditures over federal revenues is a **deficit.**
  - About 7 percent of the federal budget is allocated to pay just the interest on the federal debt.
  - Future generations will have to pay for many policies enacted today.
  - Lawmakers have considered proposing a balanced budget amendment, which would require Congress and the president to balance the budget each year.
  - Critics argue that it is too difficult to predict a balanced budget because of the uncertainties of the economy.

## Taxes and Public Policy

- Tax loopholes are any tax break that allows a person to benefit from not paying a part of his or her taxes. Deductions for specific items are considered loopholes.
- Not everyone has the same access to loopholes.
- **Tax expenditures** are the losses in federal revenues that result from tax breaks, deductions, and exemptions.
- They function as built-in subsidies—the government loses money by excusing a homeowner from paying taxes on a mortgage, but then the government does not have to pay for programs, such as a homeowners' assistance program.
- Middle- and upper-income people benefit the most because they usually have more deductions and write-offs.
- Tax reform: How much to tax is almost always a point of contention among Congress and the public.
  - President Clinton raised tax rates on the wealthy. President George W. Bush enacted a series of tax cuts across all income levels, but it particularly benefitted the wealthy.

**13.2** **Learning Objective 13.2: Analyze federal expenditures and the growth of the budget. (p. 390)**

## *Federal Expenditures*

- The government must pay its own operational costs, which make up a significant percentage of its overall expenditures.

- **National security** was a large expenditure during the Cold War and Reagan era, but it had begun to decline before September 11, 2001.

- **Social services** are now the biggest expenditure: programs for people of low income and senior citizens make up one-third of the budget.

- Social Security began with the **Social Security Act**, part of the New Deal.

- **Medicare**, initiated in 1965, extends medical coverage to senior citizens.

- Because people are living longer and the current generation of senior citizens is large, Social Security taxes have risen.

- **Uncontrollable expenditures** are a form of mandatory spending.

- Pensions and payments toward the national debt are fixed, and thus not subject to budgetary cuts or changes.

- **Entitlements** are benefits the government must pay to people who are eligible according to federal rules, such as veterans' aid, Social Security, and welfare.

- **Incrementalism** is the basis on which the budget is adjusted every year.

- A budget is calculated by assuming that the expenditures included in the budget of the previous year will rise for the next year.

- One issue is how large the increment should be, and another concern is that this creates a system of an ever-increasing budget.

## 13.3 Learning Objective 13.3: Outline the budgetary process and explain the role that politics plays. (p. 397)

### *The Budgetary Process*

- The budget affects and involves agencies and departments in the federal, state, and even local governments.

- Every year, the budget process begins with the "spring review," when the federal agencies review their programs and prepare their requests for the next fiscal year.

- Budget requests are submitted to the **Office of Management and Budget (OMB)**.

- During the "fall review," the OMB reviews the requests, and then submits the final requests to the president. Interest groups and agencies often team up when making budgetary requests.

- Based on all of the agency requests, the president formally proposes a budget plan to Congress in February.

- Since 1922, the president has been required to prepare and submit a budget to Congress.

- In 1974, the Congressional Budget and Impoundment Control Act was passed by Congress to reform and regain some control over the budgetary process.

- The **House Ways and Means Committee** and the **Senate Finance Committee** write the tax codes that will determine how much revenue the government will have for the year.

- The **Appropriations Committees** in both houses determine how federal funds within the total expenditure will be allotted among agencies and departments.

- The House and Senate Budget Committees and the **Congressional Budget Office** review the proposal for its feasibility.

- Congress must agree on a **budget resolution**, the final amount of expenditures not to be exceeded for the year.

- Congress might make changes to existing laws to meet the budget resolution.

- **Reconciliation bills** revise program authorizations.

- The **Authorization bill** allows the expenditures for discretionary programs or enacts the requirements for entitlement programs to be changed. **Approriations bills** fund programs within limits established by authorization bills. If Congress cannot pass appropriations bills they can pass **continuing resolutions** to allow agencies to spend at the level of the previous year.

- Congress must pass the final budget bill and the president must sign it for it to become law.

- The **Government Accountability Office (GAO)** audits, monitors and evaluates what agencies are doing with their budgets.

 **Learning Objective 13.4: Assess the impact of democratic politics on budgetary growth and of the budget on scope of government. (p. 404)**

## *Understanding Budgeting*

- Budgets in democracies grow because the public and organized interests demand new and larger public services.

- Some politicians compete for votes by promising to limit budgets.

- Increasing budgets increase the scope of government, but decreases in taxes and increases in debt make it more difficult to add or expand programs.

## For Additional Review

Make a table outlining the budgetary process. For each step, list the institutions involved and their specific responsibilities. Make a note of any political motivations that influence each participant's role in making the budget. Use this table when reviewing and studying for the unit test and for the AP Government and Politics exam.

Make a list of the sources of funding for the federal government. Include in this list the consequences of tax expenditures and borrowing. Use this list when reviewing and studying for the unit test and for the AP Government and Politics exam.

# Review Questions

## Multiple-Choice Questions

1. Congress's authority to levy an income tax comes from which of the following?
   a. interstate commerce clause
   b. Sixteenth Amendment
   c. Budget Act (1974)
   d. Bill of Rights

2. The institution responsible for compiling the president's budget proposal is the
   a. Department of the Treasury.
   b. Congressional Budget Office.
   c. Senate Appropriations Committee.
   d. Office of Management and Budget.

3. The largest contribution to federal revenue comes from
   a. taxes on businesses.
   b. interest on foreign debt.
   c. entry fees at national parks.
   d. individual income taxes.

**Question 4 refers to the graph below.**

Federal Revenues

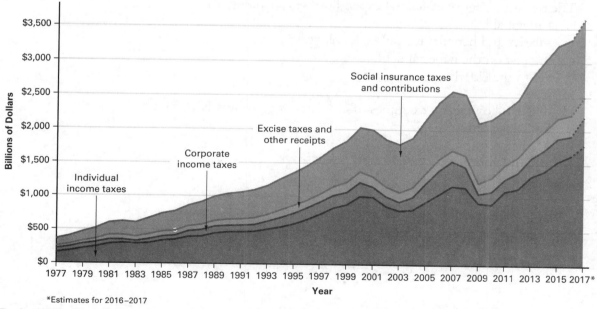

*Estimates for 2016–2017

*Budget of the United States Government, Fiscal Year 2017: Historical Tables (Washington, D.C.: U.S. Government Printing Office, 2016), Table 2.1.*

4.  All of the following statements accurately describe the data in the graph EXCEPT
    a.  individuals pay far more income taxes than corporations.
    b.  social insurance taxes are the fastest-growing source of federal revenue.
    c.  excise taxes are the smallest source of federal revenue.
    d.  federal revenue increased very little between 2008 and 2010.

5.  Which of the following statements is true about U.S. budget deficits?
    a.  The first federal budget deficit did not occur until the 1990s.
    b.  The Constitution requires a balanced federal budget.
    c.  Large budget deficits make the U.S. government more financially dependent on foreign investors.
    d.  Budget deficits have no practical effect on individual citizens.

6.  Two conditions associated with the dramatic government growth in the United States over the past half century are
    a.  growth in the national security state and growth in the social service state.
    b.  accelerated global warming and the rising cost of energy.
    c.  growth in the number of cabinet offices and growth in the number of unfunded mandates.
    d.  increased immigration and a growing birth rate.

7.  Which of the following initiates the budget process?
    a.  the House Ways and Means Committee
    b.  the president
    c.  the Senate Finance Committee
    d.  the Congressional Budget Office

8.  The biggest category of federal expenditures is spending for
    a.  foreign aid.
    b.  salaries and benefits for public employees.
    c.  interest on the national debt.
    d.  aid to the elderly and the poor.

9.  All of the following are examples of entitlement programs EXCEPT
    a.  Social Security.
    b.  Medicare.
    c.  defense contracts.
    d.  veterans' benefits.

**Questions 10-11 refer to the graph below.**

Fluctuating Deficits

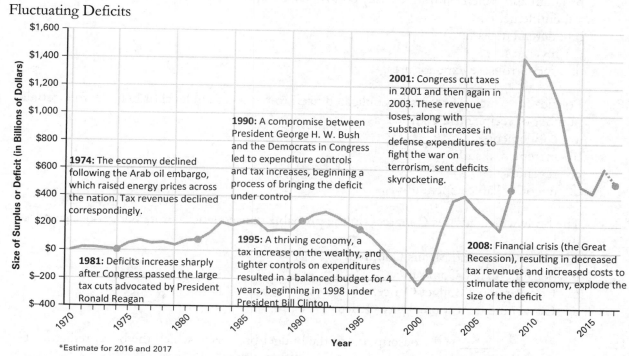

*Estimate for 2016 and 2017

*Budget of the United States Government, Fiscal Year 2017: Historical Tables (Washington, D.C.: U.S. Government Printing Office, 2016), Table 1.1*

10. Which of the following conclusions may be drawn from the graph?
    a. The Clinton administration closed the budget deficit to reach a balanced budget in 1998.
    b. The federal deficit decreased dramatically during the Reagan administration.
    c. Between 1972 and 1992, the deficit grew by about five times the 1972 deficit.
    d. The federal deficit decreased significantly between 1975 and 1980.

11. Which of the following describes a trend in the graph?
    a. Deficits decreased dramatically between 1970 and 1980.
    b. Deficits increased dramatically in 2010.
    c. Deficits remained steady between 1995 and 2005.
    d. Deficits cannot be effectively measured.

12. Government spending determined by how many eligible beneficiaries there are for a program and which cannot be easily controlled are known as
    a. entitlements.
    b. incrementalism.
    c. revenues.
    d. uncontrollable expenditures.

13. Policies for which Congress has obligated itself to pay a certain level of benefits to a certain number of recipients are known as
    a. entitlements.
    b. incrementalism.
    c. revenues.
    d. uncontrollable expenditures.

14. The body which advises Congress on the probable consequences of its budget decisions is the
    a. House Ways and Means Committee.
    b. Senate Finance Committee.
    c. Congressional Budget Office.
    d. Government Accountability Office.

15. _____ is the description of the budget process in which the best predictor of this year's budget is last year's budget, plus a little more.
    a. Estimation
    b. Revenue sharing
    c. Deficit spending
    d. Incrementalism

16. _____ is the congressional process through which program authorizations are revised to achieve savings.
    a. Estimation
    b. Revenue sharing
    c. Deficit spending
    d. Reconciliation

17. When Congress is unable to pass appropriation bills, these allow agencies to continue spending at the level of the previous year.
    a. income taxes
    b. appropriation bills
    c. continuing resolutions
    d. budget resolutions

18.  An act of Congress that establishes, continues, or changes a discretionary government program or entitlement is known as
  a.  reconciliation.
  b.  appropriation bills.
  c.  continuing resolutions.
  d.  authorization bills.

19.  Losses in revenue which result from special exemptions, exclusions, or deductions are known as
  a.  tax expenditures.
  b.  tax reductions.
  c.  uncontrollable expenditures.
  d.  entitlements.

20.  Tax expenditures were established by
  a.  the Constitution.
  b.  1974 Budget Act.
  c.  the Social Security Act.
  d.  16th Amendment.

## Free-Response Questions

1.  The rise of the national security state and the rise of the social service state have long been associated with government growth and budget deficits in the United States.

    a.  Briefly describe what is meant by "growth in the national security state."

    b.  Briefly describe what is meant by "growth in the social service state."

    c.  Identify one piece of legislation passed by Congress since 1970 that was designed to reform the budget process and control deficit spending by the government.

    d.  For the legislation you identified in "c," briefly explain one goal it was designed to accomplish.

2.    Budget deficits and increasing federal debt are perennial concerns for national policymakers. Using the graphs below, and your knowledge of the budget, answer the following questions:

The Federal Budget: An Overview
Note: Data are estimates for fiscal year 2017

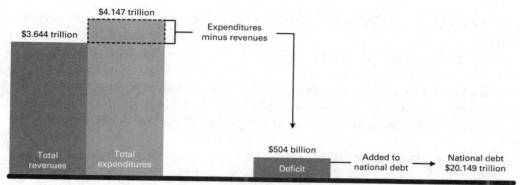

*Budget of the United States Government, Fiscal Year 2017: Historical Tables (Washington, D.C.: U.S. Government Printing Office, 2016), Tables 1.1 and 7.1.*

Total National Debt

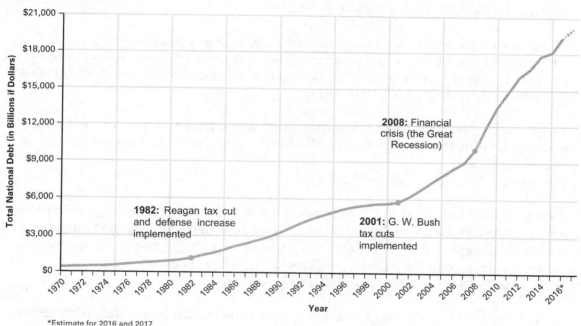

*Estimate for 2016 and 2017

*Budget of the United States Government, Fiscal Year 2017: Historical Tables (Washington, D.C.: U.S. Government Printing Office, 2016), Table 7.1.*

a.   Compare budget deficit and federal debt.

b.   Describe two negative consequences of a large federal debt.

c.   Analyze the possible impact of a balanced budget amendment on the government's ability to perform its budgetary functions.

# Answers and Explanations

## Multiple-Choice Questions

1. B   The Sixteenth Amendment, ratified in 1913, explicitly gives Congress the authority to levy a tax on income.
   *Page reference: 384, AP Big Ideas: PMI, PRD*

2. D   The Office of Budget and Management was established to coordinate the budget proposals of all government agencies into the president's final proposal. It has a significant amount of budgetary power, but this is checked by Congress's approval of the president's nominee for its director.
   *Page reference: 398, AP Big Ideas: PMI, PRD*

3. D   The three major sources of federal revenue are individual income, corporate, and social security insurance taxes. Of these, the individual income tax provides the most revenue for the federal government. Nearly half of all federal revenues are generated by personal income taxes.
   *Page reference: 384-390, AP Big Ideas: PRD, PMI*

4. D   The projected portion of the graph (with dashed lines) shows all sources of revenue increasing. The rapid rise in social insurance taxes is demonstrated by its greater slope compared to other sources of revenue. Federal revenue declined between 2001 and 2004.
   *Page reference: 385, AP Big Ideas: PMI, PRD*

5. C   Large budget deficits make the U.S. government more financially dependent on foreign investors, governments, and individuals. Foreign investors currently hold one-fifth of the U.S. national debt.
   *Page reference: 386, AP Big Ideas: PMI, PRD*

6. A   Two conditions associated with government growth in the U.S. are the rise in the national security state and the rise in the social service state. New military challenges and the cost of advanced technology are factors in the rising cost of the military state. Social service entitlements represent the largest expenditure in the federal budget.
   *Page reference: 390-395, AP Big Ideas: PMI, PRD*

7. B   Budgets are produced through a long and complex process that begins and ends with the president and has Congress squarely in the middle. The president submits a budget to Congress for consideration and decides whether to accept or reject the budget that ultimately emerges from Congress.
   *Page reference: 397-403, AP Big Ideas: PMI, PRD*

8. D   The biggest category of federal expenditures is spending for the elderly and the poor.
   *Page reference: 392-395, AP Big Ideas: PMI, CIV*

9. C    Entitlement programs are a form of mandatory spending, as everyone entitled to the benefits of the program must be paid. Congress cannot control these expenditures unless it changes the eligibility requirements of the program, which it is unlikely to do unless such measures are absolutely necessary. Defense contracts clearly do not fit this definition.
*Page reference: 396, AP Big Ideas: PMI, PRD*

10. A   The deficit was at its peak when President Clinton was elected in 1992. It decreased dramatically throughout the 1990s, however, and disappeared completely in 1998, when the United States experienced its first budget surplus in 30 years. The deficit fluctuated significantly under President George W. Bush.
*Page reference: 402, AP Big Ideas: PMI, PRD*

11. B   Deficits increased dramatically in 2010.
*Page reference: 402, AP Big Ideas: PMI, PRD*

12. D   Uncontrollable expenditures are expenditures that are determined by how many eligible beneficiaries there are for a program or by previous obligations of the government and that Congress therefore cannot easily control.
*Page reference: 396, AP Big Idea: PMI*

13. A   Entitlements are a claim for government funds that cannot be changed without violating the rights of the claimant. Social Security benefits are an example.
*Page reference: 396, AP Big Ideas: PMI, PRD*

14. C   The Congressional Budget Office is an agency of Congress that analyzes presidential budget recommendations and estimates the costs of proposed legislation. It is a counterweight to the president's Office of Management and Budget.
*Page reference: 399, AP Big Ideas: PMI, PRD*

15. D   Incrementalism is the process of preparing a budget using the previous year's budget or actual performance as a basis with incremental amounts added for the new budget period.
*Page reference: 395, AP Big Ideas: PMI, PRD*

16. D   Reconciliation is the Congressional process through which program authorizations are revised to achieve required savings. It usually also includes tax or other revenue adjustments. This usually comes near the end of the budgetary process, although occasionally the president and Congress have sought to use it in place of the regular lawmaking process.
*Page reference: 402, AP Big Ideas: PMI, PRD*

17. C   When Congress has not been able to reach agreement and pass appropriations bills at all, it has instead resorted to continuing resolutions, which are laws that allow agencies to spend at the previous year's level.
*Page reference: 403, AP Big Ideas: PMI, PRD*

18. D   An authorization bill is an act of Congress that establishes or changes a government program. Authorizations specify program goals and, for discretionary programs, set the maximum amount that they may spend.
*Page reference: 402, AP Big Ideas: PMI, PRD*

19. A   Tax expenditures are revenue losses that result from special exemptions, exclusions, or deductions allowed by federal tax law. These expenditures represent the difference between what the government actually collects in taxes and what it would have collected without special exemptions.
*Page reference: 388-389; 396, AP Big Ideas: PMI, PRD*

20. B   The Budget Act of 1974 defined tax expenditures, which amount to the subsidies for different activities.
*Page reference: 388 AP Big Ideas: PMI, PRD*

# Free-Response Questions

*This rubric provides examples of many, but not all, of the possible correct responses to the free-response questions.*

1. The rise of the national security state and the rise of the social service state have long been associated with government growth and budget deficits in the United States.

    a. Briefly describe what is meant by "growth in the national security state."

       - "Growth in the national security state" refers to the costs of supporting the military and national security establishment. The U.S. devoted a large share of its budget to military expenditures during World War II, the Cold War, and the immediate post–9/11 period.

    b. Briefly describe what is meant by "growth in the social service state."

       - "Growth in the social service state" refers to dramatic increases in social welfare expenditures since the 1960s. Social welfare entitlement programs now make up the largest share of the federal budget.

    c. Identify one piece of legislation passed by Congress since 1970 that was designed to reform the budget process and control deficit spending by the government.

       - The Congressional Budget and Impoundment Act and the Gramm-Rudman-Hollings Act were designed to reform the budget process and control deficit spending by the government. The Congressional Budget and Impoundment Act was designed to make Congress less dependent on the president by giving it some independent expertise on budget matters. It allows Congress to set and meet its own budget goals and bring spending in line with revenues.

    d. For the legislation you identified in "c," briefly explain one goal it was designed to accomplish.

       - The Balanced Budget and Emergency Deficit Control Act was an attempt by Congress to gain control over growing budget deficits. It set maximum allowable deficits for each year. If Congress failed to meet the deficit goals, automatic across-the-board spending cuts were to be ordered by the president.

2.  Budget deficits and increasing federal debt are perennial concerns for national policymakers. Using the graphs, and your knowledge of the budget, answer the following questions:

a.  Compare budget deficit and federal debt.

    ■ A budget deficit occurs when expenditures exceed revenues.

    ■ The federal debt is the cumulative amount of money borrowed by the federal government that is still outstanding.

b.  Describe two negative consequences of a large federal debt.

    ■ A large federal deficit can cause several problems:

        □ Government borrowing to service the debt may make it harder for individuals and businesses to get loans at favorable rates. The competition to borrow money increases interest rates, which makes it more difficult for businesses to invest in new equipment and buildings and create more jobs. Higher interest rates raise the costs to individuals of financing mortgages and credit card purchases.

        □ Large deficits make the American government dependent on foreign investors, individuals, and governments to fund its debt. This is not a favorable position for a global superpower.

c.  Analyze the possible impact of a balanced budget amendment on the government's ability to perform its budgetary functions.

    ■ If the Constitution required a balanced budget, the federal government could not borrow money to provide increased services during an economic downturn, nor could it cut taxes to stimulate the economy in such a situation.

# 14

# The Federal Bureaucracy

## Chapter Overview

A **bureaucracy,** according to Max Weber, is a hierarchical authority structure that uses task specialization, operates on the merit principle, and behaves with impersonality. Bureaucracies are probably the most misunderstood system of the American government. Most of the public views bureaucracies in negative terms, yet the work of the bureaucracy is essential to meeting all of the needs and requirements demanded by the American public. In this chapter, we examine the role and functions of the federal bureaucracy and consider the growth and evolution of the bureaucracy over time. Next, we evaluate the role of the bureaucracy in public policymaking. We conclude by exploring contending approaches for overseeing and reforming the federal bureaucracy. By the end of the chapter, students should have a solid understanding of the historical and contemporary nature and debates surrounding the federal bureaucracy.

# Study Outline

 **Learning Objective 14.1: Describe the federal bureaucrats and the ways in which they obtain their jobs. (p.411)**

## *The Bureaucrats*

Bureaucrats are hired in one of two ways:

- Bureaucrats are hired through the **civil service system**. The system relies on entrance exams, and civil servants are promoted by **merit** rather than **patronage (Pendleton Civil Service Act)**.

- Civil servants must be politically impartial and treated as such (**Hatch Act**).

- The Civil Service Reform Act of 1978 created the **Office of Personnel Management (OPM)**, which recruits and recommends individuals and oversees promotions and other employee issues. **The GS (General Schedule) rating** is a schedule by which salaries are keyed to rating and experience. The **Senior Executive Service** is an elite group of about 9,000 federal government managers at the top of the civil service system.

- Bureaucrats are hired through presidential recruitment. Each new administration fills about 3,000 of the top posts; the president chooses people who will support the administration's policies.

- Cabinet department heads are presidential nominees who must be approved by the Senate.

- The Department of Defense has the largest number of civil employees, followed by the U.S. Postal Service.

- Overall, federal civilian employment has not increased in decades, indicating that the federal bureaucracy is not actually growing.

**Learning Objective 14.2: Differentiate the four types of agencies into which the federal bureaucracy is organized. (p. 416)**

### *How the Federal Bureaucracy Is Organized*

- Fifteen **cabinet departments** oversee and administer various policy areas, and each is supervised by a secretary (with the exception of the Justice Department, which is headed by the attorney general).

- **Independent Regulatory commissions** oversee a particular aspect of the economy, creating regulations that protect people.

- They can enforce regulations by judging disputes, and are usually headed by a commission (confirmed by Congress) rather than a secretary and they are often closely involved with interest groups that want to influence regulations.

- **Government corporations** perform services for a fee, like a private business (the U.S. Postal Service is the largest). Other examples include Amtrak and the Tennessee Valley Authority.

- **Independent executive agencies** include all other executive bodies and most are created for specific purposes, such as the national Aeronautics and Space Administration (NASA).

- Heads are appointed by the president, so these usually have some partisan motivation.

**Learning Objective 14.3: Identify the factors that influence the effectiveness of bureaucratic implementation of public policy. (p. 420)**

### *Bureaucracies as Implementors*

- Bureaucracies enact and enforce rules and procedures for putting Congress's policy decisions into practice.

- Bureaucracies work out details and guidelines, assign responsibilities among bureaucrats, and oversee the day-to-day operation of the federal government.

- **Policy implementation** is not always successful for various reasons.

- Program design is sometimes flawed or Congress may not be clear enough about policy goals.

- A department may lack staff or resources to carry out implementation.

- An agency is sometimes so mired in its **standard operating procedures** that it fails to see what else needs to be done.

- **Administrators use their discretion** differently when the standard operating procedures do not sufficiently address a particular situation. **Street-level bureaucrats** are in constant contact with the public and have considerable administrative discretion.

- **Command-and-control policy:** The typical system of regulation whereby government tells business how to reach certain goals, checks that these commands are followed, and punishes offenders.

- **Incentive system:** An alternative to command-and-control, with market-like strategies such as rewards used to manage public policy.

- There can be confusion when several departments are involved in the implementation of a particular policy.

■ Reorganization of the bureaucracy for the sake of efficiency is unlikely, because this would disrupt well-established iron triangles of congressional committees, the agencies they oversee, and the affiliated interest groups.

**Learning Objective 14.4: Describe how bureaucracies regulate and assess deregulation and alternative approaches to regulation. (p. 431)**

## Bureaucracies as Regulators

- Bureaucracies oversee policies once they are in place through **regulation**.

- They establish guidelines for a program or project, and enforce guidelines through a combination of complaints registered by the public, inspections, and by issuing permits and licenses to people who meet the guidelines. **Deregulation** is the lifting of government restrictions.

- Bureaucratic institutions have the authority to change rules of a policy and apprehend violators.

- All products, and even many daily activities, are shaped by regulation.

**14.5** **Learning Objective 14.5: Identify the means of controlling the bureaucracy and assess the role of iron triangles. (p. 432)**

## Controlling the Bureaucracy

- The governmental bureaucracy hires the most civilians but is not elected by the public.

- Ultimately answering to the president, who appoints agency heads that will support his or her policies, the governmental bureaucracy issues **executive orders** to change or implement statutes, manage the budget of each agency (at least in his budget proposal), and can reorganize an agency.

- The governmental bureaucracy is partially controlled by Congress.

- Congress ultimately determines each agency's budget, can refuse to confirm a presidential appointment, performs legislative oversight through hearings, and can change the legislation behind a program.

- In 1996, Congress introduced special procedures in the Congressional Review Act, allowing them to express disapproval of the actions of agencies.

- The governmental bureaucracy is full of **iron triangles**, which may produce conflicting guidelines or regulations.

- The president and Congress can control the bureaucracy, including appointments, budgets, reorganization, investigations, and direct orders and specific legislation.

 ## Learning Objective 14.6: Assess the role of unelected bureaucrats in American democracy and the impact of the bureaucracy on the scope of government. (p. 437)

### *Understanding Bureaucracies*

*Bureaucracy and Democracy and the Scope of Government*

- Although bureaucrats are not elected, bureaucracies may be controlled by elected decision makers.
- Bureaucrats are competent and reasonably representative of Americans.
- The role of government and the size of the bureaucracy ultimately depends more on voters than bureaucrats.

## For Additional Review

Create a timeline of the bureaucracy. On this timeline, put the history and goals of the bureaucracies within the government departments under the executive office. Use this timeline when studying and reviewing this material for the unit test and for the AP Government and Politics Exam.

Create an organizational chart of the bureaucracy. Be sure to include the individual members and sub-departments, committees, or bureaus. Use this visual depiction of the bureaucracy to aid your understanding of the organization of the bureaucracy and refer to this when studying and reviewing for the unit test and the AP Government and Politics Exam.

# Review Questions

## Multiple-Choice Questions

1.  All of the following are important official services performed by the federal bureaucracy EXCEPT
    a.  implementing laws passed by Congress.
    b.  implementing the president's policy initiatives.
    c.  solving disputes between the executive and legislative branches of government.
    d.  distributing information about public programs and services.

2.  The Pendleton Civil Service Act is significant because
    a.  it instituted an affirmative action policy for hiring and promoting federal bureaucrats.
    b.  it created the federal civil service and prescribed that the hiring of civil servants be based on merit.
    c.  it gave the president more control over federal agencies.
    d.  it reduced the number of federal civil servants working outside of Washington, D.C.

3.  Bureaucracies are often criticized as being undemocratic because
    a.  they are not directly accountable to the people.
    b.  they utilize a merit system for hiring.
    c.  citizens tend to have low opinions of them.
    d.  the courts have no influence over their actions.

4.  Presidents attempt to exercise control over the bureaucracy through all of the following means EXCEPT
    a.  appointing loyal supporters as the heads of federal agencies.
    b.  issuing executive orders.
    c.  altering agencies' budgets.
    d.  providing incentive pay to senior agency administrators.

5.  All of the following statements represent a prevalent myth about the federal bureaucracy EXCEPT
    a.  the bureaucracy is growing smaller each year.
    b.  most federal bureaucrats work in Washington, D.C.
    c.  citizens are generally dissatisfied with the bureaucracy.
    d.  the bureaucracy makes government inefficient and cumbersome.

6.  An important tool Congress uses to influence the bureaucracy is
    a.  submitting *amicus curiae* briefs to the federal courts.
    b.  issuing executive orders.
    c.  hiring civil servants to head federal agencies.
    d.  requiring agency heads to routinely appear before congressional committees.

7. Iron triangles are made up of which of the following?
   a. congressional committees, independent executive agencies, and private corporations
   b. bureaucratic agencies, congressional committees, and interest groups
   c. regulatory commissions, the Office of Management and Budget, and interest groups
   d. the executive, legislative, and judicial branches of government

8. All of the following are independent regulatory commissions EXCEPT the
   a. Federal Reserve Board.
   b. National Labor Relations Board.
   c. Securities and Exchange Commission.
   d. Office of Management and Budget.

9. The Hatch Act helps maintain a nonpartisan bureaucracy because it
   a. creates a federal commission on which half the members are Democrats and half are Republican.
   b. ensures that federal employees are hired based on merit.
   c. requires all federal employees to register to vote as independents.
   d. prohibits government employees from active participation in partisan politics.

10. Implementation of public policy is most successful when
    a. the goals of the policy and the authority of the implementers are clear.
    b. there is a court order mandating compliance with the policy.
    c. the executive branch has precleared the policy with the federal judiciary.
    d. multiple agencies and bureaucrats are involved.

11. The federal bureaucracy handles all of the following activities EXCEPT
    a. issuing rules and regulations.
    b. holding hearings to obtain information about proposed policies.
    c. implementing policies passed by Congress.
    d. appropriating funds to pay for federal government programs.

12. Government entities that resemble a Cabinet department but have narrower areas of responsibility are called a(n)
    a. independent department.
    b. government corporation.
    c. independent executive agency.
    d. department.

13. The civil service is defined as
    a. a system of hiring and promotion based on the merit principle and the desire to create a nonpartisan government service.
    b. a system in which jobs and promotions are awarded for political reasons rather than for merit or competence.
    c. a system of government employment in which selection and promotion depend on seniority rather than political patronage.
    d. an independent agency that oversees merit in the federal government personnel system.

14. The spoils system is defined as
    a. the dispensing of government jobs to persons based on a competitive, non-partisan process.
    b. the dispensing of government jobs to persons who belong to the winning political party.
    c. the dispensing of government job promotions based on the seniority system.
    d. an independent agency that oversees merit in government departments.

15. Which of the following was NOT established by the Pendleton Act?
    a. higher minimum salaries for federal employees
    b. a requirement that applicants demonstrate their qualifications for employment
    c. creation of the Civil Service Commission
    d. retention and promotion of federal employees based on job performance, not political loyalty

16. The main task of the federal bureaucracy is to
    a. implement and administer federal laws and programs.
    b. interpret and apply federal laws and programs.
    c. implement and administer the orders of the president.
    d. implement and administer the orders of the cabinet.

17. The president's choice of cabinet members is limited by the fact that
    a. he must make selections based on applicants approved by his political party.
    b. he must make selections based on applicants approved by the House of Representatives.
    c. his selections must be confirmed by the House of Representatives.
    d. his selections must be confirmed by the Senate.

18. The president has the most direct control over which of the following?
    a. independent regulatory commissions
    b. government corporations
    c. departments
    d. executive corporations

**Questions 19-20 refer to the chart below.**

Organization of the Executive Branch

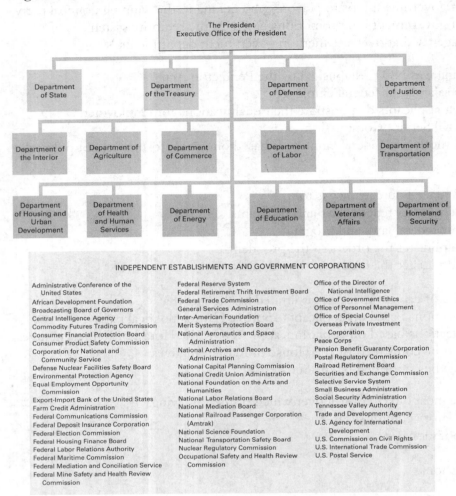

*Office of the Federal Register, United States Government Manual 2016 (Washington, DC: U.S. Government Printing Office, 2016).*

19.  The chart indicates that, though similar to independent executive agencies, independent regulatory commissions are
   a.  under direct control of the president.
   b.  under direct control of the Senate.
   c.  in operation at the state level.
   d.  free of direct control by the president.

20.  These agencies were created to engage in commercial activities that could be provided by the private sector, and they typically charge for their services.
   a.  independent executive agencies
   b.  government corporations
   c.  independent regulatory commissions
   d.  Federal Reserve banks

# Free-Response Questions

1.   Many political scientists believe that having a nonpartisan civil service increases the likelihood that government will operate in an effective and efficient manner.

     a.   Define the merit principle and explain how it helps to ensure that the civil service remains nonpartisan.

     b.   Define the Hatch Act and explain how it helps to ensure that the civil service remains nonpartisan.

     c.   Although the federal bureaucracy is nonpartisan, the president is nominally in charge of it. Identify and describe two ways a president attempts to control the bureaucracy.

2.   Policy implementation involves translating the goals and objectives of a policy into an operating, ongoing program. When policies are not successful, it is often due to problems at the implementation stage of the policy process.

     a.   Identify three reasons that policy implementation might fail.

     b.   Explain how each reason could contribute to the failure of policy implementation.

# Answers and Explanations

## Multiple-Choice Questions

1. C  The bureaucracy does not referee or solve disputes between the executive and legislative branches of government. Bureaucracies are essentially implementers of policy.
   *Page reference: 420, AP Big Ideas: PMI, PRD*

2. B  The Pendleton Civil Service Act of 1883 created the federal civil service system. Hiring and promotions in this system are based on the merit system. With regards to hiring, applicants must take an exam, and those individuals in the highest scoring group are hired. Most federal bureaucratic positions are filled this way, though the president does appoint some people to high-level positions.
   *Page reference: 414, AP Big Ideas: PMI, PRD*

3. A  Although they make vital decisions and perform essential services for government and the people, bureaucrats are not directly accountable to citizens, while the president and Congress are. This has led to the criticism that the bureaucracy is an undemocratic branch of government.
   *Page reference: 437, AP Big Ideas: PMI, PRD*

4. D  Presidents have no control over the compensation bureaucrats receive. There is a fairly rigid federal pay scale that is used to determine the level of pay and benefits to which federal employees are entitled.
   *Page reference: 432-433, AP Big Ideas: PMI, PRD*

5. D  All of the statements offered are false or misleading.
   *Page reference: 411-412, AP Big Ideas: PMI, PRD*

6. D  Congress uses oversight committee hearings as a means to ensure that federal agencies are meeting the goals and objectives set in the laws it passes, as well as to help keep federal agencies free of fraud, waste, and abuse.
   *Page reference: 433-434, AP Big Ideas: PMI, PRD*

7. B  An iron triangle is the mutually dependent relationship between bureaucratic agencies, interest groups, and congressional committees. These relationships are often detrimental to the interests of taxpayers and ordinary citizens.
   *Page reference: 434, AP Big Ideas: PMI, PRD*

8. D  The Office of Management and Budget is part of the Executive Office of the President and is not an independent regulatory commission.
   *Page reference: 418-419, AP Big Ideas: PMI, PRD*

9. D    The Hatch Act, originally passed in 1939 and amended most recently in 1993, prohibits civil service employees from actively participating in partisan politics while on duty. The act was intended to help ensure a fair and impartial bureaucracy, and to protect bureaucrats from coercion on the part of superiors or political appointees.
        *Page reference: 414, AP Big Ideas: PMI, PRD*

10. A   If the goals of a policy are not clear to those who have to implement it, and if those who have to implement it lack the authority to act definitively, then the policy in question is not likely to be well implemented or received.
        *Page reference: 420, AP Big Ideas: PMI, PRD*

11. D   Only Congress can appropriate funds to be spent by the federal government. The bureaucracy engages in all of the other activities listed.
        *Page reference: 420-432, AP Big Ideas: PMI, PRD*

12. C   Independent executive agencies are not accounted for by cabinet departments, independent regulatory commissions, and government corporations, and have a narrower area of responsibility.
        *Page reference: 419, AP Big Ideas: PMI, PRD*

13. A   Civil service is the system for hiring and promoting federal employees through a competitive, not political selection process.
        *Page reference: 412-415, AP Big Ideas: PMI, PRD*

14. B   The spoils system, also known as patronage, is a system of public employment based on rewarding political party loyalists and friends.
        *Page reference: 414, AP Big Ideas: PMI, PRD*

15. A   The Pendleton Act is a reform measure that established the principle of federal employment on the basis of open, competitive exams and created the Civil Service Commission, but it did not establish a higher minimum wage for federal employees.
        *Page reference: 414, AP Big Ideas: PMI, PRD*

16. A   A bureaucracy is a form of organization that operates through impersonal, uniform regulations which uses task specialization to implement and administer federal laws and programs.
        *Page reference: 411, AP Big Ideas: PMI, PRD*

17. D   Each of the 15 cabinet departments is headed by a secretary (except for the Department of Justice, which is headed by the attorney general), who has been chosen by the president but who must also be approved by the Senate.
        *Page reference: 416-417, AP Big Ideas: PMI, PRD*

18. D   Independent executive agencies' administrators are appointed by the president and serve at his will.
        *Page reference: 419, AP Big Ideas: PMI, PRD*

19. D   Independent regulatory commissions are agencies whose independence is protected by Congress and are therefore free from direct control by the president.
*Page reference: 418, AP Big Ideas: PMI, PRD*

20. B   Government corporations are government agencies that are designed like a business corporation and engage in commercial activities that could be provided by the private sector; they typically charge for their services.
*Page reference: 419, AP Big Ideas: PMI, PRD*

# Free-Response Questions

*This rubric provides examples of many, but not all of the possible correct responses to the free-response questions.*

1. Many political scientists believe that having a nonpartisan civil service increases the likelihood that government will operate in an effective and efficient manner.

   a. Define the merit principle and explain how it helps to ensure that the civil service remains nonpartisan.

      - The merit principle calls for the use of entrance exams and promotion ratings to hire and reward qualified civil servants. Under this principle, individuals are hired and promoted based on their qualifications, rather than patronage or partisan ties.

   b. Define the Hatch Act and explain how it helps to ensure that the civil service remains nonpartisan.

      - The Hatch Act is a federal law that prohibits government employees from participating in partisan political activities while on duty. The law helps to protect civil service employees from pressures from political appointees and others to behave in a partisan manner in carrying out their professional duties.

   c. Ways a president attempts to control the bureaucracy.

      - **Appoint the right people to head agencies.** Presidents control the appointments of federal agency heads and subheads. Appointing individuals with shared ideology and goals is one effective way presidents can influence agencies.

      - **Issue executive orders.** Executive orders carry the force of law and can be used to get agencies to take, or not take, certain actions.

      - **Alter an agency's budget.** The Office of Management and Budget (OMB) is instrumental in determining an agency's budget. Threats to cut or add to a budget usually get an agency's attention.

2. Policy implementation involves translating the goals and objectives of a policy into an operating, ongoing program. When policies are not successful, it is often due to problems at the implementation stage of the policy process.

    a. Identify three reasons that policy implementation might fail.

    b. Explain how each reason could contribute to the failure of policy implementation.

There are several reasons that policy implementation might fail.

- **Flawed program design:** It is difficult to implement a policy or program that is defective in its basic theoretical conception. In this case, policy fails because the policy itself cannot be successfully implemented even with the best effort.

- **Lack of clarity:** Congress often states a broad policy goal in legislation and leaves the implementation of the policy to bureaucrats. Congress does this so that it can claim to be responsive to its constituents, while reserving the ability to blame others if specific policies fail to meet constituents' expectations. Similarly, bureaucrats sometimes receive unclear or even contradictory instructions from Congress. This makes knowing what to implement and how best to do it quite difficult.

- **Lack of resources:** If agencies have insufficient funds to carry out assigned tasks, successful policy implementation will be difficult to achieve. For example, the IRS is required to catch people who cheat on their taxes, but this is impossible if they cannot hire enough auditors.

# 15

# The Federal Courts

## Chapter Overview

The observation that all political questions eventually move into the judicial system was made in the nineteenth century. It was a true statement at the time, and it is even more accurate today. The judicial system extends into the lives of almost all Americans. In this chapter, we explore how the judiciary operates in the United States. We begin by outlining the basic elements and structure of the courts in the United States. Then, we consider the politics of the judicial nomination and confirmation process. We examine the backgrounds and qualifications for judges, assessing how background and judicial philosophy affect judicial decision-making. Next we trace the evolution of judicial review and the dynamics of the court. We conclude by evaluating limits on the power of the courts. By the end of the chapter, students should be able to assess the role of the courts in American democracy.

# Study Outline

**15.1** Learning Objective 15.1: Identify the basic elements of the American judicial system and the major participants in it. (p. 443)

## *The Nature of the Judicial System*

- **Criminal law** is used when a person has violated a law.
- **Civil law** is used to settle disputes between private parties.
- Only about 3 percent of all cases actually go to trial; most are settled out of court.
- **Litigants** are the parties involved in a case.
- The **plaintiff** brings the charges (the plaintiff's name is listed first in the name of the case), and in matters of criminal law, the government is the plaintiff.
- The **defendant** is the party who has been charged (this name is listed second).
- Plaintiffs must have **standing to sue**, or sufficient legal reason to bring charges.
- Plaintiffs in a **class action suit** sue on behalf of all citizens who are in the same situation.
- **Justiciable disputes** are issues capable of being settled as a matter of law.
- **Interest groups** become involved with court cases to influence decisions about the law, and they may have their lawyers take up an appropriate litigant's case.
- They often submit *amicus curiae* briefs to influence a judge's decision in cases where the group is not itself a litigant, which often explain the possible effects of the judge's decision, bring new points of view to the case, or provide additional information not presented in the case.
- **Attorneys** present a case in court, and every citizen is guaranteed a lawyer in a criminal case.
- **Public interest lawyers** and **legal aid groups** may represent poor people in some civil and criminal cases.
- State and local governments hire public defenders to represent poor defendants in criminal cases.

**15.2** **Learning Objective 15.2: Outline the structure of the federal court system and the major responsibilities of each component. (p. 445)**

## *The Structure of the Federal Judicial System*

- Courts of **original jurisdiction** are the first courts to hear a case, usually when it goes to **trial**.

- The court assesses and decides a case based on the facts of the case, and most cases do not continue after their first ruling.

- There are 94 federal **district courts**, which have original jurisdiction and hold trials in which the litigants appear before the court.

- Federal district courts primarily handle cases violating federal law or involving federal civil law, civil suits in which the litigants are of different states, bankruptcy proceedings, and process of naturalization.

- The **U.S. attorney** in each district serves as the government's lawyer.

- The federal government is a plaintiff when prosecuting violators of federal laws; the government can be a plaintiff or defendant in a civil suit.

- Courts of **appellate jurisdiction** hear cases that have been **appealed**.

- The court interprets the case as it relates to the law; it does not review the facts and the litigants do not appear before the court (only their lawyers appear), and there is no jury.

- Thirteen **circuit courts of appeal** review cases appealed from the district courts; they have appellate jurisdiction.

- They do not focus on the facts of the case, but evaluate the treatment of the case in the district court in terms of errors of procedure or the law.

- Usually three judges hear a case, and their ruling sets a **precedent** for the district courts within their geographic circuit.

- The **Supreme Court** is the ultimate authority on the law.

- It has original jurisdiction in cases between two states, the federal government and a state, or a state and a foreign country, but most cases fall under its appellate jurisdiction.

- It can choose which cases to hear and it consists of nine justices who rule on cases together.

## 15.3   Learning Objective 15.3: Explain the process by which judges and justices are nominated and confirmed. (p. 450)

### The Politics of Judicial Selection

- All federal judges and justices are appointed by the president. Nominations must be confirmed by the Senate.
- Confirmation of district and circuit court judges is influenced by **senatorial courtesy**, by which senators of the president's party from the state where the district is located, or in which a circuit court nominee resides, can stop confirmation.
- Justices are carefully selected by the president when there is a vacancy on the Supreme Court.
- Justices serve much longer than a president's term.
- If the president's choice is confirmed by the Senate, the court will be more closely aligned with the president's ideology for a longer period of time.
- Nomination was routine for most of the 20th century, but since the 1960s nominations have become much more contentious, especially with regard to issues like abortion, affirmative action, and other socially divisive issues.

## 15.4   Learning Objective 15.4: Describe the backgrounds of judges and justices and assess the impact of background on their decisions. (p. 457)

### The Backgrounds of Judges and Justices

- Judges and justices are not a representative sample of the American people; they are lawyers and disproportionately white males.
- They usually share the partisan and ideological views of the president who nominated them, and these views are often reflected in their decisions.
- Other characteristics, such as gender and race, are also seen to influence decisions.

**15.5** **Learning Objective 15.5: Outline the judicial process at the Supreme Court level and assess the major factors influencing decisions and their implementation. (p. 460)**

## *The Courts as Policymakers*

- The Supreme Court shapes policy by selecting which cases to hear.

- It is most likely to choose cases involving civil rights and civil liberties, a discrepancy in the lower courts' interpretation of the law, or disagreements between justices and the lower courts.

- The **solicitor general** is a presidential appointee and the third ranking office in the Department of Justice. The solicitor general is in charge of the appellate court litigation of the federal government.

- The Supreme Court follows a regular process for making decisions.

- Justices read briefs pertaining to the case, hear **oral arguments**, meet to discuss cases, vote on the decision, and write and announce opinions.

- Opinions that have the support of the majority, called "**opinions** of the court," establish law that is binding on lower courts.

- Decisions are based heavily on **precedent**; lower courts must follow precedents set by higher courts. Justices usually rule *stare decisis*: "let the decision stand."
  **Originalism** is a view that the Constitution should be interpreted according to the original intentions or original meaning of the Framers.

- Decisions must be translated into policy, which is accomplished by policymakers, the president, lower courts, lawyers, and administrators. This process is called **judicial implementation.**

- The public must become aware of its rights under the new decision.

- Often implementers disagree with the decision and try to hinder implementation.

**Learning Objective 15.6: Trace the Supreme Court's use of judicial review in major policy battles in various eras of American history. (p. 467)**

## *The Courts and Public Policy: A Historical View*

- Some courts (usually referred to by the name of the chief justice at the time) have had a significant impact on the shaping of policy.

- **John Marshall** initiated the practice of judicial review in the case of ***Marbury v. Madison*** and expanded the power of the Supreme Court significantly.

- The **Warren court** became actively involved in expanding civil rights and civil liberties.

- The **Burger court** became somewhat more conservative than the Warren court, though it still allowed abortion in ***Roe v. Wade***.

- The **Rehnquist and Roberts courts** became even more conservative, with mainly Republican presidents' appointments, and began to limit (though not reverse) previous rulings.

- Power of the courts is checked by the president's appointments, and also by Congress's ability to amend the Constitution, despite—or in order to overrule—a Supreme Court decision.

**Learning Objective 15.7: Assess the role of unelected courts and the scope of judicial power in American democracy. (p. 513)**

## *Understanding the Courts*

- Judges and justices are not elected and are difficult to remove.

- They are not completely insulated from politics and often have acted to promote openness in the political system.

- They have a number of tools to avoid making controversial decisions.

- There are a number of means more democratically elected officials can use to overturn Court decisions.

- Some critics think the Supreme Court is too powerful, and favor **judicial restraint**.

- Others favor **judicial activism** to allow justices the freedom to forge new policies, especially concerning people largely underrepresented in the political process.
- The federal courts have developed the doctrine of **political questions** as a means to avoid deciding some cases, mainly those involving conflicts between the president and Congress.
- **Statutory construction** is the judicial interpretation of an act of Congress, and in some cases, results in Congress passing a new law to clarify existing laws.

## For Additional Review

Create a chart of the following information concerning the judiciary:

- What powers are given to the judiciary in the Constitution?
- Why is judicial independence necessary?
- What constitutional provisions assure this independence?
- Why does the federal judiciary include several levels of courts?
- What are the differences among these three levels?

Use this chart when reviewing and studying for the unit test and the AP Government and Politics Exam.

Create a diagram which demonstrates how a case finds its way to the Supreme Court. Compare and contrast judicial restraint versus judicial activism and list cases which apply to each. Use this information when reviewing and studying for the unit test and the AP Government and Politics Exam.

# Review Questions

## Multiple-Choice Questions

1. Which of the following statements is true of the judicial system in the United States?
   a. It is a unitary court system.
   b. Interest groups are forbidden from participating in criminal proceedings.
   c. The system prescribes that criminal cases be decided by juries, and civil cases be decided by judges.
   d. It is an adversarial system in which justice is supposed to emerge from the struggle between two contending points of view.

**Questions 2-3 refer to the chart below.**

Organization of the Federal Court System

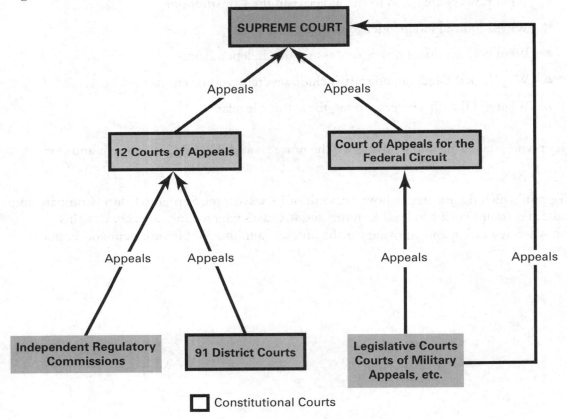

2. All of the following are part of the federal court system EXCEPT
   a. the U.S. Supreme Court.
   b. the State Supreme Courts.
   c. theCourt of Military Appeals.
   d. the U.S. Court of Appeals.

3. Federal district courts are the only federal courts in which
   a. the facts are presented by both parties in the case.
   b. *amicus curiae* briefs are registered with the court.
   c. the solicitor general appears for oral argument.
   d. juries are impaneled to decide cases.

4. Which of the following statements is true about Congress's influence over Supreme Court decision making?
   a. Congress can pass laws to prohibit judicial activism.
   b. The Senate can filibuster court decisions.
   c. Congress has significant control over the court's appellate jurisdiction.
   d. The Senate can decide which cases the Supreme Court will hear.

5. Senatorial courtesy is
   a. the custom of the Supreme Court sharing its docket with the Senate Judiciary Committee before it is made public.
   b. a tradition whereby nominees for federal judgeships must meet the approval of senators of the president's party from the state in which the nominee will serve.
   c. the tradition of the full Senate approving all judicial nominees who win a majority vote in the Judiciary Committee.
   d. the practice of the Senate filling judicial vacancies with judges who share the same judicial philosophy as their most immediate predecessor.

6. All of the following influence the selection of federal judges and Supreme Court justices EXCEPT
   a. campaign contributions.
   b. partisanship.
   c. ideology.
   d. experience.

7. Which of the following is true about the vast majority of cases decided by the Supreme Court?
   a. They are decided by unanimous decision.
   b. The decisions tend to significantly alter current policy.
   c. They tend to reverse the decision of the lower courts.
   d. They are decided based on how similar past cases have been decided.

8. One major weakness of federal courts as policymakers is that
   a. judges are term-limited, which affects their ability to implement their decisions.
   b. lower courts are not required to follow the decisions of superior courts.
   c. the courts must rely on other institutions to implement their decisions.
   d. they are shielded from the pressures of electoral politics.

9. Interest groups play a role in the federal judicial process in all of the following ways EXCEPT by
   a. running advertisements endorsing a judicial nominee.
   b. lobbying the Judiciary Committee about a judicial nominee.
   c. filing *amicus curiae* briefs.
   d. having their lawyers represent a plaintiff.

10. The power of courts to determine which acts of Congress, the executive branch, and state legislatures are constitutional is known as
    a. precedent.
    b. *stare decisis*.
    c. original jurisdiction.
    d. judicial review.

11. The doctrine developed by the federal courts and used as a means to avoid deciding some cases is known as
    a. statutory construction.
    b. judicial activism.
    c. judicial restraint.
    d. political questions.

12. All of the following are true about the Supreme Court EXCEPT
    a. cases are not allowed to be televised.
    b. cembers are seated in alphabetical order.
    c. there were originally six members in the court.
    d. there have been as many as ten members in the court.

13. The philosophy of the courts where judges play a minimal policymaking role and defer to legislatures whenever possible is known as
    a. judicial implementation.
    b. senatorial courtesy.
    c. judicial activism.
    d. judicial restraint.

14. This is a request for the Supreme Court to order up the records from a lower court to review the case.
    a. *in forma pauperis*
    b. concurrent opinion
    c. *writ of certiorari*
    d. *stare decisis*

15. The "rule of four" is a Supreme Court practice which permits four of the nine justices to
    a. overrule senatorial courtesy.
    b. grant a *writ of certiorari*.
    c. adjourn the court.
    d. establish a precedent.

16. *Stare decisis* is a judicial principle which states that the courts will decide cases largely based on
    a. earlier court decisions.
    b. economic and social conditions of the day.
    c. equality and justice.
    d. the intention of Congress when the law was written.

17. Legal briefs submitted by a "friend of the court" for the purpose of influencing the court's decision by raising additional arguments and points of view is a(n)
    a. *writ of certiorari.*
    b. *writ of habeas corpus.*
    c. *amicus curiae* brief.
    d. *stare decisis* ruling.

18. A decision written by one or more judges expressing disagreement with the majority opinion of the Supreme Court is a(n)
    a. judicial review.
    b. "rule of four."
    c. concurring opinion.
    e. dissenting opinion.

19. The Supreme Court's power is strengthened by its ability to
    a. exercise senatorial courtesy.
    b. nominate its own replacements.
    c. impeach the president.
    d. select the cases it will hear.

20. The philosophy of the courts where judges make decisions based on the spirit of the times and needs of the nation is known as
    a. *stare decisis.*
    b. a dissenting opinion.
    c. judicial activism.
    d. judicial implementation.

# Free-Response Questions

1.  The framers of the Constitution desired a federal judiciary that was removed from the pressures and direct consequences of electoral politics. Hamilton addressed this by saying:

    "The manner of constituting it seems to embrace these several objects: 1st. The mode of appointing the judges. 2d. The tenure by which they are to hold their places. 3d. The partition of the judiciary authority between different courts, and their relations to each other.

    First. As to the mode of appointing the judges; this is the same with that of appointing the officers of the Union in general, and has been so fully discussed in the two last numbers, that nothing can be said here which would not be useless repetition.

    Second. As to the tenure by which the judges are to hold their places; this chiefly concerns their duration in office; the provisions for their support; the precautions for their responsibility."

    *--The Federalist No. 78*

    a.  Identify and describe two provisions in the Constitution that were intended to shield the judiciary from electoral politics.

    b.  The framers' intent notwithstanding, the federal judiciary is not free of the influence of electoral politics. Identify and describe two ways electoral politics affect the federal judiciary.

2.  "The only answer that can be given is, that as all these exterior provisions are found to be inadequate, the defect must be supplied, by so contriving the interior structure of the government as that its several constituent parts may, by their mutual relations, be the means of keeping each other in their proper places."

    *--The United States Constitution*

    The Constitution provides each of the three branches of government with the capacity to limit and trump the powers of the other two.

    a.  Describe one way the president can check and balance the powers of the federal judiciary.

    b.  Describe one way Congress can check and balance the powers of the federal judiciary.

    c.  Describe one way the Supreme Court can check and balance the powers of the executive branch.

    d.  Describe one way the Supreme Court can check and balance the powers of Congress.

# Answers and Explanations

## Multiple-Choice Questions

1. D   A bedrock principle underlying the American court system is that justice will emerge from an adversarial system in which there is a struggle between two contending points of view.
*Page reference: 443-445, AP Big Ideas: CON, PMI*

2. B   All of the courts listed are part of the federal judiciary except the state supreme courts.
*Page reference: 445, AP Big Ideas: CON, PMI*

3. D   Federal district courts have original jurisdiction and operate as trial courts where juries may be impaneled; there are no juries in the courts of appeal, the Supreme Court, or any other federal courts.
*Page reference: 445, AP Big Ideas: CON, PMI*

4. C   In many instances, federal courts' jurisdiction derives from Congress and not the Constitution. The Constitution provides Congress with the discretion to determine which category of cases appellate courts may hear.
*Page reference: 450-456, AP Big Ideas: CON, PMI*

5. B   Senatorial courtesy is a tradition whereby nominees for federal judgeships must meet the approval of senators of the president's party from the state in which the nominee will serve. This tradition began under George Washington, and since that time the Senate has tended not to confirm nominations for district court judges when senators of the president's party from the state in which the nominee will serve oppose them.
*Page reference: 450, AP Big Ideas: CON, PMI*

6. A   There is no evidence that campaign contributions to presidential races are a major factor in determining who a president nominates for federal judgeships.
*Page reference: 450-456, AP Big Ideas: CON, PMI*

7. D   Most Supreme Court rulings uphold the decision made by the lower court. This is the principle of *stare decisis*, meaning "let the decision stand."
*Page reference: 463, AP Big Ideas: CON, PMI*

8. C   Unlike legislatures and the executive branch, the courts must always rely on other units of government to implement and enforce their rulings. This is widely viewed as a weakness for the courts as policymakers.
*Page reference: 466-467, AP Big Ideas: CON, PMI*

9. A   Interest groups do attempt to influence the appointment of federal judges, but not by running advertisements. The process of filling judgeships is far removed from the public—the only means of influence it has is by influencing the election of the president and members of the Senate, who, in turn, choose judges. Advertisements aimed at swaying public opinion therefore have little use in this case.
*Page reference: 443-445, AP Big Ideas: CON, PMI*

10. D    Judicial review is the power of the courts to determine whether acts of Congress, the executive branch, and the states are constitutional. This power was established by the Supreme Court's decision in Marbury v. Madison.
*Page reference: 468-469, AP Big Ideas: CON, PMI*

11. D    Political questions is a doctrine developed by the federal courts and is used as a means to avoid deciding some cases.
*Page reference: 474, AP Big Ideas: CON, PMI*

12. B    Members of the Supreme Court do not sit in alphabetical order, but instead, sit according to seniority.
*Page reference: 448-449, AP Big Ideas: CON, PMI*

13. D    Judicial restraint is a philosophy proposing that judges should allow the decisions of other branches of government to stand, even if they offend a judge's own principles, unless they clearly violate the Constitution.
*Page reference: 473, AP Big Ideas: CON, PMI*

14. C    A *writ of certiorari* is a formal writ used to bring a case before the Supreme Court.
*Page reference: 461, AP Big Ideas: CON, PMI*

15. B    The "rule of four" is the practice of the Supreme Court where at least four justices must vote to consider a case before a *writ of certiorari* can be issued.
*Page reference: 461, AP Big Ideas: CON, PMI*

16. A    *Stare decisis* means that court rulings will rely on past decisions or precedents to formulate decisions in new cases.
*Page reference: 463, AP Big Ideas: CON, PMI*

17. C    An *amicus curiae* brief is filed by an individual or organization urging the Supreme Court to hear a case (or discouraging it from doing so) or, at the merits stage, to present arguments in addition to those presented by the immediate parties to a case.
*Page reference: 444, AP Big Ideas: CON, PMI*

18. D    A dissenting opinion is an opinion written when justices are opposed to all or part of the majority's decision.
*Page reference: 463-466, AP Big Ideas: CON, PMI*

19. D    The power of the Supreme Court is strengthened by its ability to control its agenda. Of the approximately 8,000 cases appealed to the Supreme Court, the Court actually places fewer than 100 cases on the docket.
*Page reference: 446-449, AP Big Ideas: CON, PMI*

20. C    Judicial activism is a philosophy of judicial decision making that posits judges should use their power broadly to further justice by making decisions based on the spirit of the times and needs of the nation.
*Page reference: 473, AP Big Ideas: CON, PMI*

# Free-Response Questions

*This rubric provides examples of many, but not all of the possible correct responses to the free-response questions.*

1. The framers of the Constitution desired a federal judiciary that was removed from the pressures and direct consequences of electoral politics. Hamilton addressed this by saying:

   "The manner of constituting it seems to embrace these several objects: 1st. The mode of appointing the judges. 2d. The tenure by which they are to hold their places. 3d. The partition of the judiciary authority between different courts, and their relations to each other.

   First. As to the mode of appointing the judges; this is the same with that of appointing the officers of the Union in general, and has been so fully discussed in the two last numbers, that nothing can be said here which would not be useless repetition.

   Second. As to the tenure by which the judges are to hold their places; this chiefly concerns their duration in office; the provisions for their support; the precautions for their responsibility"

   *--The Federalist No. 78*

   a. Identify and describe two provisions in the Constitution that were intended to shield the judiciary from electoral politics.

   - **Federal judges are appointed, not elected.** This feature allows judges to make reasoned decisions based on the rule of law without the fear of losing their jobs because some of their decisions may be unpopular with a group of constituents or the general public.

   - **Lifetime appointment for federal judges.** Once confirmed by the Senate, federal judges have lifetime tenure on the bench, so long as they do not commit impeachable offenses. This lifetime tenure allows judges to make reasoned decisions based on the rule of law without the fear of losing their jobs, since some of their decisions may be unpopular with other government officials or the general public.

   - **Federal judges' salaries cannot be reduced.** The Constitution expressly prohibits the reduction of judges' salaries during their time on the bench. This constitutional provision allows judges to make decisions without fear of reprisal from the executive and legislative branches.

b. The framers' intent notwithstanding, the federal judiciary is not free of the influence of electoral politics. Identify and describe two ways electoral politics affect the federal judiciary.

- **The president, who is a political partisan, nominates federal judges.** Presidents seek to appoint judges to the bench who share their party affiliations, ideologies, judicial philosophies, and stances on specific issues. This makes federal judges products of a partisan political process.
- **The confirmation process.** The confirmation process for federal judges is sometimes highly partisan, with Democrats and Republicans seemingly using the process as a continuation of the last election or a precursor for the next.
- **Congress controls the appellate jurisdiction of federal courts.** Because of this authority, Congress has the capacity to prohibit the courts from hearing specific categories or classes of cases.

2. "The only answer that can be given is, that as all these exterior provisions are found to be inadequate, the defect must be supplied, by so contriving the interior structure of the government as that its several constituent parts may, by their mutual relations, be the means of keeping each other in their proper places."

*--The United States Constitution*

The Constitution provides each of the three branches of government with the capacity to limit and trump the powers of the other two.

a. Describe one way the president can check and balance the powers of the federal judiciary.

- **Appointment power.** The president nominates Supreme Court and other federal judges.

b. Describe one way Congress can check and balance the powers of the federal judiciary.

- **Confirmation process.** The Senate must confirm Supreme Court justices and all other federal judicial nominees.
- **Impeachment power.** Congress can impeach federal judges.

- **Jurisdiction authority over lower federal courts.** The Constitution created just one federal court, the U.S. Supreme Court. It gave Congress the authority to create any other subordinate courts that it saw fit to create. Thus, in theory, Congress could disband all federal courts except the Supreme Court. Congress also has the capacity to prohibit the courts from hearing specific categories or classes of cases.

- **Power of the purse.** Although the Constitution expressly prohibits the reduction of judges' salaries during their time on the bench, Congress determines if federal judges receive pay raises and how much any raise will be.

c. Describe one way the Supreme Court can check and balance the powers of the executive branch.

- **Judicial review.** Courts can declare acts of the president and federal agencies to be unconstitutional or unlawful.

d. Describe one way the Supreme Court can check and balance the powers of Congress.

- **Judicial review.** Courts can declare laws passed by Congress to be unconstitutional.

# 16

# Economic and Social Welfare Policymaking

## Chapter Overview

Domestic economic and social policy is at the heart of many contemporary political debates in the United States. From health care and education to Social Security and the budget deficit, American politics is often characterized by sharp differences in policy preferences. In this chapter, we examine some of these contemporary debates. We begin by exploring the economic policies of the American government. We then turn to analyze domestic social policy (**social welfare policy**) in the United States. We contrast entitlement and means-tested welfare programs. We assess the extent of economic inequality in the United States and consider the role of the government in militating against growing inequality. Next, we consider the politics of public policy, examining both the major welfare programs in the United States and the politics of Social Security and welfare reform. We conclude by distinguishing the American social welfare system from those of other established democracies and by exploring the impact of social and economic policy on democracy in the United States. By the end of the chapter, students should have a well-rounded understanding of domestic economic and social policy in the United States across a wide variety of issues.

# Study Outline

 **16.1**

**Learning Objective 16.1: Identify the main policy tools that American government can employ to address economic problems, and contrast Keynesian and supply-side economics. (p. 481)**

## *Economic Policymaking*

- The new U.S. economy is deep in the challenges and opportunities of globalization, but, through rules and regulations, the federal government plays a major role as well.

- Economic conditions affect both voting behavior and presidential approval; they are the best single predictor of voters' evaluation of how the president is doing his job.

- But voters tend to assess the overall rate of employment and unemployment more than their individual circumstances.

- Democrats are more likely to stress the importance of keeping unemployment low, whereas Republicans are worried about inflation.

- This difference in priorities reflects their constituencies.

- Unemployment occurs when there are not enough jobs and it is measured by the **unemployment rate**.

- The **underemployment rate** includes (1) people who are not working and are actively seeking a job, (2) those who would like to work but have given up looking, and (3) those who are working part-time because they cannot find a full-time position.

- The Democratic coalition consists of groups concerned with unemployment (labor and the lower classes).

- Democrats generally sacrifice higher inflation to keep unemployment down.

- **Inflation** occurs when prices rise and inflation is measured by the **Consumer Price Index (CPI)**.

- The Republican coalition includes businesspeople who are concerned about the cost of goods and services.

- Republicans generally try to prevent inflation, even at the risk of rising unemployment.

## Policies for Controlling the Economy

### Monetary Policy and the "Fed"

- **Monetary policy** is monitoring and controlling the amount of money in circulation; based on the economic theory known as monetarism, which states that controlling the money supply is the key to controlling the economy.

- **Monetarism** is an economic theory holding that the supply of money is the key to a nation's economic health; if there is too much available cash or credit, inflation occurs.

- The **Federal Reserve System** (the Fed) was created to manage monetary policy.

- Its board of governors is appointed by the president and confirmed by the Senate, but operates fairly independently.

- The Federal Open Market Committee is the most important body within the Federal Reserve; it decides how monetary policy is carried out.

- The Fed regulates monetary policy by influencing the rate at which loans are given, which influences decisions about borrowing; by controlling the amount of money banks have available, and, in turn, the rate at which people can borrow; and by adding to the money supply by selling bonds.

### Fiscal Policy: Keynesian Versus Supply-Side Economics

- **Fiscal policy** is regulating revenues and expenditures through the federal budget; determined by Congress and the president.

- **Keynesian economic theory** encourages government's active participation in the economy.

- Keynesians argue that government spending and tax cuts stimulate the economy by creating demand. This is known as expansionary fiscal policy.

- The government can decrease demand to control inflation by cutting spending and increasing taxes, which is known as contractionary fiscal policy.

- **Supply-side economics** holds that by decreasing government involvement in the economy, people will be forced to work harder and save more.

- Cutting taxes increases investment and the supply of goods, which promotes growth.

- The economic philosophy which is in direct contradiction to monetary and fiscal policy is known as **laissez-faire**, which is the principle that government should not meddle in the economy.

### Why It Is Hard to Control the Economy

- Some believe that presidents manipulate the economy for a short-run advantage to win elections, called the "political business cycle."
- It is difficult to predict the economy far enough in advance to make and implement policy.
- Also, the economy is grounded in billions of private sector decisions, which are harder to regulate than government policy.

 ## Learning Objective 16.2: Compare and contrast entitlement and means-tested social welfare programs. (p. 488)

### Types of Social Welfare Policies

- Most government funds are given through **entitlement programs** to people who are not poor.
- These programs provide benefits to individuals regardless of need.
- The two main entitlement programs, Social Security and Medicare, are the largest and most expensive social welfare programs in America.
- **Means-tested programs**, such as the Food Stamp Program and Medicaid, provide benefits only to people with specific needs.
- Eligibility for these depends on how narrowly "poverty" is defined.
- Means-tested programs generate much political controversy, with the positions taken depending largely on how people see the poor and the causes of poverty.

**16.3** Learning Objective 16.3: Assess the extent of economic inequality in America and the role of government in lessening it. (p. 489)

## Income, Poverty, and Public Policy

- **Income distribution** is the way the national income is divided into "shares" ranging from the poor to the rich.

- A perception by an individual that he or she is not doing well economically in comparison to others is known as **relative deprivation**.

- The rich have not only more **income** (the amount of money collected between two points in time) but also greater **wealth** (the value of assets including bank accounts, stocks, homes, and other assets).

- A small number of Americans—1 percent of the total population—possess more than one-third of all wealth in the United States.

- The assets of that 1 percent are actually higher than the total worth of 90 percent of Americans.

- Poverty is defined by the government as family income that falls below the **poverty line**.

- Counts underestimate poverty, because millions of people hover around the line and continually fall just below or rise just above it.

- African Americans, Hispanic Americans, people living in inner cities, and unmarried women tend to be the groups most afflicted with poverty.

- The increase in the incidents of women and their children living in poverty is referred to as the **feminization of poverty**.

### How Public Policy Affects Income

- There are three main types of taxes.
  - **Progressive** taxes tax the wealthy at a higher rate.
  - Everyone is taxed at the same rate in **proportional taxes**.
  - **Regressive taxes** tax people of lower incomes at a higher rate.

- **State sales taxes** are somewhat regressive, but the effect is counterbalanced by progressive federal income taxes.

- **Earned Income Tax Credit:** This program provides very low-income workers with a cash credit, even if they paid no federal income tax.

- Through **expenditures**, **transfer payments** are given directly to citizens by the government.

  - Examples are food stamps, financial aid grants, and Social Security and Medicare benefits.

  - The elderly receive the most in transfer payments through Social Security.

## 16.4   Learning Objective 16.4: Trace the changes over time in major federal welfare programs. (p. 496)

### *Helping the Poor? Social Policy and the Needy*

- The Great Depression proved that poverty can be beyond anyone's control and encouraged the government to become more involved in welfare.

- Social Security began under the **New Deal (Social Security Act of 1935)**; the poor become a part of the Democratic Party coalition.

- President Johnson initiated many Great Society programs to fight the War on Poverty during the civil rights era.

- President Reagan cut the growth of many of these programs in the 1980s.

- The system underwent a major overhaul during the Clinton administration **(Personal Responsibility and Work Opportunity Reconciliation Act of 1996)**.

- Under the reforms, families receive small payments with a maximum of two years to find employment, people have a lifetime maximum of five years on welfare, and states have more latitude and discretion in operating their own welfare programs.

- Welfare reform brought with it a name change for the cash payments to families from Aid to Families with Dependent Children (AFDC) to **Temporary Assistance for Needy Families (TANF)**.

**16.5** **Learning Objective 16.5: Outline how America's Social Security program works and the challenge of keeping it financially solvent in the coming years. (p. 499)**

### *Social Security: Living on Borrowed Time*

- Social Security has lifted many elderly out of poverty.

- The government taxes employees and their employers a percentage of the employee's income, up to a maximum contribution, and these are deposited into the **Social Security Trust Fund**.

- Both employee and employer contributions are paid into the Social Security Trust Fund, from which benefits are paid.

- Currently, there are about three workers per recipient, and benefits and contributions are balanced.

- But it is possible that the system will go bankrupt during the 21st century.

- More people will be of retirement age, fewer people will be working, and the cost of living is rising, so monthly payments will increase.

- Either taxes will have to be raised or benefits will have to be cut.

**16.6** **Learning Objective 16.6: Distinguish American social welfare policy from that of other established democracies. (p. 502)**

### *Social Welfare Policy Elsewhere*

- Most established democracies have more expensive and generous social welfare programs than does the United States.

- In particular, European governments provide citizens with benefits, such as paid parental leave upon the birth of a child, that are unheard of in the United States.

- Taxes in Europe have to be higher than taxes in the United States in order to pay for these benefits.

**16.7** **Learning Objective 16.7: Assess the impact of economic and social welfare policies on democracy and the scope of government in America. (p. 503)**

## *Understanding Economic and Social Welfare Policymaking*

- As in most policy arenas, groups with ample political resources tend to get more of what they want in the battle over social welfare policies.

- The elderly have been very successful in preserving their Social Security and Medicare benefits, whereas the poor have faced difficulties in preserving welfare funding.

- The growth in social welfare spending, particularly for Social Security and Medicare, accounts for much of the increase in the scope of government in recent decades.

## For Additional Review

Create a list of the main policy tools the government can use to address economic problems in the United States. For each tool, describe HOW and WHEN that tool can be used to address economic problems. Use this list when studying for the unit test and when preparing for the AP Government and Politics exam.

Create a chart demonstrating the economic inequality which exists in the United States, i.e. groups living below the poverty level. List the ways the government attempts to lessen this inequality and identify the program as an entitlement or a means-tested social welfare program. Use this list chart when studying for the unit test and when preparing for the AP Government and Politics exam.

# Review Questions

## Multiple-Choice Questions

**Questions 1-2 refer to the graph below.**

Unemployment Rates by Age and Race/Ethnicity

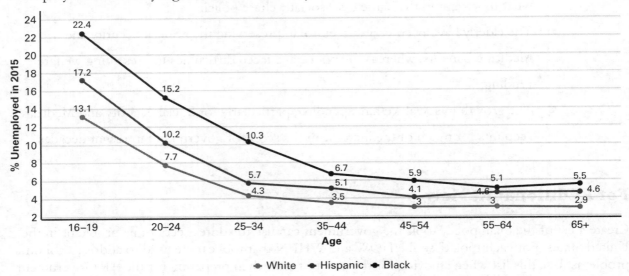

*Bureau of Labor Statistics*

1.  Which of the following best describes a trend in the line graph?
    a.  Unemployment rates tend to be higher for young Americans 16-24 than for older Americans.
    b.  Unemployment rates tend to be higher for whites, rather than Hispanics or blacks.
    c.  Unemployment rates tend to be higher for older Americans 45-54 than for younger Americans.
    d.  Unemployment rates tend to be higher for Americans 25-34 than for Americans 16-24.

2.  Which of the following is an accurate conclusion based on a comparison of trends in the line graph and your knowledge of income distribution?
    a.  Asian Americans have the highest rate of poverty.
    b.  African Americans have the highest rate of poverty.
    c.  Hispanic Americans have the highest rate of poverty.
    d.  Southern whites have the highest rate of poverty.

3. The Social Security program is endangered primarily because
   a. the U.S. birth rate has increased dramatically over the past decade.
   b. the program has lost public support in recent years.
   c. the number of contributors to the program is growing at a much slower rate than the number of recipients.
   d. large federal budget deficits have reduced the amount of tax revenue collected in support of the program.

4. All of the following are examples of means-tested programs EXCEPT
   a. Temporary Assistance for Needy Families (TANF).
   b. Children's Health Insurance Program (CHIP).
   c. Food Stamp Program.
   d. Medicaid.

5. The most expensive social welfare program in the United States is
   a. Social Security.
   b. Aid to Families with Dependent Children (AFDC).
   c. Food Stamps.
   d. Supplemental Security Income (SSI).

6. Senior citizens fare better than the poor in social welfare budget battles for which of the following reasons?
   a. The Constitution requires a certain amount of spending for senior citizens, but not the poor.
   b. Most social services for senior citizens come from state governments.
   c. Lobbyists representing the poor are not allowed to make campaign contributions.
   d. Senior citizens are more organized and better represented politically than the poor.

7. The value of all goods and services produced by an economy during a specific period of time, such as a year, is called the
   a. budget production.
   b. growth rate.
   c. economic output.
   d. gross national product.

8. One way the government attempts to overcome inflation is by
   a. decreasing loan rates to make money more available to the public.
   b. increasing the amount of credit available to the public.
   c. decreasing the amount of money in banks, which raises loan rates and discourages people from borrowing.
   d. limiting the number of bonds sold to the public.

9. The economic theory that opposes governmental interference in economic affairs beyond what is necessary to protect life and property is known as
   a. trickle-down theory.
   b. protectionism.
   c. laissez-faire economics.
   d. socialism.

10. The key measure of inflation—the change in the cost of buying a fixed basket of goods and services—is known as
    a. recession.
    b. monetary policy.
    c. fiscal policy.
    d. consumer price index.

11. All of the following are affected by actions of the Federal Reserve Board EXCEPT
    a. the federal budget deficit.
    b. the money supply.
    c. interest rates.
    d. the availability of jobs.

12. The economic theory holding that the key task for fiscal policy is to stimulate the supply of goods, as by cutting tax rates, is known as
    a. supply side economics.
    b. protectionism.
    c. laissez-faire economics.
    d. socialism.

13. Monetary policy refers to government control of
    a. the banking and computer industries.
    b. the money supply and interest rates.
    c. taxing and spending policies.
    d. equities and securities.

14. A recession is
    a. a short-term decline in the economy that occurs as investment sags, production falls off, and unemployment increases.
    b. caused by high levels of government debt.
    c. a decrease in the amount of money in banks, which raises loan rates and discourages people from borrowing.
    d. a time when monetary policy is used to increase interest rates to keep people from going further into debt.

15. Which of the following would be an example of fiscal policy?
    a. intentionally running a budget deficit to spur economic growth
    b. cutting the prime interest rate to encourage investment
    c. engaging in open market operations
    d. inflating the value of government assets to increase real estate prices

16. Government programs providing benefits to qualified individuals regardless of need are known as
    a. means tested programs.
    b. income distribution.
    c. entitlement programs.
    d. earned income tax credit.

17. A Federal Reserve open-market operation involves
    a. protecting people against loss of income because of retirement, disability, unemployment, or death or absence of the family breadwinner.
    b. government benefits that all citizens meeting eligibility criteria—such as age, income level, or unemployment—are legally "entitled" to receive.
    c. the buying and selling of government securities by the Federal Reserve Bank in the securities market.
    d. the setting of the rate of interest at which member banks can borrow money from their regional Federal Reserve Bank.

18. Which of the following indicates that the United States has a mixed economy?
    a. The Supreme Court regulates interstate commerce.
    b. The federal government owns the means of production.
    c. Congress plays no role in setting tariffs on imported goods.
    d. The Justice Department can sue monopolistic companies.

19. Which of the following statements accurately describes traditional Republican Party economic positions?
    a. Republicans place greater emphasis on full employment than Democrats do.
    b. Republicans tend to worry about inflation more than Democrats do.
    c. Republican economic positions tend to appeal to the working class and unions.
    d. Republicans tend to favor higher income tax rates.

20. One way the government attempts to overcome inflation is by
    a. decreasing loan rates to make money more available to the public.
    b. increasing the amount of credit available to the public.
    c. decreasing the amount of money in banks, which raises loan rates and discourages people from borrowing.
    d. limiting the number of bonds sold to the public.

# Free-Response Questions

*Some AP Free-Response Questions will ask you to address one specific policy area. It is, however, important that you understand the public policymaking process in general and to be able to draw appropriate examples from a variety of policy areas, because some questions will ask you to address several policy areas in one question.*

1. The two major tools for macroeconomic policy are monetary and fiscal policies.

    a. Compare monetary policy and fiscal policy.

    b. Describe how each policy is made at the federal level.

    c. Describe the major trade-offs in each policy area.

2. Benjamin Franklin said, "Nothing is certain in life but death and taxes." Taxation is as much a social policy as it is a fiscal policy and is the topic of much discussion in American society.

    a. Compare progressive and regressive taxes.

    b. Identify an example of each.

    c. Develop one argument for and one against each type of tax policy.

# Answers and Explanations

## Multiple-Choice Questions

1. A    Unemployment rates tend to be higher for young Americans 16-24 than for older Americans.
   *Page reference: 482, AP Big Ideas: PRD, PMI*

2. B    African Americans have the highest rate of poverty
   *Page reference: 482, AP Big Ideas: PRD, PMI*

3. C    The Social Security dilemma is that the number of Social Security contributors (workers) is growing slowly, while the number of recipients (the retired) is growing rapidly.
   *Page reference: 499-501, AP Big Ideas: PMI, PRD*

4. D    Social Security is an entitlement program. Entitlement programs benefit certain qualified individuals who are entitled by law, regardless of need.
   *Page reference: 488; 499, AP Big Ideas: PMI, PRD*

5. A    Social Security is the most expensive social program in the United States.
   *Page reference: 499-501, AP Big Ideas: PMI, PRD*

6. D    The elderly fare better than the poor in social welfare budget battles because they are more organized, more politically active and better represented than the poor. The elderly are also widely considered to be among the deserving poor.
   *Page reference: 499-501, AP Big Ideas: PMI, PRD*

7. D    Gross domestic product (GDP) is defined as the value of all goods and services produced by an economy during a specific period of time, such as a year.
   *Page reference: 483-484, AP Big Ideas: PMI, PRD*

8. C    One way the government attempts to overcome inflation is by decreasing the amount of money in banks, which raises loan rates and discourages people from borrowing. The Federal Reserve Board controls how much money is issued from the Federal Reserve Bank to all other banks. When it limits those available funds, banks are forced to offer loans at higher rates. This discourages people from applying for loans, which are one cause of the over-circulation of money.
   *Page reference: 484-485, AP Big Ideas: PMI, PRD*

9. C    Laissez-faire economics is a theory that opposes governmental interference in economic affairs beyond what is necessary to protect life and property.
   *Page reference: 483, AP Big Ideas: PMI, PRD*

10. D   The consumer price index is the measure of inflation.
*Page reference: 482, AP Big Ideas: PMI, PRD*

11. A   The Federal Reserve Board has either direct or indirect influence over money supply, interest rates, the availability of jobs, and inflation. It does not have control over the amount of money the government spends.
*Page reference: 484-485, AP Big Ideas: PMI, PRD*

12. A   Supply-side economics, introduced during the Reagan administration, has as its key task to stimulate the supply of goods, not their demand.
*Page reference: 485, AP Big Ideas: PMI, PRD*

13. B   Monetary policy is a form of government regulation in which the nation's money supply and interest rates are controlled to promote economic stability, as distinct from fiscal, in which tax rates and spending are used to promote economic stability.
*Page reference: 483-485, AP Big Ideas: PMI, PRD*

14. A   A recession is a short-term decline in the economy that occurs as investment sags, production falls off, and unemployment increases. It is not caused directly by high levels of government debt, increasing amounts of imports that displace American workers, or by a decrease in the amount of money in banks. It is also not a time when monetary policy is used to increase interest rates to keep people from going further into debt. Typically, the government tries to expand credit.
*Page reference: 483-486, AP Big Ideas: PMI, PRD*

15. A   Fiscal policy involves government policies on taxes, spending, and debt management. It is used to promote the nation's macroeconomic goals, particularly with respect to employment, price stability, and economic growth. Running a deficit with the goal of encouraging economic growth would be fiscal policy.
*Page reference: 485-486, AP Big Ideas: PMI, PRD*

16. C   Government benefits that all citizens meeting eligibility criteria, such as age or unemployment, are legally "entitled" to receive are known as entitlement programs.
*Page reference: 488, AP Big Ideas: PMI, PRD*

17. C   When the Federal Reserve engages in the buying and selling of government securities in the securities market, it is engaged in open market operations.
*Page reference: 484-485, AP Big Ideas: PMI, PRD*

18. D    A mixed economic system is an economic system in which the government is deeply involved but does not command or control the economy. The Justice Department's ability to sue monopolistic companies is an indication of the government's ability to be involved in the economy.
*Page reference: 481-488, AP Big Ideas: PMI, PRD*

19. B    Republicans tend to worry about inflation more than Democrats do.
*Page reference: 485-486, AP Big Ideas: PMI, PRD*

20. C    One way the government attempts to overcome inflation is by decreasing the amount of money in banks, which raises loan rates and discourages people from borrowing. The Federal Reserve Board controls how much money is issued from the Federal Reserve Bank to all other banks. When it limits those available funds, banks are forced to offer loans at higher rates. This discourages people from applying for loans, which are one cause of the over-circulation of money.
*Page reference: 482-485, AP Big Ideas: PMI, PRD*

# Free-Response Questions

*This rubric provides examples of many, but not all of the possible correct responses to the free-response questions.*

1.  The two major tools for macroeconomic policy are monetary and fiscal policies.

    a.  Compare monetary policy and fiscal policy.

        -   Fiscal policy and monetary policy are the two main policy tools for the macroeconomy. Fiscal policy is policy regarding taxing and spending. By taxing, the government takes money out of consumers' hands and reduces consumption. Spending does the opposite. By spending too much, the government might create high inflation, but spending too little would keep people from buying goods and services. Fiscal policy is established by the president and Congress through the process of making the budget.

    b.  Describe how each policy is made at the federal level.

        -   Monetary policy is policy regulating the amount of money in the economy. More money in the economy lowers interest rates, increasing borrowing and consumption. Less money reduces consumption and, if the economy is overheating, can keep inflation under control. But lowering inflation tends to increase unemployment, and vice-versa. Monetary policy is made by the Federal Reserve Board of Governors, mainly by setting interest rates.

    c.  Describe the major trade-offs in each policy area.

        -   *Note that the trade-offs for fiscal and monetary policy are not addressed in the textbook. No one source will give you all of the information that you need to answer every question. You should look at as many possible sources as you can in preparing for the AP Exam.*

2.  Benjamin Franklin said, "Nothing is certain in life but death and taxes." Taxation is as much a social policy as it is a fiscal policy and is the topic of much discussion in American society.

    a.  Compare the difference between progressive and regressive taxes.

    b.  Identify an example of each.

    c.  Develop one argument for and one against each type of tax policy.

        ■  There are several types of tax policies. Progressive taxes are taxes in which the percentage of income that one pays increases with the amount of money one makes. The individual income tax is a good example. Some people believe that progressive taxes are unfair to the rich, but others argue that the rich should pay more because they get more benefits from the government. For example, the police protect everyone's property, but the rich have more property to protect.

        ■  Regressive taxes are taxes in which the poor pay a higher percentage of their income than the rich. Sales taxes are a good example. Even though everyone pays the same tax rate, poor people spend a larger proportion of their income than the rich, who save more of their income. So poor people are taxed on more of their income. Many people believe that this is unfair, but some kinds of economic activity can only be taxed in this way.

# 17

# Policymaking for Health Care, the Environment, and Energy

## Chapter Overview

Health care, the environment, and energy represent three important areas of domestic policymaking. In this chapter, we examine how the government makes policy across these three areas. We begin by exploring the problems of health care in America and the role of government in health care, focusing in particular on the debate over the Patient Protection and Affordable Care Act (PPACA) of 2010. Then we analyze the conflicts between economic growth and environmental protection and identify the major national environmental protection policies. Along the way we evaluate the advantages and disadvantages of each of the principal sources of energy in the United States. We conclude by assessing the role of democratic politics in making health care, environmental, and energy policy and the effect of these policies on the scope of government. By the end of the chapter, students should have a well-rounded understanding of social policy in the United States across a wide variety of issues.

# Study Outline

 **Learning Objective 17.1: Outline the problems of health care in America and the role of government in health care. (p. 510)**

## *Health Care Policy*

- The cost of health care in the United States is very high and is growing.
- Funding has focused on **technological advances** that are extremely expensive.
- More health care facilities have been built than are being used, but their upkeep must be paid for.
- New drugs and procedures have been developed to treat more illnesses than ever before.
- The public is not pressed to be concerned about the cost of health care, since most of it is paid for by the government, employers, and insurance companies.
- Malpractice lawsuits are becoming more common, which raises doctors' insurance premiums and, in turn, raises the cost of their services.
- Companies feel they are bearing too much of the health care burden, but they do get significant tax breaks for contributing to their employees' insurance policies. Part-time employees are usually not eligible for benefits. Many small companies cannot afford to pay for their employees' health care.
- Americans do not all have equal access to health care. Health care and insurance are mostly privatized, not nationalized, so they are not provided for everyone. Most people get insurance through their jobs. Unemployed people have to pay for health care themselves, and most cannot afford to pay.
- **Health maintenance organizations (HMOs)** have lowered the cost of health care but have not alleviated the problem of inaccessibility.
- Accessibility is unequal among people of different races and incomes.
- A greater percentage of minorities and lower-income families do not have insurance.
- Members of minority groups and lower classes have poorer health because they often do not have regular family doctors.
- In some cases, policymakers and insurance companies choose which medical procedures to fund because the money necessary to perform just a few very

expensive procedures could be distributed more widely to provide basic services to more people.

## The Role of Government in Health Care

- Debate continues over who should pay for health care.
- The government pays for 42 percent of health care costs. The government pays for **Medicare** and part of **Medicaid**, but the Medicare system is in danger of running out of money in the next decade.
- Senior citizens actively pursue federal funding for Medicare.
- Lawmakers must fulfill the needs of their constituents, especially of those who vote.
- Interest groups representing the medical profession and insurance companies are well-funded and very active in the political arena.
- Business groups try to persuade the government to take on more responsibility for health care so that businesses do not have to pay for it.
- Many groups, particularly the poor, are largely underrepresented in the health care policy debate.

## Reform Efforts

- In the 1940s, Harry S. Truman called for **national health insurance**, a compulsory insurance program to finance all Americans' medical care.
- The idea was strongly opposed by the American Medical Association, which disparaged it as "socialized medicine."
- While every other industrial nation in the world adopted some form of national health insurance, the United States remained the exception.
- President Clinton made health care reform the centerpiece of his first administration.
- Particularly, his plan would have guaranteed health coverage for all Americans by requiring that employers provide health insurance for their employees or pay a premium into a public fund.
- Opponents labeled it a government takeover of the health care system, and the middle class felt its health care threatened. After a long and tortuous battle, the plan died in Congress.

- Early in his administration, Barack Obama made comprehensive health care reform a top priority in domestic policy.

- His plan would create a new insurance marketplace that would allow people without insurance, as well as small businesses, to compare plans and buy insurance at competitive prices, and provided new tax credits to help people buy insurance and to help small businesses cover their employees.

- It also required large employers to cover their employees and individuals who could afford it to buy insurance.

- Despite opposition from businesses and the public, the White House and the Democratic majorities in Congress pushed through a historic comprehensive health care reform bill in 2010.

 **Learning Objective 17.2: Analyze the conflicts between economic growth and environmental protection, and identify the major national environmental protection policies. (p. 517)**

## *Environmental Policy*

- **Environmental policy** and **economic policy** often conflict with each other.
- Industrial processes can harm the environment. Environmental restrictions may inhibit economic growth and expansion.
- Environmental and business interest groups lobby strongly for conflicting policies.
- Environmental groups call for preservation of wildlife and natural resources and for greater regulation of pollution.
- Business groups demand fewer regulations and restrictions that inhibit industrial expansion.
- The **EPA** was created in 1970 and is responsible for administering the government's environmental legislation.
- Under the **National Environmental Policy Act** (1969), private companies and federal agencies must file an **Environmental Impact Statement** with the EPA, citing the possible effects on the environment of every project they plan to undertake.

- Interest groups have access to the reports, and even the threat of a lawsuit brought by one of them deters many companies from proposing projects that may be challenged by the environmental lobby.

- There are around 20 major pieces of federal environmental legislation. Among them are the **Clean Air Act of 1970**, the **Water Pollution Control Act of 1972**, the **Endangered Species Act of 1973**, and the EPA's **Superfund**, which was created in 1980 to clean up toxic waste sites throughout the United States.

- One of the most intractable—and potentially most serious—environmental issues is **global warming**.

- Most scientists agree that the Earth is warming at a rapid rate, with potentially disastrous consequences.

- The principal way to reduce greenhouse gases is to burn less fuel or find alternative sources of energy, which opponents fear will cost a staggering sum.

- President Obama has proposed to stem carbon dioxide emissions through a market-based cap-and-trade system.

## Learning Objective 17.3: Evaluate the advantages and disadvantages of each of the principal sources of energy in the United States. (p. 525)

### *Energy Policy*

- Fossil fuels such as coal, petroleum, and natural gas are the bulk of America's energy sources.

- Coal is America's most abundant, but also dirtiest, fuel.

- Natural gas and petroleum are somewhat cleaner than coal, but they both contribute to global warming.

- In addition, transporting oil can result in spills that cause serious environmental damage, and refining oil pollutes the air.

- Dependence on foreign oil and natural gas also places the United States at the mercy of actions of other nations.

- One way to minimize the effects of an oil supply disruption is to ensure that our domestic production of oil is maintained.

- Oil exploration on public lands and offshore in coastal waters has the potential to increase America's oil supplies; however, this drilling also raises issues of environmental protection.

- The most controversial energy source is nuclear power.

- Nuclear energy met with increasing skepticism in the light of the accidents at Three Mile Island and Chernobyl, in 1979 and 1986, respectively.

- No new nuclear power plants have been started in the United States since 1978, but interest is growing because nuclear energy does not produce greenhouse gases.

- Renewable energy sources include water, wind, the sun, geothermal sources, hydrogen, and biomass.

- The contribution of renewable sources of energy to America's energy supply is likely to remain small for the foreseeable future.

 **Learning Objective 17.4: Assess the role of democratic politics in making health care, environmental, and energy policy and the effect of these policies on the scope of government. (p. 529)**

- High-tech issues strain the limits of public participation in a democracy, but most Americans do not leave these issues to "experts" to decide.

- The scope of the federal government has grown as it has provided health care for the elderly, the poor, and, more recently, those who simply cannot afford health insurance.

- Health is the most rapidly growing public policy area and poses a long-term challenge for budgeters.

- Concerns for environmental protection have placed additional demands on the federal government, increasing its regulatory reach.

- The public also expects the government to ensure a sufficient supply of energy and to deal with its polluting byproducts.

## For Additional Review

Make a table of the advantages and disadvantages of the current health care system. Then, in a third column, note reforms that have been attempted or suggested. Use this table when reviewing and studying for the unit test and the AP Government and Politics exam.

Make a chart depicting the steps in the policymaking process. List the possible participants for each stage of the process. Finally, put the specific information on the chart for the policymaking processes for both health care and environmental policies. Use this table when reviewing and studying for the unit test and the AP Government and Politics exam.

# Review Questions

## Multiple-Choice Questions

**Questions 1-2 refer to the graph below.**

The Rising Costs of Healthcare

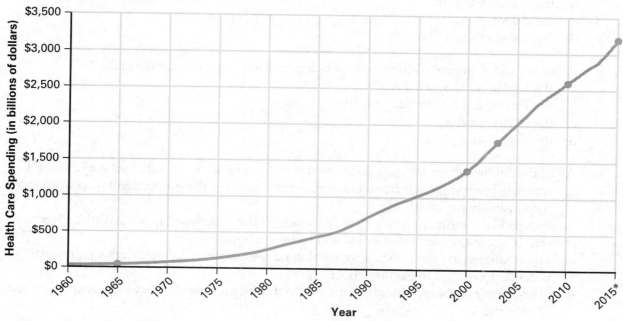

*Estimated data for 2015.

*Centers for Medicare and Medicaid Services, 2016*

1. An interesting paradox about American health care is that
   a. the U.S. spends more money on health care than any other country, yet it is far from having the healthiest population.
   b. Americans are healthier than people in most other countries, even though the U.S. devotes relatively few resources to health care.
   c. the cost of health care has been declining, even though inflation in general is becoming more of a problem.
   d. expenditures for health care for the elderly exceed expenditures for health care for the young.

2. Which of the following has NOT contributed to the rise in health care costs?
   a. new technology
   b. stronger environmental regulations
   c. unnecessary tests and procedures
   d. excessive record keeping

3. Most people in the U.S. get health insurance
   a. from the federal government.
   b. from state governments.
   c. from private policies.
   d. through their jobs.

4. Which of the following groups has the least access to health care?
   a. federal employees
   b. blue-collar workers
   c. the elderly
   d. racial and ethnic minorities

5. All of the following are major pieces of federal environmental legislation EXCEPT
   a. the Endangered Species Act.
   b. the Environmental Protection Agency.
   c. the Clean Air Act.
   d. the Superfund.

6. All of the following are accurate statements about the health care policy debate EXCEPT
   a. business interest groups represent employers who want the government to take greater responsibility for health care.
   b. groups like the American Medical Association lobby successfully for privatized health care because they are well-funded and highly organized.
   c. senior citizens are the most active portion of the electorate in the health care debate because they stand to gain the most.
   d. many new interest groups have arisen to lobby for more health care assistance to people in poverty.

7. Environmental concerns often become hotly contested political issues because
   a. the number of environmental interest groups is shrinking.
   b. the federal courts refuse to get involved in disputes involving the environment.
   c. environmental concerns often conflict with other concerns like foreign trade and economic growth.
   d. Congress has failed to enact any major environmental protection laws.

8. Which federal program was designed to provide health care for poor Americans?
   a. Medicare
   b. National Health Insurance
   c. Managed Care
   d. Medicaid

9. One major reason that many groups' health needs go unmet is
   a. there are too few well-organized groups that insist the government meets these needs.
   b. there is confusion about what their health needs are.
   c. the health care industry is overly centralized.
   d. there are too few doctors in the United States.

10. Which of the following is the United States' most abundant fuel?
    a. natural gas
    b. coal
    c. greenhouse gas
    d. oil

11. The first step of the policy process is
    a. problem recognition.
    b. agenda setting.
    c. policy implementation.
    d. policy evaluation.

12. The exchanges in the Patient Protection and Affordable Care Act of 2010 will be fully implemented in
    a. 2011.
    b. 2014.
    c. 2018.
    d. 2020.

13. In 1993, under the provisions of the Clean Air Act, an emissions trading system was created and the first sales of allowances for the discharge of sulfur dioxide were held. This illustrates which stage of the public policy process?
    a. agenda setting
    b. policy evaluation
    c. budgeting
    d. implementation

14. Which of the following programs provides medical care to elderly Social Security recipients?
    a. Old Age, Survivors, and Disability Insurance
    b. veterans disability benefits
    c. Medicare
    d. Medicaid

15. Due to the steep rise in oil prices in the early 1970s, energy policy
    a. was put on the backburner.
    b. was placed on the governmental agenda.
    c. began to focus on renewable energy over fossil fuels.
    d. relied almost exclusively on renewable portfolio standards to increase domestic production.

16. The funding for Social Security comes from
    a. individual property taxes.
    b. payroll taxes on employers and employees.
    c. individual income taxes.
    d. individual state taxes.

17. A compulsory insurance program for all Americans, first proposed by President Truman, that would have the government finance citizens' medical care is known as
   a. Medicare.
   b. Medicaid.
   c. national health insurance.
   d. affordable health care.

18. The Great Society legislation is associated with which president?
   a. Theodore Roosevelt
   b. Jimmy Carter
   c. Lyndon B. Johnson
   d. Franklin D. Roosevelt

19. A fund created by Congress in 1980 to clean up hazardous waste sites is known as
   a. the national environmental fund.
   b. the toxic waste fund.
   c. the environmental impact fund.
   d. a superfund.

20. Which of the following was NOT part of the Great Society?
   a. Social Security
   b. Medicare
   c. Medicaid
   d. Head Start

# Free-Response Questions

*Some AP Free-Response Questions will ask you to address one specific policy area. It is, however, important that you understand the public policymaking process in general and to be able to draw appropriate examples from a variety of policy areas, because some questions will ask you to address several policy areas in one question.*

1.  One of the most pressing issues in public policy is health care. Using the two graphs below and your knowledge of healthcare policy, answer the following questions:

The Costs and Benefits of Healthcare
Note: Data are for 2012 and 2013

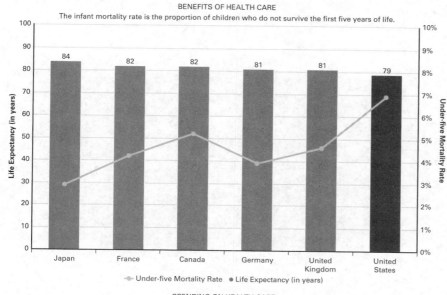

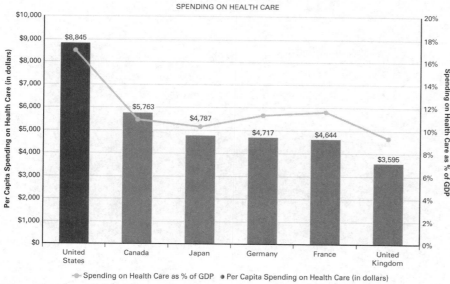

*World Health Statistics 2015 (Geneva, Switzerland: World Health Organization, 2015), 43–53, 142–149.*

a.  Describe how health care is provided in the United States, and how this shapes access to health care.

b.  Identify two advantages and two disadvantages to a national health care system.

2.  One of the biggest environmental challenges is reconciling environmental policy with policy goals in other areas.

a.  Describe two major environmental policies.

b.  Describe how environmental policies conflict with policies in two other areas.

# Answers and Explanations

## Multiple-Choice Questions

1.  A    There is a paradox about American health care: The U.S. spends more money on health care than any other country, yet it is far from having the healthiest population.
    *Page reference: 512, AP Big Ideas: PMI, PRD*

2.  B    Stronger environmental regulations are unrelated to the rising cost of health care.
    *Page reference: 512, AP Big Ideas: PMI, PRD*

3.  D    Most Americans who have health insurance get it through their job.
    *Page reference: 513-517, AP Big Ideas: PMI, PRD*

4.  D    There is uneven access to health care in the United States. Access to insurance and quality care is closely tied to race and income. Of the groups listed, racial and ethnic minorities have the worst access to health care.
    *Page reference: 513-517, AP Big Ideas: PMI, PRD*

5.  B    The Environmental Protection Agency (EPA) is not a piece of federal legislation. It is the federal agency charged with administering the government's environmental policies.
    *Page reference: 519-525, AP Big Ideas: PMI, PRD*

6.  D    Although there are many different interest groups who are extremely active in the health care debate, there has not been a significant rise in the number of such groups advocating for the poor.
    *Page reference: 510-517, AP Big Ideas: PMI, PRD*

7.  C    Environmental concerns often become heated political issues because the environmental concerns often conflict with other concerns like foreign trade and economic growth. For example, environmental restrictions may inhibit economic growth. As a consequence, business interest groups often oppose environmental groups on specific policy proposals.
    *Page reference: 517-525, AP Big Ideas: PMI, PRD*

8.  D    Medicaid is a public assistance program designed to provide health care for the poor. Medicaid is funded by both the national and state governments. It is often confused with Medicare, which is the part of the Social Security Program that provides hospitalization insurance for the elderly.
    *Page reference: 515-516, AP Big Ideas: PMI, PRD*

9.  A    One major reason that many groups' health needs go unmet is because there are relatively few advocacy groups pressuring the government to meet these needs. Single women, racial minorities, and the poor are worst off in this regard.
    *Page reference: 510-516, AP Big Ideas: PMI, PRD*

10. B   Coal is the United States' most abundant fuel. About 90 percent of the country's energy resources are in coal deposits—enough to last hundreds of years.
*Page reference: 526, AP Big Ideas: PMI, PRD*

11. A   The correct order of stages in the policymaking process is: problem recognition, agenda setting, policy formulation, policy adoption, budgeting, policy implementation, and policy evaluation.
*Page reference: 529-530, AP Big Ideas: PMI, PRD*

12. B   The primary purpose of the Patient Protection and Affordable Care Act is to establish government-operated health insurance exchanges to ensure that all Americans would have access to health care coverage. These exchanges will not be fully implemented until 2014.
*Page reference: 516-517, AP Big Ideas: PMI, PRD*

13. D   Policy implementation is the process of carrying out public policy through governmental agencies and the courts. Actually creating an emissions trading system and selling allowances for the discharge of sulfur dioxide is carrying out the policies set forth in the Clean Air Act.
*Page reference: 519-520, AP Big Ideas: PMI, PRD*

14. C   Medicare is the federal program established in the Lyndon B. Johnson administration that provides medical care to elderly Social Security recipients.
*Page reference: 515, AP Big Ideas: PMI, PRD*

15. B   The governmental agenda is the changing list of issues which government believes it should address. Prior to the steep rise in oil prices and the concomitant Arab oil embargo demonstrating America's vulnerability to heavy reliance on imported oil, energy policy was not an issue most government leaders thought needed to be on the governmental agenda, but changes in the early 1970s worked to put it there.
*Page reference: 526-527, AP Big Ideas: PMI, PRD*

16. B   Social Security is funded through payroll taxes, which are paid by employers and by employees.
*Page reference: 515, AP Big Ideas: PMI, PRD*

17. C   Harry Truman first proposed the ideas of national health insurance.
*Page reference: 514, AP Big Ideas: PMI, PRD*

18. C   President Lyndon Johnson was responsible for the adoption of the Great Society legislation, which established much of the present-day welfare system.
*Page reference: 497; 515-516, AP Big Ideas: PMI, PRD*

19. D   A superfund is the fund created by Congress in 1980 to clean up hazardous waste sites.
*Page reference: 522 AP Big Ideas: PMI, PRD*

20. A   Social Security was created through New Deal legislation and not through the legislation passed in conjunction with the Great Society.
*Page reference: 497; 510-517, AP Big Ideas: PMI, PRD*

# Free-Response Questions

*This rubric provides examples of many, but not all of the possible correct responses to the free-response questions.*

1.  One of the most pressing issues in public policy is health care. Using the two graphs and your knowledge of healthcare policy, answer the following questions:

    a.  Describe how health care is provided in the United States, and how this shapes access to health care.

        ■ In the United States, health care is provided in two ways. The government provides health care for a limited number of groups, especially children and the elderly. For most people, health care is provided through private insurance as a job fringe benefit. This means that unemployed and self-employed people often cannot get insurance. Many jobs, especially low-wage and part-time jobs, do not come with insurance. Many working poor must go without health care as a result.

    b.  Identify two advantages and two disadvantages to a national health care system.

        ■ One proposed solution to this problem is a national health care system. This would give everyone access to health care, and might be able to keep costs down because of government controls. However, many believe that this would increase waiting times for health care and would take away people's ability to choose their health care providers.

2.  One of the biggest environmental challenges is reconciling environmental policy with policy goals in other areas.

    a.  Describe two major environmental policies.

        ■ There are many policies meant to deal with the environment. The National Environmental Policy Act requires that many private actors and federal agencies complete an Environmental Impact Statement describing the effects of their projects on the environment. The federal government also provides funding for developing alternative energy sources. *There are several other policies that could be included here, including the Endangered Species Act, air and water pollution legislation, and the Superfund system.*

b. Describe how environmental policies conflict with policies in two other areas.

■ Environmental policies can conflict with both economic and energy policies. Environmental regulations can increase costs to many businesses that trade policies are trying to promote. They can also create conflicts with energy policy, as energy policies aimed at developing new sources of energy may promote the energy sources, such as nuclear or coal, that environmental policies aim to reduce. *Notice that this answer is specific about how the policies conflict, which is often necessary to receive credit for a question.*

# 18

# National Security Policymaking

## Chapter Overview

Unlike domestic policy, which receives considerable attention and debate, foreign policy usually escapes popular attention. This is largely a reflection of the general apathy toward foreign policy expressed by the American public. In this chapter, we explore U.S. foreign policy. We begin by outlining the major foreign policy instruments and decision makers in the United States. Then we outline the evolution of and major issues in American foreign policy through the end of the Cold War, focusing in particular on the post-Cold War threat of terrorism. Next, we examine the major elements of U.S. defense policy and consider the challenges for national security policy in the United States. We conclude by assessing the role of democratic politics in making national security policy and the role of national security policy in expanding government. By the end of the chapter, students should have a good understanding of the major foreign policy issues and the policymaking process.

# Study Outline

 **Learning Objective 18.1: Identify the major instruments and actors in making national security policy. (p. 535)**

## American Foreign Policy: Instruments, Actors, and Policymakers

*Instruments*

- The **military** is among the oldest instruments of **foreign policy** (policy that makes decisions about relations with the rest of the world).

- The United States has been involved in only a few full-scale wars, but it has often employed force to influence actions in other countries.

- Today, economic instruments are becoming weapons almost as potent as those of war.

- Diplomacy, the quietest instrument of influence, is the process by which nations carry on relationships with each other.

*Actors on the World Stage*

- **International organizations** are becoming more necessary in today's global political and economic arenas.

- The **United Nations** is a global legislative body.

- Nearly 200 countries are members, each with one vote in the General Assembly.

- It is mainly responsible for **peacekeeping**, but also administers international economic, education, and welfare programs.

- The **Security Council** has the real power in the United Nations and therefore makes the most pressing decisions.

- Five permanent members each hold veto power: the United States, China, Russia, France, and Great Britain. Ten other seats are rotated each session.

- **Regional organizations** combine blocs of countries in military and economic alliances.

- The **North Atlantic Treaty Organization (NATO)** is a military alliance formed by the United States and Western European countries during the Cold War.

- Since the end of the Cold War, some former Eastern bloc countries have been admitted.
- Members pledge to support each other in times of war; NATO helps prevent the threat of war in Europe.
- The **European Union** is an economic alliance.
- Most Western European countries share a common currency and there are no trade barriers or employment restrictions among countries.
- **Multinational corporations** contribute to about one-fifth of the global economy.
- They have significant influence over taxes and trade regulations, and can be as powerful as governments.
- **Nongovernmental organizations (NGOs)** such as churches, labor unions, environmental groups, and human rights groups unite people globally for common causes or goals.

## Policymakers

- The president serves as chief diplomat and as commander-in-chief of the armed forces.
- He negotiates treaties, makes executive agreements, and appoints ambassadors; he can act quickly and decisively.
- The bureaucratic arm of foreign policy is the **State Department**.
  - The **secretary of state** is the president's top foreign policy advisor.
  - American embassies fall under the jurisdiction of this department.
- The **Department of Defense** works closely with the State Department in matters of national security.
- The **Joint Chiefs of Staff** represent each branch of the armed forces in an advisory committee to the president.
- The **Central Intelligence Agency (CIA)** collects information in other countries to help the departments and the president make policy decisions.
  - It sometimes plays a covert role in the governmental affairs of other nations.
- **Congress** helps to oversee foreign policy, authorizes declarations of war, and appropriates funds for national security; the Senate ratifies treaties.

## Learning Objective 18.2: Outline the evolution of and major issues in American foreign policy through the end of the Cold War. (p. 543)

### *American Foreign Policy Through the Cold War*

- Foreign policy is made up of a nation's external policies and positions and the techniques for achieving those policies and positions.

- The goal of foreign policy is to achieve peace and prosperity in the international community.

- Foreign policy is typically a struggle to achieve a middle ground between political idealism and political realism.

- The United States practiced **isolationism** until World War I.

- During the ideological **Cold War**, the United States focused on the **containment** of **communism**.

- The Department of Defense grew in terms of size and responsibilities.

- The military-industrial complex came to play a major role in politics.

- The **arms race** between the United States and the Soviet Union caused an international arms buildup.

- The United States became involved in the **Vietnam War** to contain the spread of communism in Asia.

  - The prolonged conflict resulted in massive troop commitments and heavy bombing of North Vietnam.

  - Protests erupted at home, and Americans' faith in the government was shaken.

  - Policy stances varied after the Vietnam War.

- The policy of ***détente*** brought greater cooperation between the U.S. and U.S.S.R. Defense spending went up enormously under Reagan, higher than it had been through the previous decades of the Cold War.

- The Cold War came to an end with the fall of the Soviet bloc in the late 1980s and early 1990s, but international relations have yet to stabilize completely in a new system.

# Learning Objective 18.3: Explain the major obstacles to success in the war on terrorism. (p. 548)

## *American Foreign Policy and the War on Terrorism*

- "Terrorism" is the use of violence to demoralize and frighten a country's population or government.

- It is difficult to defend against terrorism, especially in an open society.

- Terrorists have the advantage of stealth and surprise and, often, of a willingness to die for their cause.

- Following the September 11, 2001 attacks, the United States launched a military campaign against al Qaeda and on the Taliban regime that had been harboring them in Afghanistan.

- The president also declared that Iran, Iraq, and North Korea formed an "axis of evil" and he began laying plans to remove Iraqi president Saddam Hussein from power.

- In 2003, a U.S.-led coalition toppled Hussein.

- The United States faced first chaos and then a protracted insurrection in Iraq.

- Critics responded that the war proved a boon for extremists.

- The presence of foreign, non-Muslim occupiers made the country a magnet for militants who opposed their presence and welcomed an opportunity to kill Americans and other Westerners.

- Since the war in Afghanistan, al Qaeda has transformed itself into an umbrella organization that provides an inspirational focal point for loosely affiliated terrorist groups in dozens of countries worldwide.

- Because of the increasingly decentralized nature of the terrorist threat, the military component of the global counterterrorism campaign is more likely to resemble a war of attrition on multiple fronts, and it is unlikely that the use of military force alone will suffice.

## Learning Objective 18.4: Identify the major elements of U.S. defense policy. (p. 551)

### *Defense Policy*

- Defense spending has decreased to one-sixth of the federal budget.
- There is some concern that defense spending detracts from social spending.
- Decreasing spending means fewer jobs for weapons builders.
- The standing army is large and costly.
- The extremely costly arms buildup has stopped, but new expenditures are focused on engagements in Afghanistan and Iraq, and on high-tech weapons systems.
- Treaties have reduced nuclear weapons reserves among several nations with nuclear arms.

## Learning Objective 18.5: Analyze the evolving challenges for U.S. national security policy. (p. 555)

### *The New National Security Agenda*

#### *The Changing Role of Military Power*

- As policymakers have learned that there are limits to what military strength can achieve, attention has shifted away from long wars and formal military actions and alliances.
- "Soft power," the ability of a country to persuade others to do what it wants without force or coercion, is often crucial to national security.
- On various occasions in recent decades, the United States and its allies have used military force in **humanitarian interventions**.
    - ◻ Such interventions are often controversial, because they may involve violating a nation's sovereignty with the use of force.
    - ◻ And the United States is usually hesitant to intervene, as American lives may be lost and there may be no clear ending point for the mission.
- **Economic sanctions** have become a powerful tool of foreign policy.
    - ◻ Embargoes, cutting off economic aid, and restricting imports are all forms of sanctions.

- They are safer and cheaper than military alternatives, and often initiated as a result of the efforts of human rights, environmental, and other political groups.
- Stopping the proliferation of **nuclear weapons** is high on the international agenda.

## *The International Economy*

- International trade has increased dramatically in the past few decades.
- International economic treaties have attempted to address the issue of international trade through such ideas as most favored nation status, where equitable trade and tariff policies are observed by nations.
- The use of **tariffs** has declined to allow free trade among nations.
- Capital can also move more easily across borders with the Internet and advanced communications systems.
- Labor is cheaper in other countries and this leads to unemployment in the U.S., especially in blue-collar jobs.
- In the United States, imports exceed exports, so there is a **balance of trade deficit**.
- International protests against free trade have become common, because people fear the exploitation of less-developed countries by multinational corporations and because workers fear the loss of jobs.
- The North-South divide of wealthy nations and Third World countries is becoming increasingly apparent.
- Less-developed countries are millions of dollars in debt to developed countries.
- Many countries receive foreign aid from the developed world, but aid from the United States is usually tied to military considerations; most goes to Egypt and Israel.
- **Oil** and energy supplies are making economies more **interdependent**.
- The United States imports most of its oil from the Middle East.
- The policies of the **Organization of Petroleum Exporting Countries (OPEC)** are therefore of real importance to the United States.

**18.6** **Learning Objective 18.6: Assess the role of democratic politics in making national security policy and the role of national security policy in expanding government. (p. 564)**

## *Understanding National Security Policymaking*

- There are different opinions over how much discretion to accord policymakers in national security policy, and policies at odds with the public wishes cannot be sustained.

- Congress provides a crucial check on the executive in the area of national security policymaking.

- The United States is fighting a war on terror, has treaty obligations to defend allies around the world, and participates actively in an interdependent global economy.

- As a result of these activities, the United States must deal with questions of energy supplies, global warming, and nuclear proliferation.

## For Additional Review

Create a timeline demonstrating the evolution of foreign policy in the United States. Be sure to describe the key events which led to each of the foreign policy changes. Use this timeline when studying and reviewing for the unit test and the AP Government and Politics exam.

Create a diagram listing all the major foreign policy players within and outside of the American government including the United Nations. For each player listed, describe how that player is involved with American foreign policy and how specific players might interact at any given time. Use this diagram when studying and reviewing for the unit test and the AP Government and Politics exam.

# Review Questions

## Multiple-Choice Questions

1.  Which of the following is the United Nations' most powerful policymaking entity?
    a.  Joint Chiefs of Staff
    b.  North Atlantic Treaty Organization (NATO)
    c.  European Union (EU)
    d.  Security Council

Questions 2-3 refer to the political cartoon below. Use the cartoon and your knowledge of foreign policy to answer the questions.

John Cole, *The Scranton-Times Tribune*

2.  American foreign policy is conducted mostly by the
    a.  Senate Foreign Relations Committee.
    b.  president and the Executive Branch.
    c.  National Security Agency.
    d.  Joint Chiefs of Staff.

3.  All of the following contribute directly to the development of U.S. foreign policy EXCEPT
    a.  the United Nations' General Assembly.
    b.  the Joint Chiefs of Staff.
    c.  the Central Intelligence Agency.
    d.  the State Department.

4. Congress exercises influence over foreign policy in all of the following ways EXCEPT
   a. declaring war
   b. confirming ambassadors
   c. appropriating money
   d. negotiating treaties

5. Which of the following is an accurate statement about the role regional organizations have played in U.S. defense and foreign policy?
   a. Regional organizations have contributed large sums of money to U.S. defense budgets.
   b. In times of war, regional organizations have gained complete control over U.S. armed forces.
   c. Regional organizations have largely been ignored by U.S. presidents.
   d. Regional organizations have been used to promote economic as well as national security interests.

6. All of the following can be used to characterize U.S. foreign policy at various times during the past century EXCEPT
   a. isolationism.
   b. unilateral disarmament.
   c. *détente.*
   d. containment.

7. Which of the following is a true statement about the U.S. and foreign aid?
   a. The Constitution limits the amount of money that can be spent on such aid.
   b. The U.S. can only provide nonmilitary aid.
   c. The U.S. is the world's largest donor of foreign aid.
   d. The president can provide such aid without congressional approval.

8. Which of the following is the most important national security issue the United States has faced since the end of the Cold War?
   a. the spread of terrorism
   b. a dramatic increase in nuclear proliferation
   c. an increasing isolationist State Department
   d. the inability to secure cooperation and commitments from allies

9. Which of the following bureaucratic institutions has primary responsibility for coordinating U.S. foreign and military policies?
   a. Department of Defense
   b. Federal Bureau of Investigation
   c. Central Intelligence Agency
   d. National Security Council

10. Which of the following statements best describes today's international economy?
   a. It is dominated by trade between the United States and the European Union.
   b. It is remarkably similar to the international economy prior to World War II.
   c. It is controlled and dominated by regional nongovernmental organizations.
   d. It is characterized by greater interdependency than ever before.

11. The U.S. decision to continue with the planned invasion of Iraq even after failing to gain approval from the United Nations Security Council is an example of
    a. containment.
    b. isolationism.
    c. humanitarianism.
    d. unilateralism.

12. President Jimmy Carter differed from his Cold War predecessors in operating foreign policy according to the principles of
    a. isolationism.
    b. unilateralism.
    c. moralism.
    d. containment.

13. All of the following can be used to characterize U.S. foreign policy at various times during the 20th century EXCEPT
    a. isolationism.
    b. unilateral disarmament.
    c. *détente*.
    d. containment.

14. The Constitution divided foreign policy powers between
    a. the Democrats and the Republicans.
    b. Congress and the Supreme Court.
    c. Congress and the president.
    d. the president and the Supreme Court.

15. Taxes on imports used to raise government revenue and to protect infant industries are
    a. domestication duties.
    b. excise taxes.
    c. revenue taxes.
    d. tariffs.

16. Which of the following bureaucratic institutions has primary responsibility for advising the president about foreign and defense policy and events?
    a. Department of Defense
    b. National Security Agency
    c. Central Intelligence Agency
    d. National Security Council

17. Which of the following is most consistent with the principle of isolationism?
    a. the Truman Doctrine
    b. the Marshall Plan
    c. the Bush Doctrine
    d. the Senate's refusal to join the League of Nations

18. Treaties in the United States are ratified by a(n)
    a. two-thirds vote in Congress.
    b. two-thirds vote in the House.
    c. two-thirds vote in the Senate.
    d. executive order of the president.

19. The foreign policy course the United States followed throughout most of its history, whereby it tried to stay out of other nations' conflicts, particularly European wars, is known as
    a. multilateralism.
    b. isolationism.
    c. unilateralism.
    d. multinational.

20. A foreign policy strategy that called for the United States to isolate the Soviet Union and resist its encroachments by peaceful means if possible but by force if necessary is known as
    a. deterrence.
    b. *détente.*
    c. containment.
    d. interdependency.

# Free-Response Questions

1.  Foreign policy involves choices about relations with the rest of the world. The instruments or tools presidents use to conduct foreign policy are different from the instruments or tools they use to conduct domestic policy.

    a.  Identify three types of instruments or tools most commonly used by presidents to conduct foreign policy.

    b.  Choose two of the instruments or tools you identified in "a," and describe how they are used to help accomplish foreign policy objectives.

    c.  Identify two executive branch bureaucratic institutions involved in U.S. foreign policy and describe the role they play in the foreign policy process.

2.  Congress shares with the president constitutional authority over foreign and defense policy.

    a.  Identify and describe two constitutionally derived powers Congress has in foreign policymaking.

    b.  Identify and describe two constitutionally derived powers the president has in foreign policymaking.

    c.  Identify and describe a limitation on Congress in foreign policymaking.

# Answers and Explanations

## Multiple-Choice Questions

1. **D** The Security Council is the seat of real power in the UN. Five of its 15 members (the United States, Great Britain, China, France, and Russia) are permanent members of the council; the other 10 are chosen on a rotating basis. The five permanent member states on the Security Council have veto power over all Security Council decisions.
*Page reference: 536, AP Big Idea: PMI*

2. **B** The president is the chief initiator of foreign policy in the United States. Presidents are aided in foreign policy decision making by several executive branch agencies including the State Department, the Department of Defense, the National Security Council, and the Central Intelligence Agency.
*Page reference: 540, AP Big Idea: PMI*

3. **A** The UN General Assembly plays no direct role in formulating American foreign policy.
*Page reference: 540, AP Big Idea: PMI*

4. **D** Negotiating treaties is not a way Congress influences foreign policy.
*Page reference: 538-539, AP Big Idea: PMI*

5. **D** Regional organizations have proliferated since the end of World War II. The United States has used them to help promote its economic and national security interests.
*Page reference: 536-537, AP Big Idea: PMI*

6. **B** Although the U.S. has entered into several arms control agreements over the years, it has never had a foreign policy predicated on unilateral disarmament.
*Page reference: 543-548, AP Big Idea: PMI*

7. **C** The U.S. is the world's largest donor of foreign aid. However, the U.S. ranks lower than almost all other industrialized nations in the percentage of its gross domestic product it spends on economic development aid for needy nations.
*Page reference: 562-564, AP Big Idea: PMI*

8. **A** The spread of terrorism is the most troublesome national security issue the U.S. has faced in the post-Cold War era. Terrorism takes on many forms, including bombing buildings and assassinating political leaders. It is difficult and costly to defend against terrorism, especially in an open society like the United States.
*Page reference: 548-551, AP Big Idea: PMI*

9. **D** Created in 1947, the National Security Council (NSC) is charged with the responsibility of coordinating American foreign and military policies. The NSC is composed of the president, vice president, the secretary of defense, and the secretary of state. The president's national security advisor manages the NSC staff.
*Page reference: 539-541, AP Big Idea: PMI*

10. D  Interdependency is the word that best describes today's international economy. The health of the American economy depends increasingly on the prosperity of its trading partners and on the smooth flow of trade and finance across borders.
*Page reference: 560-562, AP Big Idea: PMI*

11. D  Unilateralism is acting without consulting with or gaining support from others. Invading a country after being denied support by others can be seen as acting unilaterally.
*Page reference: 549-551, AP Big Idea: PMI*

12. C  President Carter differed from his Cold War predecessors by emphasizing support for human rights as the moral and proper course of action to follow. Moralism is the policy of emphasizing morality in foreign affairs, thus emphasizing human rights would be an example of moralism.
*Page reference: 546, AP Big Idea: PMI*

13. B  Although the U.S. has entered into several arms control agreements over the years, it has never had a foreign policy predicated on unilateral disarmament. The U.S. followed isolationism in the period between WWI and WWII. *Détente* was the policy toward the Soviet Union for most of the 1970s, replacing the more conflict-based policy of the nuclear arms race and attempts to use containment to prevent further Soviet expansion.
*Page reference: 544-547, AP Big Idea: PMI*

14. C  The Constitution divided authority for foreign and military policy functions between the president and Congress. The president is made commander-in-chief of the armed forces, but Congress has the power to fund the army and navy and to declare war. The president has authority to negotiate and sign treaties, but treaties only take effect after the Senate ratifies them by a two-thirds majority.
*Page reference: 538-543, AP Big Idea: PMI*

15. D  Tariff is defined in the root of the question.
*Page reference: 561, AP Big Idea: PMI*

16. D  Created in 1947, the National Security Council (NSC) is charged with the responsibility of advising the president about foreign and defense policy and events. The other agencies mentioned play other roles in the foreign policy process.
*Page reference: 540-541, AP Big Idea: PMI*

17. D  Isolationism is a policy of avoiding participation in foreign affairs. Refusing to join the League of Nations would be a way of avoiding participation in foreign affairs.
*Page reference: 543, AP Big Idea: PMI*

18. C  Treaties entered into by the United States must be ratified by a two-thirds vote in the Senate.
*Page reference: 542-543, AP Big Idea: PMI*

19. B   Isolationism is the desire to avoid international entanglements altogether and this philosophy characterized the foreign policy course followed by the United States for most of its history.
*Page reference: 543, AP Big Idea: PMI*

20. C   The U.S. policy of opposing Soviet expansion and communist revolutions around the world with military forces, economic assistance and political influence is known as containment.
*Page reference: 544, AP Big Idea: PMI*

# Free-Response Questions

*This rubric provides examples of many, but not all of the possible correct responses to the free-response questions.*

1.  Foreign policy involves choices about relations with the rest of the world. The instruments or tools presidents use to conduct foreign policy are different from the instruments or tools they use to conduct domestic policy.

    a.  Identify three types of instruments or tools mostly commonly used by presidents to conduct foreign policy.

        - **Military instruments**
        - **Diplomacy**
        - **Economic instruments**

    b.  Choose two of the instruments or tools you identified in "a," and describe how they are used to help accomplish foreign policy objectives.

        - **Military.** War and the threat of war are among the oldest instruments of foreign policy. Among other things, the United States has used its armed forces to help topple enemy governments, protect friendly governments, ensure the delivery of humanitarian aid, protect American business interests and prevent ethnic cleansing.

        - **Diplomacy.** Diplomacy is the least obvious instrument of foreign policy. It takes place when national leaders meet in summit talks or when less prominent negotiators meet to work out treaties covering all kinds of national contracts, such as economic relations, arms control agreements, and cease fires in armed conflicts.

        - **Economic.** Economic instruments can be as potent as war. For example, the control of oil can be a major source of power. Trade regulations, embargos, tariffs, and monetary policies can all be economic instruments of foreign policy.

    c.  Identify executive branch bureaucratic institutions involved in U.S. foreign policy and describe the role they play in the foreign policy process.

        - **State Department.** The State Department is the main foreign policy agency of the U.S. government. It is the home of the diplomatic corps, and its head, the secretary of state, is the president's chief diplomatic advisor.

        - **Department of the Defense.** The Department of Defense is a key foreign policy actor. It is the administrative home to the U.S. military, the army, air force, and navy.

U.S. strategic and tactical military planning take place at the Department of the Defense.

- **National Security Council (NSC).** The NSC is the committee that links the president's key foreign and military policy advisors. Its formal members are the president, vice president, secretary of defense, and secretary of state. The NSC coordinates U.S. national security policy for the president.

- **Central Intelligence Agency (CIA).** The CIA is responsible for collecting and analyzing military, economic, and political data and information from foreign countries. This information can be used for both military and diplomatic planning. Information gathered by the CIA can also be used to prevent attacks on U.S. interests.

2. Congress shares with the president constitutional authority over foreign and defense policy.

   a. Identify and describe two constitutionally derived powers Congress has in foreign policymaking.

- **Power to declare war.**
- **Power of the purse.** A president's national security agenda requires a willingness on the part of Congress to appropriate the necessary funds to support it.
- **Treaty ratification.** Treaties that presidents negotiate with foreign countries must be approved by a two-thirds vote in the Senate.
- **Approval of key personnel.** The secretaries of state and defense, the director of the CIA, and ambassadors to foreign nations must be confirmed by the Senate.

   b. Identify and describe two constitutionally derived powers the president has in foreign policymaking.

- **Commander-in-chief.** Because the framers wanted civilian control of the military, they made the president commander-in-chief of the armed forces. As commander in chief, the president controls where and how the military is deployed. The president also commands the vast arsenal of weapons of mass destruction.
- **Appointment power.** The president selects the persons who serve in key foreign policy decision-making positions like the secretaries of state and defense, the national security advisor, and the director of the CIA.

- **Diplomatic powers.** The president alone extends diplomatic recognition to foreign governments. The president can also terminate relations with other countries. The president is also responsible for choosing U.S. ambassadors to foreign countries.
- **Power to make treaties with other nations.** The president has the sole power to negotiate treaties with other countries, although the Constitution requires the Senate to approve them by a two-thirds vote.

c. Identify and describe a limitation on Congress in foreign policymaking.

- Congress is a relative large and decentralized institution, which makes it difficult for it to speak with one unified voice.
- There is a common perception that the Constitution vests foreign policy decision making solely in the president. This often makes it difficult for Congress to effectively assert itself in matters of foreign policy.
- Congress has to rely on the president for important intelligence information about other countries. This can sometimes result in Congress receiving misleading or wrong information, as in the period leading up to the 2003 invasion of Iraq.

# Government and Politics: United States AP Exam Practice Test 1

## Government and Politics: United States

**Section I**
**Time: 80 minutes**
**55 Questions**

*Directions*: *Each of the questions or incomplete statements below is followed by four suggested answers or completions. Select the statement that is best in each case.*

Questions 1-2 refer to the chart below.

| Political Action Committees—Number of Committee Type: 1980 to 2001 (As of December 31) | | | | | | | | | |
|---|---|---|---|---|---|---|---|---|---|
| Committee type | 1980 | 1985 | 1990 | 1995 | 1997 | 1998 | 1999 | 2000 | 2001 |
| **Total** | 2,55 | 3,99 | 4,17 | 4,01 | 3,84 | 3,79 | 3,83 | 3,70 | 3,90 |
| Corporate | 1,20 | 1,71 | 1,79 | 1,67 | 1,59 | 1,56 | 1,54 | 1,52 | 1,54 |
| Labor | 297 | 388 | 346 | 334 | 332 | 321 | 318 | 316 | 317 |
| Trades/membership/healt | 576 | 695 | 774 | 815 | 825 | 821 | 844 | 812 | 860 |
| Nonconnected | 374 | 1,00 | 1,06 | 1,02 | 931 | 935 | 972 | 902 | 1,02 |
| Cooperative | 42 | 54 | 59 | 44 | 42 | 39 | 38 | 39 | 41 |
| Corporation without stock | 56 | 142 | 136 | 129 | 117 | 115 | 115 | 114 | 118 |

*U.S. Federal Election Commission, press release of January 2002.*

1. Political action committees (PACs) were created by campaign reform laws to

   a. involve the public more directly in presidential campaigns.
   b. regulate how groups such as business and labor contribute to campaigns.
   c. finance challengers' campaigns to eliminate the advantages of incumbency.
   d. pay for candidates' air time because it has become the most expensive feature in a campaign.

2.  Which of the following generalizations is supported by the information in the chart above?

    a.  Nonconnected PACs grew in number more sharply between 1980 and 2001 than any other kind of PAC.
    b.  The most dramatic change in the number of PACs occurred between 1985 and 1990.
    c.  There are only a few cooperative PACs because these are the most difficult type to meet the approval of the Federal Election Commission.
    d.  Business PACs spend the most money on congressional elections.

Questions 3-4 refer to the graph below.

## Entitlements and Discretionary Spending, 1963-2007

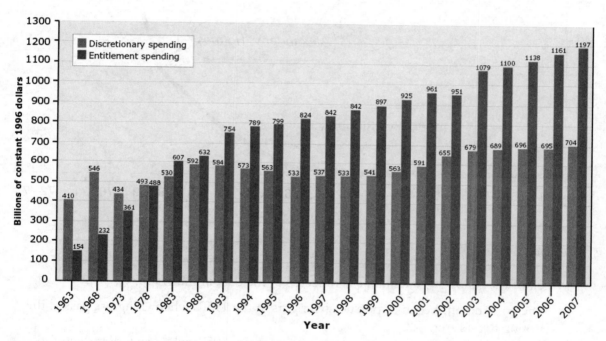

*United States Budget, Fiscal Year 2007, www.gpo.gov.*

3.  Which of the following are true of the data in the figure above?

    a.  In recent years, the government has spent considerably more on entitlements than on discretionary spending.
    b.  Discretionary spending has declined over time.
    c.  Entitlement spending has increased by more than 900 percent.
    d.  Entitlement and discretionary spending are at relatively equal levels.

4.  All of the following are examples of entitlement programs EXCEPT

    a.  Social Security.
    b.  Medicare.
    c.  defense contracts.
    d.  veteran's benefits.

Questions 5-6 refer to the graph below.

**Percentage of Black Students Attending School with Any Whites in Southern States**

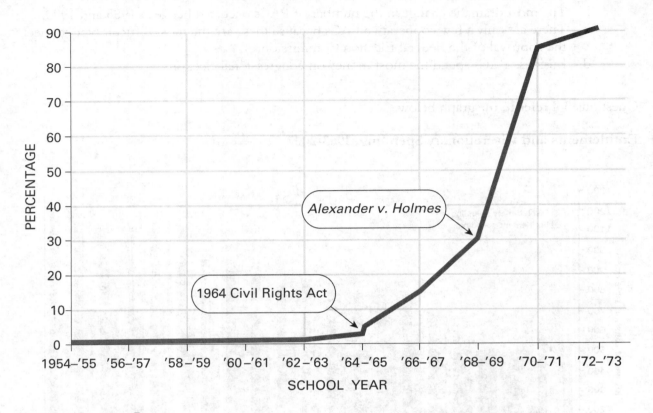

*Data from Lawrence Baum*

5.    Which of the following statements is reflected in the data in the graph?

a.  The government began to pursue civil rights in the 1950s when Congress passed the Voting Rights Act.

b.  The government began to pursue civil rights in the 1950s when civil rights activists marched on Washington to demand government action.

c.  The government began to pursue civil rights in the 1950s when the Supreme Court declared public school segregation unconstitutional.

d.  The government began to pursue civil rights in the 1950s when states agreed to discontinue their use of poll taxes as a means of preventing people from voting.

6.   Which of the following best describes a trend in the line graph above?

   a.   The percentage of Black students attending school with white students in the South began to increase in the 1964-65 school year due to the Brown v. Board of Education decision.

   b.   The percentage of Black students attending school with white students did not begin to increase until the 1970-71 school year.

   c.   The percentage of Black students attending school with white students began to increase in the 1964-65 school year due to the passage of the 1964 Civil Rights Act.

   d.   The percentage of Black students attending school with white students began to increase in the 1964-65 school year, but declined after that.

Questions 7-8 refer to the graph below.

**Who Were the Framers?**

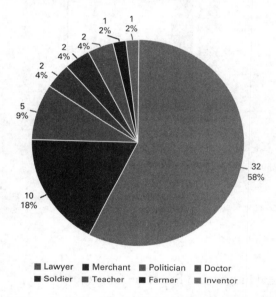

*Charters of Freedom, National Archives and Records Administration*

7.   Which of the following accurately describes the information presented in the pie chart?

   a.   The educated elite represented the largest percentage of the framers.
   b.   Merchants represented a very small percentage of the framers.
   c.   Politicians represented the second largest percentage of the framers.
   d.   Teachers represented the smallest percentage of the framers.

8.   The framers' distrust of the public when writing the Constitution is best illustrated by the

   a.   Electoral College.
   b.   Bill of Rights.
   c.   process of electing members to the House of Representatives.
   d.   creation of a bicameral legislature.

Questions 9-10 refer to the graph below and your knowledge of judicial appointments.

**Who Are Federal Judges?**

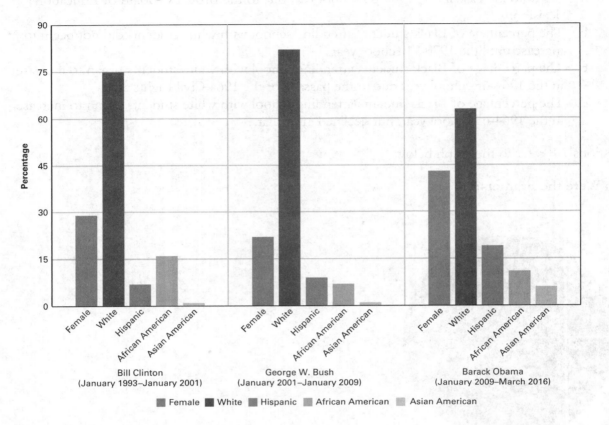

*Federal Judicial Center, Biographical Directory of Federal Judges*

9.   All of the following influence the selection of federal judges and Supreme Court justices EXCEPT

   a.   campaign contributions.
   b.   partisanship.
   c.   ideology.
   d.   judicial philosophy.

10.   The chart above suggests presidents use judicial appointments

   a.   to increase gender and racial diversity of the U.S. government.
   b.   to eliminate judges who are too liberal or too conservative.
   c.   to limit participation by underrepresented groups.
   d.   to appoint judges who will hear only those cases on which judges are likely to agree with the president's point of view.

Questions 11-13 refer to the passage below.

"If an act of the Legislature repugnant to the Constitution is void, does it, notwithstanding its invalidity, bind the Courts and oblige them to give it effect? …It is emphatically the province and duty of the Judicial Department to say what the law is. Those who apply the rule to particular cases must, of necessity, expound and interpret that rule. If two laws conflict with each other, the Courts must decide on the operation of each…

The judicial power of the United States is extended to all cases arising under the Constitution.

Could it be the intention of those who gave this power to say that, in using it, the Constitution should not be looked into? That a case arising under the Constitution should be decided without examining the instrument under which it arises?

This is too extravagant to be maintained."

--*Marbury v. Madison*

11. The Supreme Court asserted which of the following principles in *Marbury* v. *Madison?*

   a. The Fourteenth Amendment guarantees all individual freedoms under state laws.
   b. Freedom of religion is guaranteed, but some religious practices may violate the establishment clause.
   c. Under the Tenth Amendment, the federal government can regulate commerce among states.
   d. The Supreme Court has the power to declare laws passed by Congress unconstitutional.

12. Which of the following regarding judicial review is correct?

   a. The framers likely assumed Congress would abolish the judiciary and therefore judicial review would not be necessary.
   b. The framers most likely did not include judicial review in the Constitution because they believed that power could be inferred from interpreting and applying the Constitution.
   c. The framers never intended the Supreme Court would have the power of judicial review.
   d. The framers intended for the Supreme Court to only preside over criminal trials, making judicial review unnecessary.

13. Which of the following constitutional provisions is the power of judicial review based upon?

   a. Article IV
   b. Article III
   c. Article I
   d. Article V

Questions 14-16 refer to the passage below.

"…Ambition must be made to counteract ambition. The interest of the man must be connected with the constitutional rights of the place. It may be a reflection on human nature, that such devices should be necessary to control the abuses of government. But what is government itself, but the greatest of all reflections on human nature? If men were angels, no government would be necessary. If angels were to govern men, neither external nor internal controls on government would be necessary. In framing a government which is to be administered by men over men, the great difficulty lies in this: you must first enable the government to control the governed; and in the next place oblige it to control itself. A dependence on the people is, no doubt, the primary control on the government; but experience has taught mankind the necessity of auxiliary precautions."

*--James Madison, The Federalist No. 51*

14.  Which of the following statements best summarizes Madison's argument?
     a.  The government must be strong enough to control the masses.
     b.  The government must be able to control itself.
     c.  The government must be directly controlled by the people.
     d.  The government must be directly controlled by the states.

15.  To achieve the purpose stated above, the Constitution created

     a.  universal white male suffrage.
     b.  the practice of judicial review.
     c.  the system of checks and balances.
     d.  full faith and credit.

16.  Based on the text, Madison would most likely agree that the accumulation of all powers; legislative, executive, and judiciary; in the same hands is called

     a.  federalism.
     b.  a strong government.
     c.  democracy.
     d.  tyranny.

Questions 17-18 refer to the chart below.

**Iron Triangles: One Example**

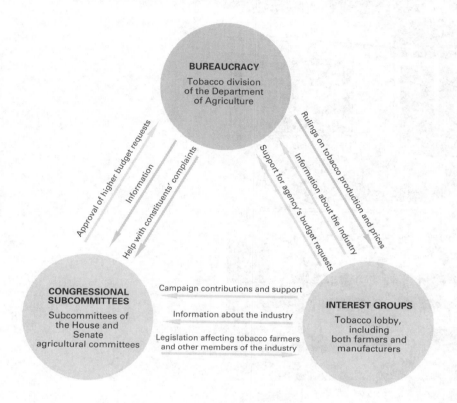

17. Which of the following statements accurately describes iron triangles as shown in the chart?

   a. Iron triangles are composed of members of the military-industrial complex, Congress, and the Department of Defense.
   b. Iron triangles are formed in specific policy areas to advance policies among groups that benefit each other mutually.
   c. Iron triangles are formed to generate support for presidential proposals in Congress.
   d. Iron triangles help coordinate policy among the executive, legislative, and judicial branches.

18. Which of the following statements is accurately reflected in the chart?

   a. Bureaucracies are often criticized as being undemocratic because they are not directly accountable to the people.
   b. Bureaucracies are often criticized as being undemocratic because they utilized a merit system for hiring.
   c. Bureaucracies are often criticized as being undemocratic because citizens tend to have low opinions of them.
   d. Bureaucracies are often criticized as being undemocratic because the courts have no influence over their actions.

Questions 19-20 refer to the cartoon below.

"Mr. Speaker, will the gentleman from Small Firearms
yield the floor to the gentleman from Big Tobacco?"

*JB Handelsman/The Cartoon Bank*

19.   Which of the following best describes the message in the political cartoon?

    a.   Interests groups have no influence in the legislative process.
    b.   Interests groups play a central role in the legislative process.
    c.   Interest groups represent all people equally.
    d.   Interest groups typically represent individuals and not corporations.

20.   James Madison urged the control of factions in

    a.   Federalist #51.
    b.   Federalist # 70.
    c.   Federalist # 10.
    d.   Federalist # 78.

Questions 21-22 are based on the graph below.

## The Incumbency Factor in Congressional Elections

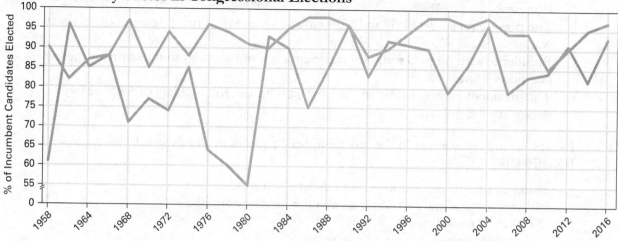

*Data compiled by the authors. Figures reflect incumbents running in both primary and general elections. The blue line represents Senate incumbents; the red line represents House incumbents.*

21.    Which of the following statements is accurately reflected in the graph?

   a.   Incumbents have no more of an advantage in winning an election than any other candidate.
   b.   In Congressional elections, incumbents usually win.
   c.   Incumbents get re-elected in the Senate, but not in the House.
   d.   Incumbents get re-elected to the presidency, but not to Congress.

22.    Each of the following helps explain the incumbency advantage of members of Congress EXCEPT

   a.   the franking privilege.
   b.   the pattern of campaign contributions.
   c.   casework.
   d.   the low standing of Congress in public opinion.

23. Which of the following statements about the president as commander in chief is true?

    a. The president has the authority to declare war for up to 60 days without consulting Congress.
    b. The president can decide if and when to use weapons of mass destruction in times of war.
    c. Presidents with no prior military experience are not allowed to make major military decisions alone.
    d. The president is required by law to consult with the Joint Chiefs of Staff before deploying the military.

24. Interest groups play a role in the federal judicial process in all of the following ways EXCEPT by

    a. giving campaign contributions to judicial nominees.
    b. lobbying the Judiciary Committee about a judicial nominee.
    c. filing *amicus curiae* briefs.
    d. having their lawyers represent a plaintiff.

25. The electoral votes of most states are allocated by which of the following methods?

    a. Each party's candidate receives electoral votes based on his or her percentage of the state's popular vote.
    b. Each elector chooses the candidate whom he or she feels is best suited to represent the needs of the state.
    c. The winner of the popular election in the state receives 75 percent of the state's electoral votes and the loser receives 25 percent.
    d. All of the state's electors cast their votes for whichever candidate won the state's popular vote.

26. Which of the following groups is most likely to vote in elections?

    a. people under the age of 21
    b. senior citizens
    c. people without a college degree
    d. people with no party affiliation.

27. In the process of political socialization, individuals

    a. form their political beliefs.
    b. participate in a direct democracy.
    c. attend functions organized by political parties.
    d. evaluate and select their representatives.

28. The failure of the Articles of Confederation and necessity for a new Constitution were made evident by the

    a. success of the American Revolution.
    b. legislature's inability to select a president.
    c. need for a bicameral legislature.
    d. government's inability to subdue Shays' Rebellion.

29.     Voter turnout in the United States is low in part because

    a.   minority groups still struggle for the right to vote in Southern states.
    b.   registering to vote has become more difficult.
    c.   voters see little difference between the platforms of the two parties' candidates.
    d.   many low-income people are not able to pass the literacy test required to vote.

30.     Which of the following statements is true about U.S. budget deficits?

    a.   The first federal budget deficit did not occur until the 1990s.
    b.   The Constitution requires a balanced federal budget.
    c.   Large budget deficits make the U.S. government more financially dependent on foreign investors.
    d.   Budget deficits have no practical effect on individual citizens.

31.     Congress performs legislative oversight over executive departments by

    a.   hiring and firing department heads.
    b.   determining departments' budgets.
    c.   vetoing department proposals.
    d.   issuing impoundment bills.

32.     Members of Congress most often vote according to

    a.   their own policy preferences.
    b.   the needs of their constituents.
    c.   their relationship with the president.
    d.   their party affiliation.

33.     Which of the following is NOT specifically prohibited by the Constitution?

    a.   gender bias in the workplace
    b.   self-incrimination
    c.   slavery
    d.   national religion

34.     Regulatory agencies are most likely to turn to the industries they oversee when they

    a.   have leaders who need campaign contributions.
    b.   want to deregulate.
    c.   have an unambiguous policy to implement.
    d.   are making budget proposals to Congress.

35.     The largest federal expenditure is

    a.   national defense.
    b.   public education.
    c.   Social Security.
    d.   grants to the states.

36. The two main responsibilities of congressional committees are

   a. making and implementing policies.
   b. setting the dates for federal elections and confirming the appointment of federal judges.
   c. writing guidelines for federal programs and educating the public.
   d. reviewing proposed legislation and performing legislative oversight.

37. All of the following are recent trends in presidential nominations and campaigns EXCEPT

   a. declining party identification among voters.
   b. increasing costs of campaigning.
   c. decreasing importance of national conventions.
   d. infrequency of presidential primaries among states.

38. Single-issue groups, as opposed to other types of groups, represent people in the electorate who

   a. have little political access and influence.
   b. donate money to political campaigns.
   c. pressure candidates to be less ambiguous about their ideology.
   d. feel strongly about a certain cause.

39. Which of the following presidential appointments requires Senate confirmation?

   a. the National Security Council
   b. the Chief of Staff
   c. the White House Counsel
   d. the Secretary of State

40. According to the Constitution, the vice president

   a. chairs all cabinet meetings.
   b. is ineligible to run for president after two terms as vice president.
   c. is the president of the Senate.
   d. must be of the same party as the president.

41. The Social Security program is endangered primarily because

   a. the U.S. birth rate has increased dramatically over the past decade.
   b. the program has lost public support in recent years..
   c. the number of contributors to the program is growing at a much slower rate than the number of recipients.
   d. large federal budget deficits have reduced the amount of tax revenue collected in support of the program.

42. The Supreme Court has upheld which of the following in its interpretation of the freedom of speech?

   a. All forms of speech, including obscenity, are protected under the First Amendment.
   b. The government cannot under any circumstances censor information.
   c. Protests against the government are not protected under the First Amendment.
   d. Forms of symbolic speech are protected under the First Amendment.

43. The rise of the primary election system has led to

   a. the increasing role of political parties in presidential elections.
   b. the public's more direct involvement in the election of the president.
   c. a decline in media coverage of presidential campaigns.
   d. a shift in power from national to state party organizations.

44. Unlike members of the House of Representatives, senators can influence policy debates by

   a. relying on partisan support.
   b. calling for a vote.
   c. using a filibuster.
   d. forming a presidential coalition.

45. A president can be removed from office in which of the following ways?

   a. The Supreme Court rules that he is incompetent or has violated the law.
   b. In a recall, citizens can vote to remove the president from office.
   c. The House votes to impeach him, and the Senate tries and convicts him.
   d. The Senate votes to impeach him, and the Supreme Court tries the president.

46. Third parties rarely last in the American system because

   a. they encourage moderation in policymaking and discourage change.
   b. they offer voters no choice among ideologies.
   c. the rules of the U.S. political system make it hard for third parties to win elections.
   d. they deal with unimportant issues and political figures.

47. All of the following are true of two-party systems, EXCEPT

   a. they encourage extremism in policymaking and encourage change.
   b. they offer voters no choice among ideologies.
   c. they usually include a liberal and a conservative party.
   d. they rely on popular elections to change the party in power.

48. The media has the most influence over which of the following aspects of the presidential selection process?

   a. the way electoral votes are distributed
   b. the outcome of the popular election
   c. who decides to run for office
   d. the outcome of primary elections

49. Congress increased the power of the federal government to enforce regulations in employment by passing the

   a. Fourteenth Amendment.
   b. Civil Rights Act.
   c. Fifteenth Amendment.
   d. Equal Rights Amendment.

50. The Hatch Act helps maintain a nonpartisan bureaucracy because it

    a. creates a federal commission on which half the members are Democrats and half are Republican.
    b. ensures that federal employees are hired based on merit.
    c. requires all federal employees to register to vote as independents.
    d. prohibits government employees in their official capacities from active participation in partisan politics.

51. The principle that the Constitution gives states all powers that are neither granted to the federal government nor denied to the states refers to

    a. states' rights.
    b. reserved powers.
    c. federal supremacy.
    d. concurrent powers.

52. Which of the following statements is true about Congress' influence over Supreme Court decision making?

    a. Congress can pass laws to prohibit judicial activism.
    b. The Senate can filibuster court decisions.
    c. Congress has significant control over the court's appellate jurisdiction.
    d. The Senate can decide which cases the Supreme Court will hear.

53. Implementation of public policy is most successful when

    a. the goals of the policy and the authority of the implementers are clear.
    b. there is a court order mandating compliance with the policy.
    c. the executive branch has precleared the policy with the federal judiciary.
    d. multiple agencies and bureaucrats are involved.

54. Which of the following is true of relationships between the president and Congress?

    a. Presidents usually have little success in forming presidential coalitions in Congress.
    b. Presidents work mostly with minority party leaders to win minority support.
    c. Policy gridlock results when the president's party is not the majority in Congress.
    d. Members of Congress almost always vote in favor of presidential initiatives.

55. The establishment clause, as interpreted by the Supreme Court, prevents

    a. states from passing laws that conflict with federal laws.
    b. the government from violating the rights of individuals.
    c. Congress from exercising any powers beyond those necessary to execute the law.
    d. the incorporation of religion into policy.

**END OF SECTION I.**

**IF YOU FINISH BEFORE TIME IS CALLED, YOU MAY CHECK YOUR WORK ON THIS SECTION.**

**DO NOT GO ON TO SECTION II UNTIL YOU ARE TOLD TO DO SO.**

# Government and Politics: United States

## Section II
## Time: 100 minutes

*Directions: You have 100 minutes to answer all four of the following questions. It is suggested that you take a few minutes to plan and outline each answer. Spend approximately one-fourth of your time (25 minutes) on each question. Illustrate your essay with substantive examples where appropriate. Make certain to number each of your answers as the question is numbered below.*

1. "In the American democracy, political parties use two different systems for selecting delegates to the national party conventions that nominate presidential candidates. In 1968, The McGovern-Fraser Commission established new rules for this process including state parties to adopt explicit written Party rules which provide for uniform times and dates of all meetings involved in the delegate selection process. These meetings and events include caucuses, conventions, committee meetings, primaries, filing deadlines, and Party enrollment periods. Rules regarding time and date should be uniform in two senses. First, each stage of the delegate selection process should occur at a uniform time and date throughout the State. Second, the time and date should be uniform from year to year…"

*--McGovern-Fraser Commission Report*

After reading the above passage, respond to a, b. and c, below:

   a. Describe how caucuses select delegates to the national convention.

   b. Describe how primaries select delegates to the national convention.

   c. Explain one consequence of "frontloading" the delegate selection process.

2. In the 1920s, the state of Minnesota had a law subjecting newspapers to official approval before publication. Publishers had to show "good motives and justifiable ends" for what they were about to print. If they could not, the paper could be censored in advance. Additionally, it was a crime to publish "obscene, lewd, and lascivious" or "malicious, scandalous and defamatory" materials.

Jay Near published a "scandal sheet" in 1920's Minneapolis. This paper was devoted to sensational news and "exposé" reports on corruption. Near regularly criticized elected officials and accused them of dishonesty. He asserted that Jews were "practically ruling" the city, that the chief of police was taking bribes, and that the governor was incompetent. Near was eventually stopped from publishing his newspaper in 1925 on the basis of the Minnesota law.

In 1931, the Supreme Court in *Near v. Minnesota* ruled in a 5-4 vote that prior restraint on publication (censoring newspapers in advance) in Minnesota was "the essence of censorship" and the heart of what the First Amendment was designed to prevent. Even in cases where printed statements could be punished after the fact (libelous statements, for example), neither federal nor state governments could stop the publication of materials in advance. The Court cautioned that prior restraint may be constitutional during wartime: "No one would question but that a government might prevent actual obstruction to its recruiting service or the publication of the sailing dates of transports or the number and location of troops."

*--Bill of Rights Institute*

After reading the above passage, respond to a, b. and c, below:

a. Identify the constitutional principles in common in both *Near V. Minnesota (1931)* and *New York Times Company v. United States (1971)*.

b. Based on the constitutional principles in common identified in part (a.), explain how these cases differ.

c. Explain how *New York Times v. US* is related to the concept of executive privilege.

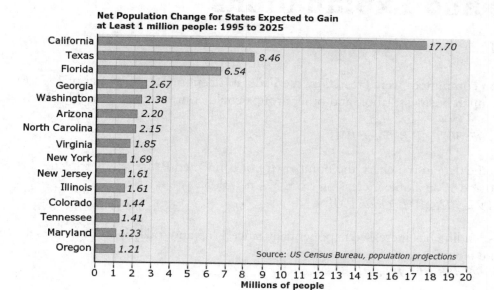

**Net Population Change for States Expected to Gain at Least 1 million people: 1995 to 2025**

California 17.70
Texas 8.46
Florida 6.54
Georgia 2.67
Washington 2.38
Arizona 2.20
North Carolina 2.15
Virginia 1.85
New York 1.69
New Jersey 1.61
Illinois 1.61
Colorado 1.44
Tennessee 1.41
Maryland 1.23
Oregon 1.21

Source: *US Census Bureau, population projections*

Millions of people

*U.S. Bureau of the Census, population projections.*

3. The above graph shows population projections for the first quarter of the 21st century. All of the states listed are expected to gain at least a million people in the next few decades.

   Using the data above and your knowledge of U.S. government and politics, identify and explain THREE ways that these shifting populations will have an impact on government and politics.

4. The Tenth Amendment reserves for the states all powers neither denied nor designated to the federal government in the Constitution. For decades, this afforded states a good deal of freedom in writing their state laws. However, the ratification of the Fourteenth Amendment allowed the Supreme Court to exercise its authority over the states in an attempt to advance the civil liberties of all Americans.

   Develop an argument that explains how the Fourteenth Amendment allows the Supreme Court to exercise its authority over the states.

   In your essay you must:

   - Articulate what provision of the Fourteenth Amendment has been used by the Supreme Court to exercise its authority over the states for the purpose of advancing civil liberties.

   - Identify two areas in which civil liberties protections have been extended to the states, and discuss the specific case(s) that accomplished this task in each area.

   - Use reasoning to explain why your evidence supports your thesis.

   - Respond to an opposing or alternative perspective.

## END OF EXAMINATION

# Answers and Explanations

## Practice Test 1

1. B   Political action committees were created by the Federal Election Campaign Act of 1974 to regulate how much business, labor, and other groups could contribute to a candidate's election.
*Page reference: 295, 302, AP Big Idea: PMI*

2. A   According to the data in the chart, the number of nonconnected PACs nearly tripled between 1980 and 1985 alone, increasing from 374 to 1,003.
*Page reference: 295, 302, AP Big Idea: PMI*

3. A   Entitlement spending has increased exponentially since 1963 and today it encompasses a majority of the federal budget.
*Page reference: 396, 488, 495-496, AP Big Idea: PMI*

4. C   Entitlement programs are a form of mandatory spending because everyone entitled to the benefits of the program must be paid. Congress cannot control these expenditures unless it changes the eligibility requirements of the program. Defense contracts clearly do not fit this definition.
*Page reference: 396, 488, 495-496, AP Big Idea: PMI*

5. C   The Supreme Court's 1954 landmark decision in Brown v. Board of Education overturned segregation in public education which began "the Second Reconstruction," in which the Court, Congress, and the executive took steps to advance civil rights.
*Page reference: 63, 133-140, AP Big Idea: PRD*

6. C   The percentage of Black students attending school with white students did begin to increase in 1964-1965 due to the passage of the Civil Rights Act.
*Page reference: 63, 133-140, AP Big Idea: PRD*

7. A   The educated elite represented the largest percentage of the framers.
*Page reference: 33-34, 43, AP Big Idea: CON*

8. A   The Electoral College illustrated the framers' distrust of the public.
*Page reference: 33-34, 43, AP Big Idea: CON*

9. A   Campaign contributions do not influence the selection of the federal judges and Supreme Court justices.
*Page reference: 41, 450-457, AP Big Idea: PMI*

10. A   Presidents try to use appointments to increase the gender and racial diversity of the U.S. government.
*Page reference: 41, 450-457, AP Big Idea: PMI*

11. D   The Supreme Court has the power to declare laws passed by Congress unconstitutional.
*Page reference: 42, 50, 468-469, 474, AP Big Idea: CON*

12. B  The framers most likely did not include judicial review in the Constitution because they believed that power could be inferred from interpreting and applying the Constitution.
*Page reference: 42, 50, 468-469, 474, AP Big Idea: CON*

13. B  Article III established the judiciary.
*Page reference: 42, 50, 468-469, 474, AP Big Idea: CON*

14. B  Madison believed the government must be able to control itself.
*Page reference: 42, 44, 230, AP Big Idea: CON*

15. C  The purpose stated is the system of checks and balances.
*Page reference: 42, 44, 230, AP Big Idea: CON*

16. D  Based on the text, Madison would most likely agree that the accumulation of all powers, legislative, executive, and judiciary, in the same hands is called tyranny.
*Page reference: 42, 44, 230, AP Big Idea: CON*

17. B  Iron triangles are formed in specific policy areas to advance policies among groups that benefit each other mutually.
*Page reference: 288-289, 434-437, AP Big Idea: PMI*

18. A  Bureaucracies are often criticized as being undemocratic because they are not directly accountable to the people.
*Page reference: 411, AP Big Idea: PMI*

19. B  Interests groups play a central role in the legislative process.
*Page reference: 335-336, AP Big Idea: PMI*

20. C  James Madison urged the control of factions in Federalist # 10
*Page reference: 335-336, AP Big Idea: CON*

21. B  In Congressional elections, incumbents usually win.
*Page reference: 313-317, AP Big Idea: PRD*

22. D  The low standing of Congress in public opinion does not explain the incumbency advantage.
*Page reference: 313-317, AP Big Idea: PRD*

23. B  As commander in chief of military forces, the president decides if and when American armed forces use weapons of mass destruction in times of war.
*Page reference: 348-350, AP Big Idea: CON*

24. A  Federal judges are appointed, not elected, and therefore do not receive campaign contributions from interest groups.
*Page reference: 444, AP Big Idea: PMI*

25. D  Most states award their electoral votes in a "winner-take-all" system which means the candidate who wins the popular vote in the state receives all of that state's electoral votes.
*Page reference: 49-50, 53, 273-276, AP Big Idea: PMI*

26. B  Senior citizens tend to be the most active and informed group in the electorate, especially because Social Security and health care have become major political issues, therefore they have the highest voter turnout.
*Page reference: 263-274, AP Big Idea: MPA*

27. A  Political socialization is the process through which citizens learn about government and form their political beliefs. Family, school, the media, and religion play major parts in influencing how people see the government and with which party they identify themselves.
*Page reference: 170-171, AP Big Idea: MPA*

28. D  Under the Articles of Confederation, the national government was not able to raise a militia to stop Shays' Rebellion, and so the event was an embarrassing failure for the new government. It served as the final proof that the government established by the Articles lacked centralized power and legitimacy.
*Page reference: 30-31, 33, 60, 69, AP Big Idea: CON*

29. C  People who have not voted often cite the generally indistinguishable ideologies of the candidates of the two parties as one major reason for their inaction.
*Page reference: 4-5, 8-9, 172, 264-265, 267-269, AP Big Idea: MPA*

30. C  Large budget deficits make the U.S. government more financially dependent on foreign investors, other governments, and individuals.
*Page reference: 386,388, AP Big Idea: PMI*

31. B  One of the ways Congress oversees the activities of the departments in the executive branch is by determining their budgets and deciding how much each department can spend on its programs and activities.
*Page reference: 327-329, AP Big Idea: PMI*

32. D  Members of Congress most often vote according to their party affiliation based on the presumption that in doing so, they may also be voting according to their constituency's preferences.
*Page reference: 331-336, AP Big Idea: PMI*

33. A  Gender discrimination is not specifically addressed in the Constitution or its amendments; however, it is prohibited by law as a form of civil rights discrimination.
*Page reference: 52-53, 131-132, AP Big Idea: LOR*

34. D  Industries increase their lobbying pressure during the budgetary process to convince the relevant committees of their need for the money they have requested.
*Page reference: 430-432, AP Big Idea: PMI*

35. C  In the past few decades, Social Security has become the largest federal expenditure. It alone accounts for nearly a quarter of all expenditures.
*Page reference: 390-397, 499, AP Big Idea: PMI*

36. D   Congressional committees review and assess bills for their feasibility and consequences and revise, kill, or pass them with a recommendation. Congressional committees also perform oversight of all the federal departments and agencies by setting their budgets and assessing their performance and activities in committee hearings.
*Page reference: 327-329, 322-323, AP Big Idea: PMI*

37. D   The use of presidential primaries has been increasing, not decreasing.
*Page reference: 50, 52-53, 208-209, 226, 265, 272-274, 346, AP Big Idea: PMI*

38. D   Single-issue groups attract people who feel very strongly about one particular issue, such as abortion or gun control, which often incite emotional responses.
*Page reference: 9, 285, 291, 334, AP Big Idea: PMI*

39. D   The secretary of state is a member of the president's cabinet and nominees for this post must be confirmed by the Senate.
*Page reference: 350-351, 433-434, AP Big Idea: PMI*

40. C   The Constitution assigns vice presidents the relatively minor tasks of presiding over the Senate and voting in case of a tie among the senators.
*Page reference: 321, 346, 351, AP Big Idea: CON*

41. C   The Social Security dilemma is that the number of Social Security contributors (the workers) is growing slowly, while the number of recipients (the retired) is growing rapidly.
*Page reference: 169, 499, 501, AP Big Idea: PMI*

42. D   In the 1989 case of Texas v. Johnson, the Supreme Court determined that flag burning, a form of symbolic speech, is protected under the First Amendment.
*Page reference: 17, 25, 86, 93, AP Big Idea: CON*

43. B   Primary elections give voters the opportunity to participate more directly in the presidential election process which circumvents the traditional role of political parties in the nomination process, especially when a blanket primary is used.
*Page reference: 226-228, 246-247, 250, 248-252, AP Big Idea: PMI*

44. C   Only senators have the ability to use a filibuster to hold up debate on a bill. The Senate imposes no restrictions on the length of time for debate over a piece of legislation, so senators are free to talk as long as it takes for their colleagues to lose interest and choose not to vote on the bill.
*Page reference: 310-313, 329, AP Big Idea: PMI*

45. C   The impeachment process set forth in the Constitution provides that the House votes to impeach the president then the Senate tries the president and can convict and remove with a two-thirds vote.
*Page reference: 347-348, AP Big Idea: PMI*

46. C   The winner-take-all system used in American legislative elections and in apportioning most states' Electoral College votes makes it very hard for third parties to win substantial representation in government.
*Page reference: 236-237, AP Big Idea: PMI*

47. A  With only two parties offering policy alternatives, there is little opportunity or incentive for political change. Each party, to draw in a majority of the electorate, stays toward the middle of the road and maintains the status quo.
*Page reference: 49, 220, AP Big Idea: PMI*

48. D  One of the major criticisms held against the primary system is that it allows the media too much influence over election results, particularly in the early primaries. Media attention skews the results by branding winners and losers so early in the campaign process that losers have little chance to score victories in later primaries.
*Page reference: 226, 254-256, 374-377, AP Big Idea: PMI*

49. B  By passing the Civil Rights Act of 1964, Congress outlawed discrimination in the workplace, and consequently, the Justice Department was granted authority to enforce equality in employment and to pursue violators of the Civil Rights Act.
*Page reference: 73, 94, 137, 142, 148, 150, 152, 329, AP Big Idea: PRD*

50. D  The Hatch Act, originally passed in 1939 and amended most recently in 1993, prohibits civil service employees from actively participating in partisan politics while on duty.
*Page reference: 414, AP Big Idea: PMI*

51. B  The Tenth Amendment articulates the reserved powers of the states by stating all powers not denied by the Constitution or specifically designated to the federal government are held by the states.
*Page reference: 63-64, AP Big Idea: CON*

52. C  In many instances federal courts' jurisdiction derives from Congress and not the Constitution due to the fact that the Constitution provides Congress with the discretion to determine which category of cases appellate courts may hear.
*Page reference: 442-443, 452-457, AP Big Idea: PMI*

53. A  If the goals of a policy are not clear to those who have to implement it, and if those who have to implement lack the authority to act definitively, then the policy in question is not likely to be well implemented or received.
*Page Reference: 420, 433-434, 466-467, AP Big Idea: PMI*

54. C  The relationship between the president and Congress tends to be strained when the president's party is not the majority party in Congress. The two often have conflicting policy goals and work together less often than do a president and Congress of the same political party.
*Page reference: 229, 358-361, 364-365, 369-370, AP Big Idea: PMI*

55. D  The establishment clause, located in the First Amendment of the Constitution, establishes the separation of church and state in all levels of government which means that religious qualifications cannot be imposed on public officials, and the government cannot regulate, restrict, or endorse religious worship.
*Page reference: 89-93, AP Big Idea: CON*

# Free-Response Questions

*This rubric provides examples of many, but not all of the possible correct responses to the free-response questions.*

1.

   a.  Describe how caucuses select delegates to the national convention.

   In some states, delegates are chosen for the national conventions by caucuses. Caucuses are when members of political parties meet (i.e., caucus) in town hall-like meetings to discuss and debate about their party's nominees for the presidency. Individuals attending the caucus vote for their preferred candidate. Candidates are awarded delegates to the state and national party conventions based on the number of votes they receive.

   b.  Describe how primaries select delegates to the national convention.

   In some states, delegates are elected for the national party conventions in a primary vote. In states that have primaries, voters go to the poll to vote for a particular candidate. When people vote for the presidential candidate they prefer, they are most often voting for a delegate to the state or national convention who, at the convention, is obligated to vote for the candidate they represent.

   c.  Discuss one consequence of "frontloading" the delegate selection process.

   Frontloading is when several states hold their primary or caucus early in the primary election cycle. With frontloading, one candidate often is able to gain an insurmountable lead in the delegate count long before primaries and caucuses are held in other states. Frontloading has led to a race to the front of the line, with many states moving their primary or caucus to earlier dates.

2.

   a.  The constitutional principle involved in both *Near v. Minnesota* and *New York Times Company v. United States* was that of prior restraint.

   b.  In *Near v. Minnesota,* the case dealt with a state law which allowed newspapers to be censored in advance, which was declared prior restraint by the Court. *New York Times v. U.S.* dealt with leaked government documents given to the New York Times which concerned the war in Vietnam. Even though the government argued the documents breached national security and sought an injunction to block publication, the Supreme Court ruled the injunction would be prior restraint.

   c.  The Nixon administration tried to obtain the injunction and block the publication by claiming executive privilege, which was denied.

3. Identify and explain three ways that shifting populations will have an impact on government and politics.

- The graph clearly indicates that Florida, Texas, and especially California are expected to see the largest increase in population in the next 20 to 25 years. These states will therefore experience a significant increase in political clout as well. With more seats in the House, they will have more influence over national policy and may bring new issues that are pertinent to them to the federal agenda.

- A state's number of electors is equal to the total of its representatives and senators, so if these states gain seats, they will also gain electoral votes. As a result, presidential candidates will focus their campaign efforts on these states.

- The increasing power as a result of migration to these three states in particular may have other political consequences, because all three of these states have sizable populations of Hispanic Americans. This minority group, which is itself growing, may therefore win a greater voice in government. More Hispanic Americans may be elected to public office to represent largely Hispanic constituencies. They may also bring new social and economic issues particular to Hispanic Americans to the political agenda.

4.

a. What provision of the Fourteenth Amendment has been used by the Supreme Court to advance civil liberties?

- The due process clause of the Fourteenth Amendment was used to make the provisions of the federal Bill of Rights applicable to state governments.

b. Identify two areas in which civil liberties protections have been extended to the states, and discuss the specific case that accomplished this task in each area.

- **Freedom of speech** (*Gitlow* v. *New York*)

- **Freedom of press** (*Near* v. *Minnesota*)

- **Right to Privacy** (*Griswold* v. *Connecticut*)

- **Right to Counsel in felony cases** (*Gideon* v. *Wainwright*)

# Government and Politics: United States AP Exam Practice Test 2

## Government and Politics: United States

**Section I**
**Time: 80 minutes**
**55 Questions**

*Directions: Each of the questions or incomplete statements below is followed by four suggested answers or completions. Select the statement that is best in each case.*

Questions 1-2 refer to the chart below.

**The Policymaking System**

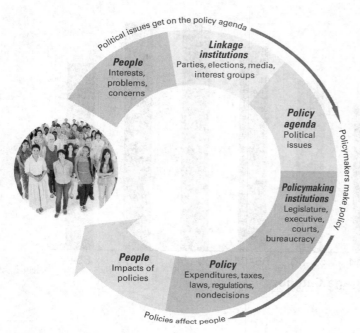

*Rawpixel.com/Fotolia*

1. Which of the following statements is reflected in the data in the chart?

   a. People have no role in the policymaking system.
   b. People's concerns get transmitted to linkage institutions in the policymaking system.
   c. Political institutions are the only participants in the policymaking system.
   d. Political institutions have only an advisory role in the policymaking system.

2. Which of the following is an accurate conclusion based on the graph?

   a. The president exercises the most influence over policymaking by vetoing legislation passed by Congress.
   b. The president exercises the most influence over policymaking by setting the congressional agenda.
   c. The president exercises the most influence over policymaking by introducing legislation for debate.
   d. The president exercises the most influence over policymaking by participating in committee hearings.

Questions 3-4 refer to the graph below.

**Turnout Increases with Age**

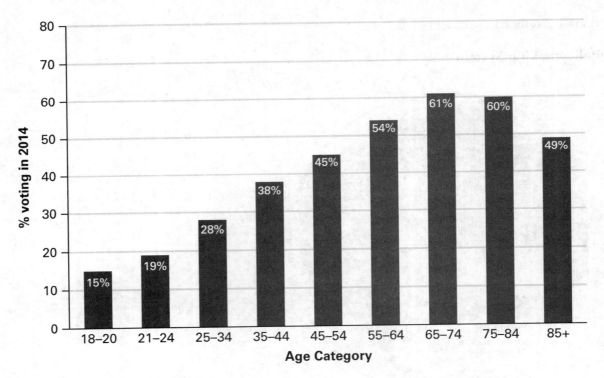

Authors' analysis of 2014 Census Bureau data.

3.    Which of the following is an accurate conclusion based on the graph?

    a.  65- to 75-year-olds are least likely to participate in the political process.
    b.  high school graduates are least likely to participate in the political process.
    c.  women are least likely to participate in the political process.
    d.  18- to 25-year-olds are least likely to participate in the political process.

4.    Which of the following is a potential consequence of the information illustrated in the graph?

    a.  Politicians are much more likely to listen to the concerns of the 18-25 age group.
    b.  Politicians are much less likely to listen to the concerns of the 65-75 age group.
    c.  Politicians are much more likely to listen to the concerns of women.
    d.  Politicians are much less likely to listen to the concerns of the 18-25 age group.

Questions 5-6 refer to the graph below.

**Realignment in the South**

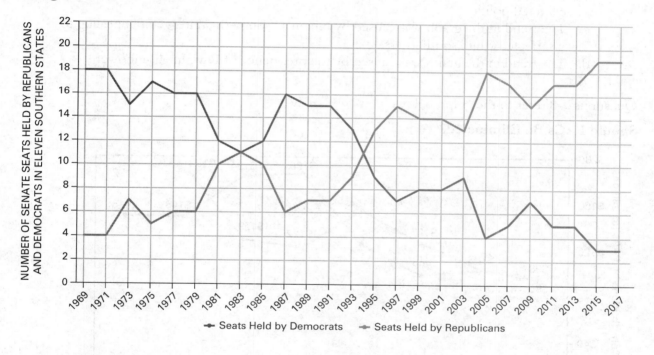

5. Which of the following is an accurate statement about the information in the line graph?

    a. There has been a significant increase in the number of seats held by Democrats in the southern states since 1969.

    b. There has not been a significant shift in the number of seats held by either Democrats or Republicans in the southern states since 1969.

    c. There has been a significant increase in the number of seats held by Republicans in the southern states since 1969.

    d. There has been a significant increase in the number of seats held by third parties in the southern states since 1969.

6. Which of the following is an accurate conclusion based on the information in the graph above?

    a. The trend in the graph was caused by the Great Depression and subsequent New Deal programs.

    b. The trend in the graph was caused by the rise of political party machines and candidate-centered politics.

    c. The trend in the graph was caused by Nixon's "southern strategy" of appealing to disaffected white southerners.

    d. The trend in the graph was caused by the presidency of Dwight Eisenhower.

Questions 7-8 refer to the graph below.

**Should PACs Be Eliminated?**

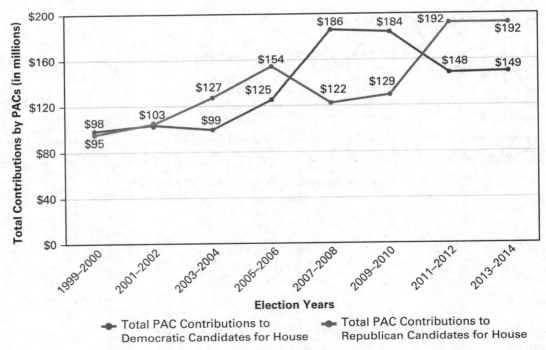

Harold Stanley and Richard Niemi, *Vital Statistics on American Politics, 2015–2016 (Los Angeles: CQ Press, 2015), 102–104.*

7. Which of the following best describes a trend in the line graph above?

   a. Contributions by PACs have not significantly increased since 1999.
   b. Contributions by PACs increased for Republican candidates in 2007-2008.
   c. Contributions by PACs decreased for Democratic candidates in 2007-2008.
   d. Contributions by PACs increased for Republican candidates between 2009-2010 and 2011-2012.

8. Which of the following is an accurate conclusion based on the information in the graph.

   a. Electioneering is an entirely negative development of PACs.
   b. Electioneering by PACs has introduced obvious biases into the electoral process.
   c. Electioneering by PACs has led to more objective participation in the electoral process.
   d. Electioneering by PACs has been eliminated by law.

Questions 9-10 refer to the graph below.

**How Does the Federal Government Spend Money?**

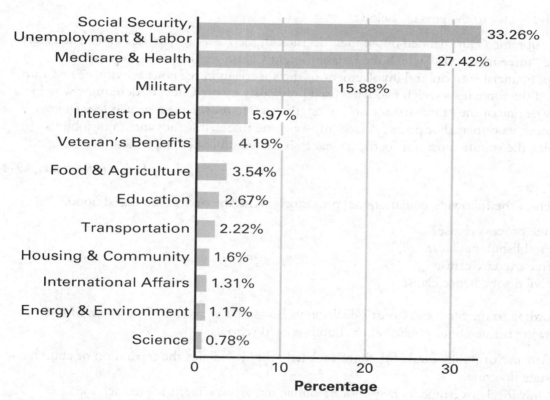

*Data from the National Priorities Project*
*www.nationalpriorities.org/budget-basics/federal-budget 101/revenues/*
*www.nationalpriorities.org/budget-basics/federal-budget-101/spending.*

9. Which of the following can be assumed from the information in the chart?

   a. The rise of the Social Security system has led to cutbacks in defense spending and the building of new weapons.
   b. The rise of the Social Security system has become the largest federal expenditure.
   c. The rise of the Social Security system has increased Americans' trust in a government that provides for all Americans.
   d. The rise of the Social Security system has caused income tax rates to double since its initiation.

10. Which of the following statements is reflected in the data in the chart?

   a. Medicare and health spending is not a high priority in the budget.
   b. Education and transportation spending together represent the majority of the budget.
   c. The military is not an important priority when planning the budget.
   d. Spending for the social security and other social welfare programs are the most important items in the budget.

Questions 11-13 refer to the passage below.

In 1971, the Supreme Court handed down their decision in the *Lemon v. Kurtzman* case. The Court described the "three main evils" which the Establishment Clause was intended to prevent: "sponsorship, financial support and involvement of the sovereign in religious activity." The Court then described the three tests which had been used previously by the Court to determine whether a State is guilty of one of the "three main evils". First, the statute must have a secular legislative purpose; second, its principal or primary effect must be one that neither advances nor inhibits religion; finally, the statute must not foster "an excessive government entanglement with religion".

--*Lemon v. Kurtzman*, 1971

11. Which of the following constitutional provisions is the above decision based upon?

   a. due process clause
   b. establishment clause
   c. free exercise clause
   d. civil disobedience clause

12. According to the Supreme Court's decision in *Lemon* v. *Kurtzman* (1971), which of the following is true about public aid to church-related schools?

   a. Any use of public funds for church-related schools violates the separation of church and state doctrine.
   b. Only local governments may allocate public money to church-related schools.
   c. Public aid to church-related schools must be matched by an equal amount of privately raised funds.
   d. Public aid to church-related schools must have a primary effect that neither advances nor inhibits religion.

13. Freedom of religion is NOT protected by which of the following?

   a. allowing the free exercise of religion
   b. the Supreme Court's encouragement that states maintain a position of neutrality toward religion
   c. prohibiting laws that would encourage "establishment of religion"
   d. not allowing Americans to hold any religious belief they choose

Questions 14-16 refer to the passage below.

"An Act to enforce the fifteenth amendment to the Constitution of the United States, and for other purposes. Be it enacted by the Senate and House of Representatives of the United States of America in Congress assembled, That this Act shall be known as the "Voting Rights Act of 1965."
SEC. 2. No voting qualifications or prerequisite to voting, or standard, practice, or procedure shall be imposed or applied by any State or political subdivision to deny or abridge the right of any citizen of the United States to vote on account of race or color…"

*--Voting Rights Act 1965*

14. Which of the following statements is most consistent with the ideas in the above passage?

   a. Legislation enacted in 1965 was designed to ensure no person would be deprived of due process based on race or color.
   b. Legislation enacted in 1965 was designed to ensure no person would be deprived of the right to vote based on race or color.
   c. Legislation enacted in 1965 was designed to ensure no person would be deprived of the right to a fair trial based on race or color.
   d. Legislation enacted in 1965 was designed to ensure no person would be deprived of the right of freedom of religion based on race or color.

15. Which of the following authorized the Justice Department to send federal officials to oversee state elections?

   a. Fifteenth Amendment
   b. Voting Rights Act
   c. Motor Voter Act
   d. Thirteenth Amendment

16. Which of the following is a true statement about the Voting Rights Act of 1965?

   a. It resulted in increased discrimination against women voters.
   b. It allowed literacy tests to be administered as a prerequisite for voting.
   c. It gave the states more control over federal elections.
   d. It resulted in dramatic increases in the number of African American voters.

Questions 17-18 refer to the map below.

**Where is Union Membership Highest?**

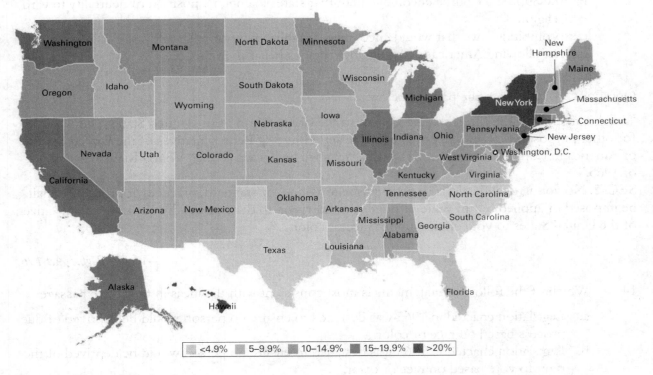

*Data from Bureau of Labor Statistics*

17.    Which of the following statements is a correct interpretation of the map?

    a.  Union membership is relatively constant throughout the United States.

    b.  Union membership is highest in the Midwest.

    c.  Union membership is lowest in the South.

    d.  Union membership is very low throughout the United States.

18.    Legislation that forbids labor contracts from requiring workers to join unions in order to hold their jobs is known as

    a.  unfair labor practice legislation.

    b.  right-to-work laws.

    c.  right-to-choose laws.

    d.  right-to-unionize laws.

Questions 19-20 refer to the cartoon below.

19. Which of the following best describes the message in the political cartoon?

    a. Congress rewards special interest groups for their work on the legislative agenda.
    b. Interest groups buy legislation from Congress to advance their causes.
    c. Congress must take "pay offs" because they are unable to accept campaign contributions from interest groups.
    d. There is a funding problem in Congress, therefore, members must take money from questionable sources.

20. Despite their influence over the political agenda, interest groups may be seen as democratic institutions in that they

    a. help voters decide how to cast their ballots in an election.
    b. fund campaigns through political action committees.
    c. run advertisements to generate public support for a presidential proposal.
    d. promote equal representation of citizens' political beliefs.

21.	In which of the following elections are voters allowed to choose candidates from either party for different offices?

a.	open primary
b.	initiative
c.	closed primary
d.	blanket primary

22.	All of the following play a role in the impeachment of a president, EXCEPT the

a.	court of appeals.
b.	Judiciary Committee.
c.	U.S. House of Representatives.
d.	chief justice of the United States.

23.	In general, Democrats are more likely than the Republicans to advocate for which of the following?

a.	lower capital gains tax rates
b.	reduced spending for social services
c.	prayer in public schools
d.	restrictions on handgun ownership

24.	The federal bureaucracy handles all of the following activities EXCEPT

a.	issuing rules and regulations.
b.	holding hearings to obtain information about proposed policies.
c.	implementing policies passed by Congress.
d.	appropriating funds to pay for federal government programs.

25.	The elastic clause grants Congress the authority to

a.	amend the president's budget proposal as it sees fit.
b.	make any laws that enable it to carry out its assigned responsibilities.
c.	raise taxes.
d.	create any number of legislative committees and subcommittees.

26.	The most common way that ordinary citizens participate in politics is by

a.	participating in political protests.
b.	writing letters to the editor of a local newspaper.
c.	voting in elections.
d.	contacting their elected representatives.

27.	The Constitution authorizes Supreme Court justices to be appointed for life for which of the following reasons?

a.	to shield judges from political influence and pressure
b.	to reward judges for their distinguished careers
c.	to create a strong relationship between the court and Congress
d.	to allow politicians to use the patronage system

28. One common criticism of the media's participation in politics is

   a. its bias in favor of outsiders and third parties.
   b. its focus on the Supreme Court to the exclusion of the other branches.
   c. its live and uncensored coverage of committee hearings.
   d. its tendency to focus more on personalities than on issues.

29. Which of the following statements about the budgetary process is true?

   a. The president submits a budget proposal to Congress, which ultimately decides how to allocate money.
   b. The president assigns a spending minimum and maximum to each agency in the executive branch.
   c. Interest groups have little influence over this aspect of policymaking.
   d. The Office of Management and Budget handles the entire budgetary process.

30. In which of the following cases is a congressional candidate most likely to be elected?

   a. if he or she has a good television presence
   b. when a state has just gained seats due to reapportionment
   c. if he or she is new to politics
   d. if he or she is an incumbent

31. Which of the following is true of iron triangles?

   a. An iron triangle is composed of the president, the Speaker of the House, and the chief justice.
   b. Iron triangles inhibit the policy process by interfering with the debate over a piece of legislation.
   c. Iron triangles help unify the three branches of government in pursuit of a single, clear policy agenda.
   d. Iron triangles help advance legislation and implementation in a particular policy area.

32. An environmental lobby would be LEAST likely to exert its influence by meeting with a

   a. federal judge hearing a case on the constitutionality of an environmental regulation.
   b. member of the House committee that authorizes money for the building of power plants.
   c. staff member of the Environmental Protection Agency.
   d. newspaper in the town where environmental laws are being violated.

33. A voter's choice of candidate is most influenced by

   a. campaign finance laws.
   b. political advertisements.
   c. party identification.
   d. the media.

34. Many Supreme Court cases of the 1960s involved issues of

   a. gender discrimination.
   b. economic regulation.
   c. constitutional powers of the president.
   d. rights of the accused.

35. If the Supreme Court rules that a newly passed law is unconstitutional, Congress can

   a. ask the president to appoint new justices.
   b. try to amend the Constitution to override the Supreme Court's interpretation.
   c. appeal the Court's decision to the Senate Judiciary Committee.
   d. issue a referendum to allow the public to vote on the Supreme Court's decision.

36. If the House and Senate pass two different versions of a bill,

   a. the Senate version has seniority and is sent to the president.
   b. the Supreme Court chooses the better version.
   c. the two versions are sent to a conference committee to work out a compromise bill.
   d. the president has the authority to choose which version will be signed into law.

37. One tool that allows the president to sidestep congressional approval of his diplomatic duties is the

   a. power to negotiate treaties.
   b. authority to enter into executive agreements.
   c. ability to send troops into war.
   d. freedom to appoint ambassadors.

38. Which of the following is an accurate statement about the caseload of the Supreme Court?

   a. Only a small portion of cases seeking review are heard by the Supreme Court.
   b. The Senate Judiciary Committee selects which cases will be placed on the docket.
   c. Most cases that reach the Supreme Court are appealed from state courts.
   d. The solicitor general is responsible for assigning cases to the Supreme Court.

39. The Supreme Court has extended federal supremacy over state laws through its interpretation of the

   a. Tenth Amendment.
   b. eminent domain clause.
   c. First Amendment.
   d. Fourteenth Amendment.

40. Which of the following is an incumbent's greatest advantage during an election?

   a. automatic endorsement from the president
   b. a clean political record
   c. name recognition
   d. more campaign resources and funding

41. Television has had which of the following effects on political parties?

    a. It has helped lower the cost of campaigning, thereby saving the parties money.
    b. It has forced candidates to rely more heavily on their parties.
    c. It has caused a decrease in party identification among the electorate.
    d. It has led to the declining importance of national conventions.

42. Articles of impeachment must be passed by

    a. either the House or the Senate.
    b. both the House and the Senate.
    c. just the Senate.
    d. just the House.

43. What happens if no presidential candidate receives an Electoral College majority?

    a. The election is decided by the U.S. House of Representatives.
    b. The winner is decided by a conference of the state governors.
    c. A run-off election is held to determine the winner.
    d. The U.S. Supreme Court determines the winner.

44. Which of the following is a trend in American elections?

    a. Fewer candidates are seeking elective office.
    b. Campaigns are becoming less expensive to run.
    c. Political pundits are becoming more influential.
    d. More states are allowing early voting.

45. Article II of the Constitution grants the president power to do all of the following EXCEPT

    a. authorize troop movements during war.
    b. appropriate funds for agencies.
    c. veto proposed legislation.
    d. appeal to Congress and make legislative requests in a state of the union address.

46. The Civil Rights Act of 1964 articulated which of the following?

    a. the requirement that all public schools desegregate
    b. a prohibition of states' institution of poll taxes or literacy tests when administering elections
    c. the illegality of discrimination in employment and public accommodations
    d. the creation of the Justice Department to investigate civil rights violations

47. Which of the following statements accurately describes the procedure of debate in the House?

    a. The Rules Committee determines the order in which bills will be heard and the length of debate for each one.
    b. Representatives who are introducing a bill are allowed the privilege of unlimited debate.
    c. The Speaker and the sergeant at arms together determine the schedule of debate.
    d. The minority party is allowed an automatic 10 minutes of debate time to refute legislation introduced by the majority party.

48. In *Texas* v. *Johnson,* the Supreme Court determined that

    a. the drawing of unreasonable school district lines cannot be used as a means of integrating schools.
    b. symbolic speech is protected under the First Amendment.
    c. affirmative action quotas are unconstitutional.
    d. the death penalty is not a form of cruel and unusual punishment.

49. A weakness of the Articles of Confederation was that they established a government that was unable to

    a. remain a democracy.
    b. be recognized by foreign governments.
    c. represent the views of the various states.
    d. centralize its powers.

50. The Federal Reserve Board oversees which of the following policy areas?

    a. social welfare policy
    b. foreign policy
    c. monetary policy
    d. health care policy

51. Which of the following is a major difference between the Democratic and Republican parties?

    a. The Democratic Party campaigns fairly, but the Republican Party does not.
    b. A wider variety of groups in the electorate vote for Republican candidates.
    c. The Republican Party is much older than the Democratic Party.
    d. The Democratic Party has a more liberal ideology, whereas the Republican Party has a more conservative ideology.

52. One way federal agencies regulate an industry is by

    a. hiring corporate leaders in the industry.
    b. issuing bonds to the industry.
    c. fixing stock prices in the industry.
    d. sending inspectors to investigate an industry's regular activity.

53. Which of the following is a basic weakness inherent in the presidency?

    a. Except in military affairs, presidents must rely on the support of other people to influence policy decisions.
    b. Because they are limited to only two terms, presidents rarely have enough time to achieve any of their policy goals.
    c. Media attention focuses heavily on the president, which leads the public to hold him accountable and, in turn, deprives him of power.
    d. The president is commander in chief, yet he cannot act in military situations without congressional approval.

54. Which of the following is true of federal systems of government?

    a. The central government completely regulates the activities of state governments.
    b. Citizens vote for central government officials only.
    c. The central government shares power with the states.
    d. Most democracies are federal systems.

55. The House of Representatives differs from the Senate in all of the following ways EXCEPT

    a. House seats are distributed according to each state's population, whereas each state has the same number of senators.
    b. House debates are scheduled, whereas the Senate allows unlimited debate.
    c. representatives tend to act more independently, whereas senators usually vote according to party lines.
    d. power is distributed more hierarchically in the House than it is in the Senate.


*END OF SECTION I.*

*IF YOU FINISH BEFORE TIME IS CALLED, YOU MAY CHECK YOUR WORK ON THIS SECTION.*

*DO NOT GO ON TO SECTION II UNTIL YOU ARE TOLD TO DO SO.*

# Government and Politics: United States

## Section II
## Time: 100 minutes

*Directions:* *You have 100 minutes to answer all four of the following questions. It is suggested that you take a few minutes to plan and outline each answer. Spend approximately one-fourth of your time (25 minutes) on each question. Illustrate your essay with substantive examples where appropriate. Make certain to number each of your answers as the question is numbered below.*

1.  The writers of the Constitution favored the ideals of democracy, yet they feared putting too much power in the hands of the people. "From this view of the subject, it may be concluded, that a pure democracy, by which I mean, a society consisting of a small number of citizens, who assemble and administer the government in person, can admit of no cure for the mischiefs of faction…there is nothing to check the inducements to sacrifice the weaker party, or an obnoxious individual. Hence it is, that such democracies have ever been spectacles of turbulence and contention; have ever been found incompatible with personal security, or the rights of property; and have, in general, been as short in their lives, as they have been violent in their deaths."

    *--The Federalist No. 10*

After reading the above passage, respond to a, b, and c below:

   a.  Identify TWO changes from the original Constitution that increased the democratic nature of government.

   b.  Explain how each of the two factors identified in part *a*, above, has resulted in a more democratic nation.

   c.  Explain how this relates to the concepts of public opinion and political action.

## 2. Harris v. McRae (1980)

### The issue before the Court:

In 1976, Congress passed an amendment, known as the Hyde Amendment, which prohibited using federal Medicaid funds for abortion except to save the woman's life. A lawsuit argued that the Hyde Amendment, by denying public funding for medically necessary abortions, violated the Fifth Amendment's due process clause and the First Amendment's religion clauses (the argument was that the Hyde Amendment incorporated Catholic doctrine about when life begins). In a 5-4 vote, the Court ruled that the Hyde Amendment was constitutional.

### The Court's ruling:

"... [R]egardless of whether the freedom of a woman to choose to terminate her pregnancy for health reasons lies at the core or the periphery of the due process liberty recognized in *Wade*, it simply does not follow that a woman's freedom of choice carries with it a constitutional entitlement to the financial resources to avail herself of the full range of protected choices... Nor is it irrational that Congress has authorized federal reimbursement for medically necessary services generally, but not for certain medically necessary abortions. Abortion is inherently different from other medical procedures, because no other procedure involves the purposeful termination of a potential life."

*--Harris v. McRae,* 448 U.S. 297 (1980)

a.  Identify the constitutional issue that is common in *Roe v. Wade* (1973) and *Harris v. McRae* (1980).

b.  Based on the constitutional issue identified in a., explain why the facts of *Harris v. McRae* led to a different holding than *Roe v. Wade*.

c.  Describe an action which could be taken by opponents of the *Harris v. McRae* decision.

## Race and Ethnicity in America, 1967–2008

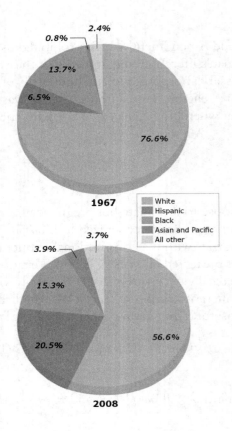

*U.S. Census Bureau, Statistical Abstract of the United States*

3. The above graph details how the composition of the American population has changed over the last 40 years.

Using the data above and your knowledge of U.S. government and politics, identify and explain THREE ways that these shifting populations will have an impact on government and politics.

   a. Identify one way the geographic distribution of the population has changed and explain why that shift occurred.

   b. Describe THREE ways that these shifting populations will have an impact on government and politics.

4. During the budgetary process, Congress weighs revenues and expenditures to determine how to allocate money within the federal government. Social spending has become a major component of the federal budget in recent decades, but in some cases Congress is not able to adjust spending for it. Develop a thesis that explains the role of uncontrollable expenditures and entitlements in the budgetary process, the impact of democratic politics on budgetary growth, and the impact of the budget on the scope of government.

In your essay you must:

- Articulate a defensible thesis that responds to the prompt.

- Support your thesis by identifying TWO items in the budget that cannot usually be amended during the budgetary process.

- For each one, explain why spending is not cut.

- Use reasoning to explain why your evidence supports your claim.

- Respond to an opposing or alternative perspective.


**END OF EXAMINATION**

# Answers and Explanations

## Practice Test 2

1. B  People's concerns get transmitted to linkage institutions in the policymaking system.
   *Page reference: 9-12, 50, 460-467, AP Big Idea: PMI*

2. A  The veto is one of the president's strongest legislative tools and most of the time it allows him the final say on every piece of legislation.
   *Page reference: 9-12, 50, 460-467, AP Big Idea: PMI*

3. D  Young people (18- to 25-year-olds) are the least likely group in the electorate to vote and this is partially because young people have not yet formed their political beliefs or determined their needs from government.
   *Page reference: 2-5, 171, 183-188, AP Big Idea: PRD*

4. D  Politicians are much less likely to listen to the concerns of the 18-25 age group.
   *Page 2-5, 171, 183-188, AP Big Idea: PRD*

5. C  There has been a significant increase in the number of seats held by Republicans in the southern states since 1969.
   *Page reference: 233, 310-319, 320-322, AP Big Idea: PRD*

6. C  The trend in the graph was caused by Nixon's "southern strategy" of appealing to disaffected white southerners.
   *Page reference: 233, 310-319, 320-322, AP Big Idea: PRD*

7. D  Contributions by PACs increased for Republican candidates between 2009-2010 and 2011-2012.
   *Page reference: 16, 258, 261, 295-297, 302, 305, 332, AP Big Idea: PMI*

8. B  Electioneering by PACs has introduced obvious biases into the electoral process.
   *Page reference: 16, 258, 261, 295-297, 302, 305, 332, AP Big Idea: PMI*

9. B  Social Security has replaced national defense as the government's biggest expenditure.
   *Page reference: 390, 396, 488, 495-496, 499, AP Big Idea: PMI*

10. D  Spending for the social security and other social welfare programs are the most important items in the budget.
    *Page reference: 390, 396, 488, 495-496, 499, AP Big Idea: PMI*

11. B  The establishment clause is the basis of the *Lemon v. Kurtzman* decision.
    *Page reference: 89-93, AP Big Idea: CON*

12. D   In *Lemon* v. *Kurtzman* the Supreme Court ruled that aid to church-related schools must (1) have a secular purpose (2) must have a primary effect that neither advances nor inhibits religion and (3) not foster excessive government entanglement with religion.
*Page reference: 89-93, AP Big Idea: CON*

13. D   Not allowing Americans to hold any religious belief they choose does not protect freedom of religion.
*Page reference: 89-93, AP Big Idea: CON*

14. B   Legislation enacted in 1965 was designed to ensure no person would be deprived of the right to vote based on race or color.
*Page reference: 52, 137-138, 427-428, AP Big Idea: PRD*

15. B   The Voting Rights Act was passed to enable the government to enforce African Americans' right to vote as guaranteed by the Fifteenth Amendment and as a result of its new power to enforce the law, the Justice Department sent in federal officials to oversee elections in Southern states.
*Page reference: 52, 137-138, 427-428, AP Big Idea: PRD*

16. D   The Voting Rights Act of 1965, a law designed to help end formal and informal barriers to African American suffrage, resulted in dramatic gains in African American voter registration, voting, and engagement in politics more generally.
*Page reference: 52, 137-138, 427-428, AP Big Idea: PRD*

17. C   Union membership is lowest in the South.
*Page reference: 300-301, AP Big Idea: PMI*

18  B   Right-to-work laws are a key tactic of businesses in trying to weaken labor unions by preventing mandatory membership.
*Page reference: 300-301, AP Big Idea: PMI*

19. B   The message is that interest groups buy legislation from Congress to advance their causes.
*Page reference: 302, 335, AP Big Idea: PMI*

20. D   Interest groups play a role in democratizing government by serving as linkage institutions between politicians and the public and thereby represent the needs of different groups of people to lawmakers, so these groups help the constituency to be heard.
*Page reference: 302, 335, AP Big Idea: PMI*

21. D   In a blanket primary, candidates of all parties are listed on the ballot and a voter may choose a candidate from one party for one office and a candidate from another party for a different office.
*Page reference: 226-228, 246-247, 248-252, AP Big Idea: PMI*

22. A   The court of appeals plays no role in the impeachment process.
*Page reference: 374-348, 447, AP Big Idea: PMI*

23. D   Democrats more than Republicans tend to favor polices like background checks and mandatory safety classes that make it more difficult for individuals to own handguns.
*Page reference: 221, 230, 253, AP Big Idea: PMI*

24. D   Only Congress can appropriate funds to be spent by the federal government.
*Page reference: 411, AP Big Idea: PMI*

25. B   Located in Article I of the Constitution, the elastic clause enumerates the implied powers of Congress and it gives the legislature full authority to make any laws "necessary and proper" to carry out those responsibilities assigned to it by the Constitution.
*Page reference: 65, AP Big Idea: CON*

26. C   Voting is the most common way people express their political views and by participating in an election, voters choose those candidates whom they feel agree with their political beliefs.
*Page reference: 263-274, AP Big Idea: PRD*

27. A   Supreme Court justices are granted life terms which allows them to make judicial decisions objectively without the pressures of political influence.
*Page reference: 442, 452-457, AP Big Idea: PMI*

28. D   The media tends to focus more heavily on candidates' personality than their policy platforms for the sake of achieving higher viewer ratings and this may distort the public's perception both of candidates and the party they represent.
*Page reference: 192-196, AP Big Idea: PRD*

29. A   The president sends his proposed budget to Congress, which, through its committees, ultimately decides how much money each department or agency gets to spend in the coming year.
*Page reference: 397-403, AP Big Idea: PMI*

30. D   Incumbents have better exposure, a political record with the constituency, and more campaign money with which to eliminate any chance of their challengers' success, and as a result of these advantages, usually more than 50 percent of congressional incumbents are reelected.
*Page reference: 313-317, AP Big Idea: PMI*

31. D   Iron triangles, or subgovernments, often work like well-oiled machines to produce and implement policies in a specific policy area.
*Page reference: 287-289, 434-437, AP Big Idea: PMI*

32. A   Lobbyists have the least influence over judges because they have no leverage with which to influence judges who hold their offices for life. However, interest groups can file amicus curiae briefs to try to influence a judge's decision.
*Page reference: 73, 284, 292-294, 335-336, AP Big Idea: PMI*

33. C   Political science research has consistently found party identification to be the strongest predictor of vote choice.
*Page reference: 263-274, 316, AP Big Idea: PRD*

34. D Many important and controversial Supreme Court cases in the 1960s addressed the rights of the accused such as extending the right of protection from self-incrimination, the right of counsel to the poor, and confirmed the exclusionary rule which prevents the use of evidence gained through unreasonable search and seizure from being used in trials.
*Page reference: 109-121, 462, AP Big Idea: CON*

35. B If the Supreme Court finds a law unconstitutional, Congress has the authority to amend the Constitution to suit the law, and the Supreme Court has no choice but to interpret the law in light of the amendment to the Constitution.
*Page reference: 309-310, 462-467, AP Big Idea: CON*

36. C It is often the case that the two houses pass different versions of the same bill and when this happens, the bill is sent to a conference committee composed of members of both houses. The committee works to develop a compromise between the bill's two versions.
*Page reference: 322, 325, AP Big Idea: PMI*

37. B The president has the power to negotiate executive agreements as well as treaties. Treaties are more formal and require the approval of Congress. Executive agreements, however, deal with smaller matters, so it is often easier for the president to handle them independently.
*Page reference: 366, 417, AP Big Idea: PMI*

38. A Thousands of cases are appealed to the Supreme Court each year, but only a few are actually placed on the docket due to the fact that the justices choose to hear only those cases they feel are most deserving of appeal or may have the greatest impact on the interpretation of the law.
*Page reference: 460-462, AP Big Idea: PMI*

39. D The Fourteenth Amendment offered the Supreme Court the opportunity to assert federal supremacy over state laws in order to grant to all people the right to due process of the law. The court has cited the Fourteenth Amendment in numerous civil liberties and civil rights cases.
*Page reference: 62-68, 462-467, 474, AP Big Idea: PMI*

40. C The *greatest* advantage of an incumbent in an election is name recognition due to the fact that incumbents receive a great deal of press coverage from local media outlets, and as a consequence, their names are more easily recognized by voters.
*Page reference: 313-317, AP Big Idea: PMI*

41. C Television allows viewers to see and judge political candidates without the structure of a political party and candidates too can address the public directly without having to channel their campaigns through the party machine.
*Page reference: 25, 49, 103-104, 197-198, AP Big Idea: PRD*

42. D Articles of Impeachment are the formal charges brought by the House.
*Page reference: 347-348, AP Big Idea: PMI*

43. A  If no candidate receives an Electoral College majority, then the election moves to the House of Representatives, which must choose from among the top three electoral vote winners.
*Page reference: 49, 50, 53, 273-276, AP Big Idea: PMI*

44. D  More and more states are allowing early voting, which is voting that takes place before the announced Election Day and allows registered voters to either vote by mail or show up at specially designated polling places to cast their votes.
*Page reference: 244, 253-256, 269, AP Big Idea: PRD*

45. B  Even though residents do have a significant amount of influence over the federal budget, Article II does not grant them the power to appropriate funds for agencies.
*Page reference: 52, 348-349, AP Big Idea: CON*

46. C  The Civil Rights Act officially prohibited discrimination in any public facilities and in employment and it authorized the Justice Department to enforce the act by investigating and suing any company that violated civil rights as outlined by the law.
*Page reference: 73, 94, 137, 142, 148, 150, 152, 329, AP Big Idea: CON*

47. A  The Rules Committee is very influential on legislation because it determines the length of debate for each piece of legislation and the order in which the bills will be heard.
*Page reference: 319-320, 327, AP Big Idea: PMI*

48. B  In *Texas* v. *Johnson* the court ruled that flag burning is protected under the First Amendment as a form of speech. This ruling set a precedent that symbolic speech is considered "free speech" in the eyes of the law.
*Page reference: 25, 102, AP Big Idea: CON*

49. D  The Articles did prevent the new United States from raising militias and paying its war debts and these were consequences of the fact that the government simply was too weak—it did not have enough centralized power to give it legitimacy and, ultimately, to allow it to function.
*Page reference: 30-31, 33, 60, 69, AP Big Idea: CON*

50. C  The Federal Reserve Board is an executive institution that oversees monetary policy by controlling the flow of currency.
*Page reference: 418, 483, AP Big Idea: PMI*

51. D  Democrats tend to favor liberal policies such as social spending, whereas Republicans usually endorse more conservative policies, such as those that limit the role of the federal government.
*Page reference: 221, 223-224, 231-232, AP Big Idea: PRD*

52. D  Regulatory agencies set industry standards to ensure both the quality of products and the safety of industrial workers. To oversee industries, agencies often send inspectors to determine whether specific companies are complying with industry standards.
*Page reference: 11, 430-432, AP Big Idea: PMI*

53. A   Presidents are not legislators, so they may propose policies indirectly or try to influence the policy process, but this means they must rely heavily on the support of other people to help them pursue their political agenda.
*Page reference: 342, 348-350, AP Big Idea: PMI*

54. C   Federalism imposes a tiered structure on government where more than one level shares authority over the people.
*Page reference: 59-60, 61-82, AP Big Idea: CON*

55. C   Senators actually act more independently of their party due to the fact that they have longer terms than representatives do and party affiliations and party leadership are also much stronger in the House, so representatives tend to vote along party lines.
*Page reference: 319-320, 347, AP Big Idea: PMI*

# Free-Response Questions

*This rubric provides examples of many, but not all of the possible correct responses to the free-response questions.*

1.

    a. Identify changes from the original Constitution that increased the democratic nature of government.

- Seventeenth Amendment.
- Nineteenth Amendment.
- Twenty-third Amendment.

    b. Explain how each of the two factors identified in part *a*, above, has resulted in a more democratic nation.

- **Seventeenth Amendment.** Under the original Constitution, U.S. senators were selected by state legislators. The Seventeenth Amendment, ratified in 1913, provides for the direct election of senators by the people.
- **Nineteenth Amendment.** Women were disenfranchised in the original Constitution. The Nineteenth Amendment, ratified in 1920, gave women the right to vote.
- **Twenty-third Amendment.** The Twenty-third Amendment, ratified in 1961, provided the District of Columbia with Electoral College votes in presidential elections. This gave the citizens of the District of Columbia a voice and influence in presidential politics.

2.

    a. Identify the constitutional issue that is common in *Roe v. Wade* (1973) and *Harris v. McRae* (1980).

- The cases have the due process clause of the $14^{th}$ Amendment and a broad right to privacy based on the $1^{st}$, $4^{th}$, $5^{th}$, and $9^{th}$ Amendments.

    b. Based on the constitutional issue identified in a., explain why the facts of *Harris v. McRae* led to a different holding than *Roe v. Wade*.

- Even though a woman's freedom to choose to terminate her pregnancy is constitutionally protected, she does not have a constitutional entitlement to financial resources to pay for the termination of the pregnancy.

c. Describe an action which could be taken by opponents of the *Harris v. McRae* decision.

- Individuals opposed to the Harris decision can protest and organize in an attempt to possibly have the decision overturned in the future.

3. Identify and explain ways that shifting populations will have an impact on government and politics.

- Changes in the demographics of the nation place new demands on the government. As the percentage of Latino/as in the population increases, for example, the prevalence of the Spanish language increases. This necessitates more English-as-a-second-language (ESL) programs and increases the cost to government to print materials in multiple languages. Other issues, such as immigration, may also become more salient in light of these changes.

- The increasing percentage of minority groups in the population makes changing the representativeness of Congress increasingly important. Right now, minority groups are significantly underrepresented in our nation's legislatures.

- Changes in the composition of society may change the partisan composition of the country. African Americans and most Hispanics (except Cubans) are more likely to identify as Democrats than Republicans. This has an effect on electoral politics in localities, states, and the nation at large.

4.

a. Identify items in the budget that cannot usually be amended during the budgetary process.

- Social Security
- Medicare

b. For each of the items in part *a*, above, explain why spending is difficult to cut.

- **Social Security** pays benefits to senior citizens who have paid into the system during their careers because they no longer work to earn an income. The government must pay benefits to those entitled. Not only are Social Security recipients more likely to vote than other citizens, there are also a number of well-organized interest groups that oppose reductions in spending for Social Security. This makes it difficult for members of Congress to go on record supporting cuts in this program.

- **Medicare:** Medicare is an entitlement program that helps pay for medical care for the elderly. The number of recipients has grown steadily. Congress, again, finds it difficult, if not impossible, to amend Medicare funding during the budgetary process. Senior citizens are very protective of their claim to health care benefits, which places members of Congress under significant pressure to not cut Medicare services.

# Government and Politics: United States AP Exam Practice Test 3

## Government and Politics: United States

Section I
Time: 80 minutes
55 Questions

**Directions:** *Each of the questions or incomplete statements below is followed by five suggested answers or completions. Select the statement that is best in each case.*

Questions 1-2 refer to the graph below.

**Percentage Registering and Voting by Race and Hispanic Origin: Congressional Elections**

Note: Percent of the citizen civilian noninstitutionalized population, age 18 and over.

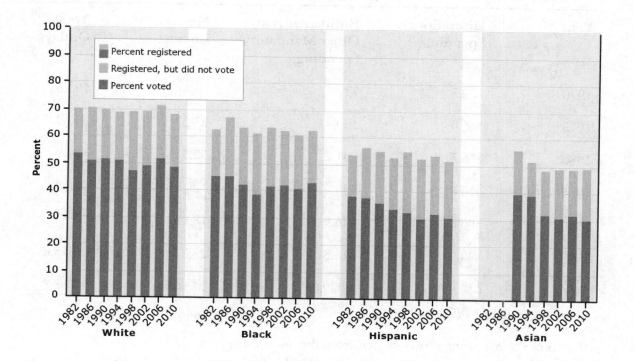

*United States Census Bureau, Current Population Survey, Voting and Registration Supplements, historical table A-4. http://www.census.gov/hhes/www/socdemo/voting/index.html*

1. Which of the following generalizations is supported by the information in the graph above?
   a. The proportion of the registered electorate has declined sharply across all racial/ethnic groups.
   b. The number of Asians voting in Congressional elections has consistently exceeded the number of Hispanics.
   c. Voter registration consistently yields political success.
   d. Despite growing minority populations, non-Hispanic Whites maintain political supremacy in most Congressional elections.

2. Which of the following statements is reflected in the graph?
   a. Hispanics actually voted more than all other groups depicted.
   b. Black voter registration has remained relatively steady since 1998.
   c. Asian voter registration has increased sharply since 1990.
   d. Non-Hispanic voter registration has declined steadily since 1990.

Questions 3-4 refer to the table below.

## OUTLAYS BY MAJOR SPENDING CATEGORY, 1970–2002
### (in billions of dollars)

| Year | Discretionary Spending | Entitlements and Other Mandatory Spending | Net Interest | Total Outlays |
|------|------------------------|-------------------------------------------|--------------|---------------|
| 1970 | 120.3 | 72.5 | 14.4 | 195.6 |
| 1975 | 158.0 | 169.4 | 23.2 | 332.3 |
| 1980 | 276.3 | 291.2 | 52.5 | 590.9 |
| 1985 | 415.8 | 448.2 | 129.5 | 946.4 |
| 1990 | 500.6 | 626.9 | 184.3 | 1,253.2 |
| 1995 | 544.9 | 818.5 | 232.1 | 1,515.8 |
| 2000 | 614.8 | 1,029.8 | 223.0 | 1,788.8 |

*Congressional Budget Office*

3. Which of the following can be drawn from the table above?
   a. For the time period covered, it would require congressional action not to spend a majority of federal outlays.
   b. States significantly affect the national budget.
   c. Interest is an insignificant part of the national budget.
   d. The national deficit is a significant public policy problem.

4. Based on the chart above, and your knowledge of the budgetary process, which of the following statements is accurate?
   a. Entitlement spending has no effect on discretionary spending.
   b. Discretionary spending must be factored into the budget before entitlements because it is determined by law.
   c. Increases in entitlement spending can lead to cuts in discretionary spending.
   d. Increases in discretionary spending will automatically result in cuts to entitlement spending.

Questions 5-6 refer to the graph below.

## How Much Money Do Top PACs Spend on National Elections?

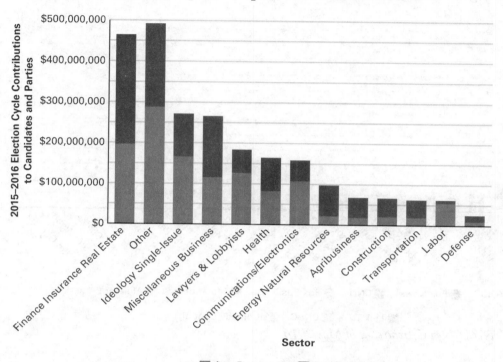

Center for Responsive Politics, *www.opensecrets.org*

5. Which of the following statements is reflected in the data in the chart?
   a. Overall, more money was donated to Republicans than to Democrats during the 2015-2016 election cycle.
   b. Overall, more money was donated to Democrats than to Republicans during the 2015-2016 election cycle.
   c. More money is donated by energy and natural resources PACs than any others.
   d. PACs do not play an important role in the electoral process.

6. Which of the following is an accurate conclusion based on the graph?
   a. Political Action Committees (PACs) support challengers more than incumbents.
   b. Political Action Committees (PACs) are a means of legally buying votes.
   c. Political Action Committees (PACs) are organized by candidates.
   d. Political Action Committees (PACs) raise money to support campaigns of candidates they would like to see win.

Questions 7-8 refer to the graph below.

## How did Media Coverage of the 2017 Presidential Candidates Influence the Election?

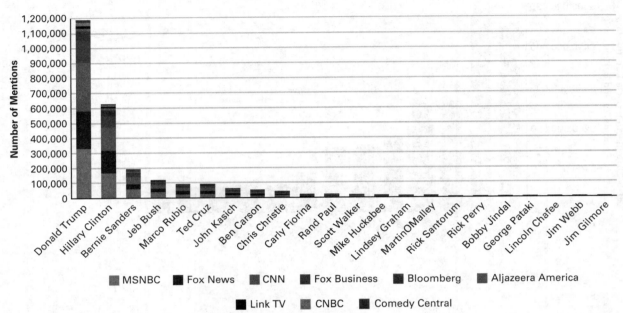

Data from Internet Archive TV News Archive, as of May 2016

7. What concept employed by the media best describes the information in the chart?
   a. framing
   b. media effects
   c. narrowcasting
   d. agenda setting

8. Which of the following is an accurate conclusion based on the chart?
   a. Mass media coverage of election campaigns often focuses on who is ahead in the polls.
   b. Mass media coverage of election campaigns often focuses on the parties' conventions.
   c. Mass media coverage of election campaigns often focuses on the parties' platforms.
   d. Mass media coverage of election campaigns often focuses on the full range of candidates running under the parties' banners.

Questions 9-10 refer to the graph below.

**The Increase in Income Inequality and the Rise of the Top 1 Percent**

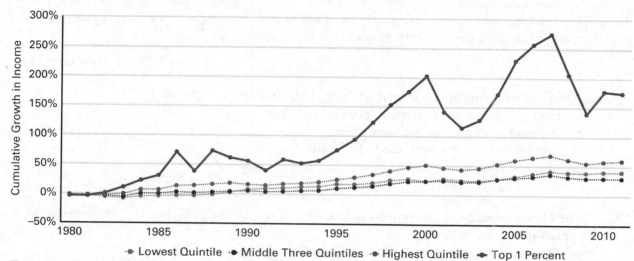

*From data underlying figures in the Congressional Budget Office, The Distribution of Household Income and Federal Taxes, 2011, November 2014, 21, Fig. 11.*

9.    Which of the following best describes a trend in the line graph above?
      a.    People below the 80th percentile saw their real income rise 50 percent during this period.
      b.    The major gains were reserved for the 81st through 99th percentiles during this period.
      c.    The top 1 percent saw a decline in income during this period.
      d.    The top 1 percent saw a 275 percent increase in income during this period.

10.   This increasing inequality in the distribution of income can contribute to a situation known as
      a.    poverty line.
      b.    relative deprivation.
      c.    laissez-faire.
      d.    inflation.

Questions 11-13 refer to the passage below.

Amendment I

"Congress shall make no law respecting an establishment of religion, or prohibiting the free exercise thereof; or abridging the freedom of speech, or of the press; or the right of the people peaceably to assemble, and to petition the government for a redress of grievances."

*--The United States Constitution*

11.    All of the following are protected by the right to free speech EXCEPT
       a.   the right to express unpopular political opinions.
       b.   the right to engage in symbolic speech.
       c.   the right to disagree with elected officials.
       d.   obscene speech.


12.    The First Amendment protection for free speech is most limited when the Supreme Court applies the
       a.   Clear and Present Danger Test.
       b.   Dangerous Tendency Test.
       c.   Child Benefit Theory.
       d.   Symbolic Speech Doctrine.


13.    The burning of the American Flag as a means of political protest has been ruled
       a.   speech not protected by the First Amendment.
       b.   a matter for state courts.
       c.   an issue that does not relate to the First Amendment.
       d.   symbolic speech protected by the First Amendment.

Questions 14-16 refer to the passage below.

The proposed Constitution, therefore, even when tested by the rules laid down by its antagonists, is, in strictness, neither a national nor a federal Constitution, but a composition of both. In its foundation it is federal, not national; in the sources from which the ordinary powers of the government are drawn, it is partly federal and partly national; in the operation of these powers, it is national, not federal; in the extent of them, again, it is federal, not national; and, finally in the authoritative mode of introducing amendments, it is neither wholly federal nor wholly national.

--*The Federalist No. 39*

14. Constitutionally, the federal system consists of the national government and
    a. the state senates.
    b. the national judiciary.
    c. only the 50 states.
    d. the bureaucracy.

15. Political scholars believe federalism is best suited to people who are all of the following EXCEPT
    a. opponents of concentrated power
    b. located on a large land mass
    c. diverse
    d. supporters of anarchy

16. The Supreme Court defined the division of power between the national and state governments in 1819 in
    a. *Marbury v. Madison.*
    b. *McCulloch v. Maryland.*
    c. *Fletcher v. Peck.*
    d. *Mapp v. Ohio.*

Questions 17-18 refer to the map below.

**Equal Employment Opportunity Commission**
**15 Districts**

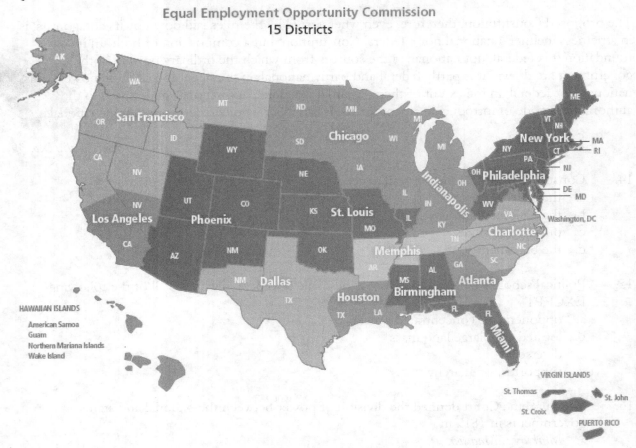

*U.S. Equal Employment Opportunity Commission, https://www.eeoc.gov/field/*

17.    The Equal Employment Opportunity Commission is organized into 15 districts located
       throughout the United States, the Virgin Islands and Puerto Rico. This organization model
       illustrates
       a.   the impact of federalism on public policy.
       b.   that the law enforced by the Equal Employment Opportunity Commission differs across
            the country.
       c.   that the Equal Employment Opportunity Commission is independent of partisan
            politics.
       d.   that the implementation of public policy can be decentralized.

18.    The Equal Employment Opportunity Commission was created by
       a.   the Voting Rights Act of 1965.
       b.   the Civil Rights Act of 1964.
       c.   the Fifteenth Amendment.
       d.   the Equal Rights Amendment.

Questions 19-20 refer to the cartoon below.

*"Do you ever have one of those days when every-*
*thing seems unconstitutional?"*

*Joseph Mirachi/The New Yorker Collection/The Cartoon Bank*

19.    The power to decide the constitutionality of a law was assumed by the Supreme Court in
    a.  *Marbury v. Madison.*
    b.  *McCullouch v. Maryland.*
    c.  *Plessy v. Ferguson.*
    d.  *Barron v. Baltimore.*

20.    "Judicial activism" means that
    a.  the Supreme Court hears more cases each succeeding year.
    b.  judges actively seek cases to hear.
    c.  judges lobby Congress for more funding.
    d.  judges interpret the Constitution according to their own attitudes.

21.    The Constitutional requirement that the Senate advise and consent on presidential
appointments to the Supreme Court is an example of
    a.  full faith and credit.
    b.  federalism.
    c.  selective incorporation.
    d.  checks and balances.

22. In a primary election, voters
    a. nominate a candidate for the party in whose primary they are voting.
    b. elect a candidate to office.
    c. nominate candidates for both major political parties.
    d. are only expressing a preference. The outcome has no effect on political parties.

23. Supreme Court Justices can leave the Court in all of the following ways EXCEPT
    a. death.
    b. retirement.
    c. impeachment.
    d. being fired by the President.

24. To produce identical bills to send to the President for his consideration, the House and Senate use
    a. the Rules Committee.
    b. the Ways and Means Committee.
    c. a Conference Committee.
    d. a Joint Committee.

25. All of the following make it more likely that the Supreme Court will hear a case EXCEPT if
    a. four Justices think it should be heard.
    b. different U.S. Courts of Appeals have reached different interpretations of the Constitution.
    c. Congress fails to certify a case for review.
    d. multiple interest groups file *amicus curiae* briefs.

26. Presidents may not be successful in getting a judiciary that agrees with them because
    a. federal judges are often swayed by the media or public.
    b. Congress may pass laws overriding the Supreme Court's constitutional decisions.
    c. federal judges serve for life during good behavior.
    d. federal judges change when the party in the White House changes.

27. The innovative system of distributing power adopted in the Constitution is
    a. a unitary form of government.
    b. federalism.
    c. a confederation.
    d. libertarianism.

28. States have an impact on national government by
    a. ratifying proposed constitutional amendments.
    b. selecting U.S. Senators.
    c. regulating political campaign spending.
    d. paying taxes based on population.

29. Protection against self-incrimination was applied to the states in
   a. *Miranda v. Arizona.*
   b. *Mapp v. Ohio.*
   c. *Gideon v. Wainwright.*
   d. *Gitlow v. New York.*

30. Establishing an educational system is
   a. specifically listed in the Tenth Amendment.
   b. a concurrent power of the national and state governments.
   c. a reserved power.
   d. an implied power granted to the states.

31. Turnout in presidential elections
   a. is highest among young voters.
   b. is at the same level across all age groups.
   c. is highest among independents.
   d. is highest among older voters.

32. Political parties in the United States
   a. are strongly organized from the national through the local levels.
   b. control who runs under their party label.
   c. have strict membership requirements.
   d. are focused on winning elections.

33. The national government's power has been greatly expanded by its expressed power to
   a. establish post offices and post roads.
   b. establish a national educational system.
   c. establish Social Security.
   d. regulate interstate commerce.

34. The group of advisors closest to the president is
   a. the Cabinet.
   b. the Executive Office of the President.
   c. the Speaker of the House and the President pro tempore of the Senate.
   d. the Vice President and his staff.

35. Bureaucratic power arises from
   a. federalism.
   b. generally positive public opinion.
   c. discretion to implement vague Congressional mandates.
   d. PAC funds.

36. Clarence Gideon argued that he had the right to
   a. place Bibles in motel rooms.
   b. counsel.
   c. privacy.
   d. speech.

37. The right to privacy is based on
    a. implied powers.
    b. enumerated powers.
    c. Supreme Court decisions.
    d. Executive Orders.

38. Protecting property rights
    a. is undemocratic, and therefore was rejected by the Framers of the Constitution.
    b. is reflected in the expressed powers in the Constitution.
    c. is left to state governments in the Constitution.
    d. is solely a function of the courts.

39. The "Rule of Four"
    a. sets the minimum number of electoral votes each state has.
    b. sets a precedent in Supreme Court cases.
    c. sets the maximum number of terms a president may serve.
    d. generally is sufficient for the Supreme Court to hear a case.

40. If your right against unreasonable search and seizure is violated, the remedy is
    a. the exclusionary rule.
    b. the plea bargaining.
    c. an *ex post facto* law.
    d. *habeas corpus*.

41. Cloture
    a. removes a President or Justice who has been impeached.
    b. is a Constitutional provision to protect minority rights.
    c. is used only in the Senate.
    d. is used only in the House.

42. The number of interest groups has grown because
    a. "organization begets counterorganization."
    b. political parties charge more to join.
    c. interest groups get good media coverage.
    d. interest groups are subsidized by the government.

43. The group most closely associated with voting for the Democratic Party is
    a. Black Americans.
    b. Asian Americans.
    c. Hispanic Americans.
    d. Southerners after 1964.

44. State and local party organizations have less control over who their candidates are than in the past. This is because of the growth in the use of
    a. public campaign financing.
    b. partisanship.
    c. ideology.
    d. primaries.

45. The fact that members of Congress serve on committees that allow them to contribute to their constituencies contributes to
    a. the party in the electorate.
    b. the incumbency effect.
    c. the committee effect.
    d. corruption.

46. Budget preparation by the Office of Management and Budget is a function of the
    a. legislative branch of government.
    b. executive branch of government.
    c. judicial branch of government.
    d. independent regulatory commissions.

47. Most protections in the "Bill of Rights" have been extended to the states through a process known as
    a. cooperative federalism.
    b. selective incorporation.
    c. the legislative veto.
    d. dual federalism.

48. Congress affects the power of the courts by all of the following EXCEPT
    a. establishing new federal courts.
    b. creating new federal judgeships.
    c. determining the jurisdiction of federal courts.
    d. reducing the pay of sitting federal judges.

49. The winner-take-all electoral system in the U.S. is a primary reason for
    a. only two major political parties.
    b. the high costs of electoral campaigns.
    c. the way states allocate Electoral College votes.
    d. "third" parties that routinely win elections.

50. All of the following are reasons an interest group would have a great deal of influence in the policy area in which they are interested EXCEPT
    a. a monopoly on relevant information.
    b. a large membership.
    c. cohesion.
    d. high levels of Congressional expertise and commitment in the area.

51. If you were trying to predict the outcome of an upcoming congressional election, the most valuable information you could have is
    a. a candidate's incumbency status.
    b. the amount of money each candidate has to spend.
    c. how the President performed in the district in the last election.
    d. the number of voters who voted in the last election.

52. In striking down discrimination in public accommodations, e.g. hotels and restaurants, Congress, upheld by the Supreme Court, relied on
    a. the interstate commerce clause.
    b. the First Amendment's right to freedom of assembly.
    c. the Equal Protection Clause.
    d. the expressed powers of Congress.

53. The Framers of the Constitution, compared to the Articles of Confederation,
    a. gave more power to the states.
    b. gave more power to the people.
    c. did not change the relationship between the national government and the states.
    d. gave more power to the national government.

54. Pluralist theory emphasizes the role of
    a. individuals.
    b. competition among groups.
    c. wealth.
    d. the limited number of access points to government.

55. If one wanted to insulate decisions from partisan political influence, one might house the policy responsibility in
    a. a cabinet department.
    b. state governments.
    c. the bureaucracy.
    d. an independent regulatory commission.


*END OF SECTION I.*

*IF YOU FINISH BEFORE TIME IS CALLED, YOU MAY CHECK YOUR WORK ON THIS SECTION.*

*DO NOT GO ON TO SECTION II UNTIL YOU ARE TOLD TO DO SO.*

# Government and Politics: United States

## Section II
## Time: 100 minutes

*Directions: You have 100 minutes to answer all four of the following questions. It is suggested that you take a few minutes to plan and outline each answer. Spend approximately one-fourth of your time (25 minutes) on each question. Illustrate your essay with substantive examples where appropriate. Make certain to number each of your answers as the question is numbered below.*

1.  In 2010 the Supreme Court ruled in *McDonald v. Chicago* that the Second Amendment applied to the states. The holding of the court ruled the right to keep and bear arms for self-defense in one's home as protected under the Second Amendment, and is incorporated against the states through the Due Process Clause of the Fourteenth Amendment.

    a.  Identify the term that is used to describe the application of one of the amendments in the Bill of Rights to the states.

    b.  Explain why it is necessary for the Supreme Court to render such a decision if the Second Amendment is to be applied to the states.

    c.  Identify two (2) other Supreme Court cases that applied one of the amendments in the Bill of Rights to the states and describe which right was extended by the case.

2.  Catherine Kuhlmeier was a student at East High School. She was a member of the student newspaper 'The Spectrum' and the Principal of the high school had the ability to review the content of the paper before publication. The Principal discovered news stories reflecting teen pregnancy and divorce and he decided to eliminate the stories from the publication. The student editors of the paper said the Principal had violated their respective 1st Amendment rights The Supreme Court ruled in favor of the Hazelwood School District in 1988, in a 5-3 ruling, stating that public settings may differ by locale. With regard to a school, the nature of the public sector within publically-funded institutions - such as public schools - is defined with regard to the nature of the respective form of media, its adherence to legislation, and the discretion of school administration. As a result, schools are not entitled to the breadth of the 1st Amendment as is entitled to jurisdictions existing outside of publically-funded educational facilities.

    *--Hazelwood School District et al. v. Kuhlmeier et al.*

a. Identify the constitutional clause that is common in both *Hazelwood v. Kuhlmeier* (1988) and *Tinker v. Des Moines* (1969)

b. Based on the constitutional clause identified in part a, explain why the holdings in these two cases are different.

c. Describe actions that can be taken by the members of the public who might disagree with the ruling in *Hazelwood v. Kuhlmeier*.

**Percent Voting by Educational Attainment**

Note: Percent of the citizen civilian noninstitutionalized population, age 18 and over.

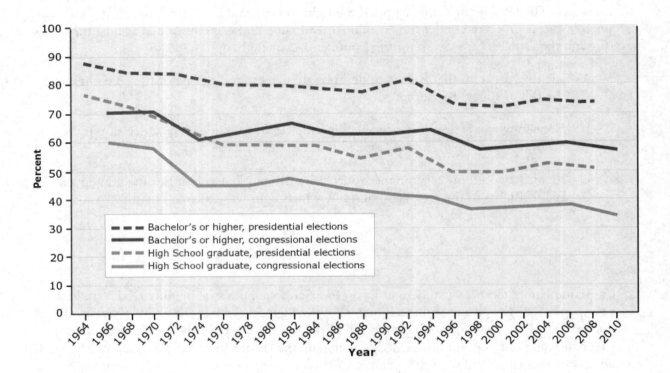

*United States Census Bureau, Current Population Survey, Voting and Registration Supplements, historical table A-4. http://www.census.gov/hhes/www/socdemo/voting/index.html*

3. The graph shows the proportion of the civilian, noninstitutionalized population, age 18 and over voting in various elections. Using this information and your knowledge of U.S. politics:

   a. Briefly describe two trends depicted in this graph.

   b. Identify two factors that may have produced the trends you describe.

   c. Explain why there are differences between the levels of voting for presidential and congressional elections.

   d. Explain why there are differences based on educational attainment.

4. The Framers of the Constitution were concerned that power would be too concentrated in government. Some citizens today complain that government cannot get anything done.

   Develop a thesis that responds to the prompt and establish a line of reasoning.

   Support your thesis by:

   • Identifying three mechanisms that the Framers adopted to make sure power was not too concentrated in government.

   • Explaining how each of these mechanisms was meant to make sure power was not too concentrated in government.

   • Identifying one mechanism used today to try to make sure government accomplishes something.

   • Explaining how this mechanism used today is meant to make sure government accomplishes something.

**END OF EXAMINATION**

# Answers and Explanations

## Practice Test 3

1. D   The graph indicates that non-Hispanic whites are more politically active than minority populations, regardless of the population growth in the minority populations.
*Page reference: 264, 266-267, 277, AP Big Idea: PRD*

2. B   Black voter registration has remained relatively steady since 1998.
*Page reference: 264, 266-267, 277, AP Big Idea: PRD*

3. A   Entitlements and other mandatory spending have increased since 1970 and not spending that money would require action from Congress.
*Page reference: 396, 488, 495-496, AP Big Idea: PMI*

4. C   Increases in entitlement spending can lead to cuts in discretionary spending.
*Page reference: 396, 488, 495-496, AP Big Idea: PMI*

5. A   Overall, more money was donated to Republicans than to Democrats during the 2015-2016 election cycle.
*Page reference: 292-304, 335-336, AP Big Idea: PMI*

6. D   The purpose of a PAC is to raise money and distribute the funds to candidates the group supports.
*Page reference: 292-304, 335-336, AP Big Idea: PMI*

7. A   Framing best describes the information in the chart.
*Page reference: 254-256, 374-377, AP Big Idea: PRD*

8. A   Mass media focuses on the front runners to the almost exclusion of other candidates.
*Page reference: 254-256, 374-377, AP Big Idea: PRD*

9. D   The top 1 percent saw a 275 percent increase in income during this period.
*Page reference: 18-19, 489-490, AP Big Idea: PMI*

10. B   Increasing inequality in the distribution of income contributes to a situation known as relative deprivation.
*Page 18-19, 489-490, AP Big Idea:  PMI*

11. D   Obscene speech is not of form of speech protected by the First Amendment.
*Page reference: 87, 89-107, 124-125, 204 AP Big Idea: CON*

12. B   The Dangerous Tendency Test permits legislatures to forbid speech that tends to encourage people to engage in illegal activities.
*Page reference: 87, 89-107. 124-125, 204 AP Big Idea: CON*

13. D  Symbolic speech is protected by the First Amendment.
*Page reference: 87, 89-107, 124-125, 204, AP Big Idea: CON*

14. C  The federal system consists of the national government and only the 50 states.
*Page reference: 59-60, 61-68, AP Big Idea: CON*

15. D  Federalism is not suited to supporters of anarchy.
*Page reference: 59-60, 61-68, AP Big Idea: CON*

16. B  *McCulloch v. Maryland* did define the division of power between the national and state governments.
*Page reference: 59-60, 61-68, AP Big Idea: CON*

17. D  The organization of the locations of the EEOC districts indicates that this area of public policy has been decentralized.
*Page reference: 137, 148, 150, 431-432, AP Big Idea: LOR*

18. B  The EEOC was created by the Civil Rights Act of 1964
*Page reference: 137, 148, 150, 431-432, AP Big Idea: LOR*

19. A  *Marbury v. Madison* established the Supreme Court's right to declare the acts of Congress unconstitutional.
*Page reference: 42, 50, 468-470, 474, AP Big Idea: CON*

20. D  Judicial activism is an approach to decision making where judges sometimes make bold policy decisions often based on their own attitudes.
*Page reference: 42, 50, 468-470, 474, AP Big Idea: PMI*

21. D  The Constitution creates a system of checks and balances and the Senate's ability to advise and consent is an example of that.
*Page reference: 35, 40, 42-43, 53-54, AP Big Idea: CON*

22. A  A primary election allows voters to nominate a candidate for the party conducting the primary.
*Page reference: 226-228, 246-247, 248-252, AP Big Idea: PMI*

23. D  Supreme Court Justices are appointed by the President, but cannot be fired by the President.
*Page reference: 442, 452-457, AP Big Idea: PMI*

24. C  A Conference Committee is created by party leadership from both houses to iron out the differences and bring back a single bill.
*Page reference: 322, AP Big Idea: PMI*

25. C  Congress does not have to certify a case in order for the Supreme Court to hear it.
*Page reference: 460-467, AP Big Idea: CON*

26. C   Federal judges serve for life and a president may not have the opportunity to make appointments to the federal courts during his term of office.
*Page reference: 442, 462-467, AP Big Idea: PMI*

27. B   The Constitution divides power between national and state governments, thus creating a federal government.
*Page reference: 59-689, AP Big Idea: CON*

28. A   States must ratify constitutional amendments before they become part of the Constitution which allows the states to have an impact on the national government.
*Page reference: 25, 68-76, AP Big Idea: CON*

29. A   The *Miranda* case set guidelines for police questioning to protect accused persons against self-incrimination.
*Page reference: 114-115, 470, AP Big Idea: LOR*

30. C   The 10th Amendment reserved powers for the states and establishing an educational system is one of those reserved powers.
*Page reference: 61-70, 78-82, AP Big Idea: CON*

31. D   The group with the highest voter turnout in presidential elections is the 65 and older group.
*Page reference: 50, 52-53, 208-209, 264-265, 272-274, 346, AP Big Idea: PRD*

32. D   A political party's main goal is to control the governing institutions by getting their candidates elected to office.
*Page reference: 50, 219-220, 225-236, AP Big Idea: PMI*

33. D   Commerce clause, and all the implied powers related to it, have greatly increased the power of the national government.
*Page reference: 59-76, AP Big Idea: CON*

34. B   The Cabinet, which is selected by the president, is the group of advisors who work closest to the president.
*Page reference: 351-352, AP Big Idea: PMI*

35. C   The bureaucracy was created to implement the mandates of the government and as the size and power of the government grew, so did the size and power of the bureaucracy.
*Page reference: 411, AP Big Idea: PMI*

36. B   Clarence Gideon appealed his conviction on the basis of his constitutional right to an attorney.
*Page reference: 115, AP Big Idea: LOR*

37. C   The right to privacy is not specifically stated in the Constitution but is based on Supreme Court decisions.
*Page reference: 121-124, 135-137, AP Big Idea: CON*

38. B  The basis for protecting property rights is found in Article I of the Constitution, such as the guidelines for taxing property.
*Page reference: 28, 34, 121, AP Big Idea: CON*

39. D  It takes only four Supreme Court justices to agree to hear a case and this is known as the "rule of four."
*Page reference: 460-467, AP Big Idea: PMI*

40. A  The exclusionary rule says that evidence that is not constitutionally obtained cannot be introduced as evidence in court.
*Page reference: 112-113, AP Big Idea: LOR*

41. C  Cloture, a procedure for terminating debate, can only be used in the Senate to stop a filibuster.
*Page reference: 329, AP Big Idea: PMI*

42. A  For each interest group that is created, an opposite interest group will be created in response, causing the number of interest groups to grow dramatically.
*Page reference: 285, 317-319,299-304, AP Topic: PMI*

43. A  Black Americans tend to vote for Democrats more than the other groups listed.
*Page reference: 223-224, 296-297, AP Topic: PRD*

44. D  Primaries have moved the control of party candidates more to the national party organization away from the state and local organizations.
*Page reference: 220, 223-225, 299, 316-317, AP Big Idea: PRD*

45. B  The serving on committees gives members of Congress the opportunity to help constituents; the constituents tend to return them to Congress in order to retain that help.
*Page reference: 322-323, 327-329, AP Big Idea: PMI*

46. B  The OMB is a part of the executive branch making budget preparation a function of the executive branch.
*Page reference: 352-354, 398, 400, 433, AP Big Idea: PMI*

47. B  The process by which the Supreme Court used the 14th Amendment to make the provisions of the Bill of Rights applicable to the states is known as selective incorporation.
*Page reference: 45-46, 62, 87-89, 131, AP Big Idea: LOR*

48. D  Congress is prohibited from reducing the pay of sitting judges.
*Page reference: 443-449, 460, AP Big Idea: PMI*

49. A  The winner-take-all electoral system is the primary reason for only two major political parties because additional parties dilute the vote and make declaring a winner difficult.
*Page reference: 236-237, AP Big Idea: PRD*

50. D   If there is a high level of Congressional expertise and commitment in a particular area, an interest group would be an unnecessary source of information.
*Page reference: 285, 292-299, 335, AP Big Idea: PMI*

51. A   Incumbency is the greatest predictor of the outcome of an election.
*Page reference: 313-317, AP Big Idea: PMI*

52. A   The interstate commerce clause provided the interstate jurisdiction which allowed the Supreme Court to strike down discrimination in public accommodations in all states.
*Page reference: 133-140, 157-158, 431, AP Big Idea: LOR*

53. D   The Constitution created a central government with significantly more power compared to the Articles of Confederation.
*Page reference: 30-31, 33, 60, 69, AP Big Idea: CON*

54. B   The pluralist theory states that the policymaking process is very open to the participation of groups with shared interests, with no single group usually dominating.
*Page reference: 13-14, 15-16, 286-287, 305, AP Topic: CON*

55. D   The independent regulatory commission is by definition, independent from influence, and that independence is protected by Congress.
*Page reference: 418-419, AP Big Idea: PMI*

# Free-Response Questions

*This rubric provides examples of many, but not all of the possible correct responses to the free-response questions.*

1. In 2010 the Supreme Court ruled in *McDonald v. Chicago* that the Second Amendment applied to the states. The holding of the court ruled the right to keep and bear arms for self-defense in one's home as protected under the Second Amendment, and is incorporated against the states through the Due Process Clause of the Fourteenth Amendment.

   a. Identify the term that is used to describe the application of one of the amendments in the Bill of Rights to the states.

      ▪ "Selective incorporation" is the preferred term. Any term that communicates that the Supreme Court has never ruled that all of the Bill of Rights applies to the states merits credit. A description that indicates that this process is done on a case-by-case basis communicates this. "Nationalization of the Bill of Rights" also merits credit.

   b. Explain why it is necessary for the Supreme Court to render such a decision if the Second Amendment is to be applied to the states.

      ▪ The original interpretation of whether the Bill of Rights limited states came in *Barron v. Baltimore* (1833), in which the Supreme Court limited only what the national government, not states' governments, could do. The ratification of the Fourteenth Amendment, with its due process clause, offered hope for overturning this decision, but it took multiple cases to reach this point. Finally, in 1925, in the case of *Gitlow v. New York*, the Supreme Court ruled that the First Amendment rights of freedom of speech and press limited the states. Since then, other parts, but not all, of the Bill of Rights have been applied to the states.

   c. Identify two (2) other Supreme Court cases that applied one of the amendments in the Bill of Rights to the states and describe which right was extended by the case.

      ▪ Any two cases from the table below can be listed and the provision described.

| Provision | Case | Year |
|---|---|---|
| **1st Amendment** | | |
| Freedom of Speech & Press | *Gitlow v. New York* | 1925 |
| Freedom of Assembly | *DeJonge v. Oregon* | 1937 |
| Freedom of Petition | *Hague v. CIO* | 1939 |
| Free Exercise of Religion | *Cantwell v. Connecticut* | 1940 |
| Establishment of Religion | *Everson v. Board of Education* | 1947 |
| | | |
| **4th Amendment** | | |
| Unreasonable Search & Seizure | *Wolf v. Colorado* | 1949 |
| Exclusionary Rule | *Mapp v. Ohio* | 1961 |
| | | |
| **5th Amendment** | | |
| Payment of Compensation for Taking of Private Property | *Chicago, Burlington & Quincy Railway Co. v. Chicago* | 1897 |
| Self-Incrimination | *Malloy v. Hogan* | 1964 |
| Double Jeopardy | *Benton v. Maryland* | 1969 |
| When Jeopardy Attaches | *Crist v. Bretz* | 1978 |
| | | |
| **6th Amendment** | | |
| Public Trial | *In re Oliver* | 1948 |
| Due Notice | *Cole v. Arkansas* | 1948 |
| Right to Counsel (Felonies) | *Gideon v. Wainwright* | 1963 |
| Confrontation & Cross-Examination of Adverse Witnesses | *Pointer v. Texas* | 1965 |
| Speedy Trial | *Klopfer v. North Carolina* | 1967 |
| Compulsory Process to Obtain Witnesses | *Washington v. Texas* | 1967 |
| Jury Trial | *Duncan v. Louisiana* | 1968 |
| Right to Counsel (Misdemeanor when Jail is Possible) | *Argersinger v. Hamlin* | 1972 |
| | | |
| **8th Amendment** | | |
| Cruel & Unusual Punishment | *Louisiana ex rel. Francis v. Resweber* | 1947 |
| | | |
| **9th Amendment** | | |
| Privacy (Not Specifically Mentioned) | *Griswold v. Connecticut* | 1965 |

2. Catherine Kuhlmeier was a student at East High School. She was a member of the student newspaper 'The Spectrum' and the Principal of the high school had the ability to review the content of the paper before publication. The Principal discovered news stories reflecting teen pregnancy and divorce and he decided to eliminate the stories from the publication. The student editors of the paper said the Principal had violated their respective 1st Amendment rights The Supreme Court ruled in favor of the Hazelwood School District in 1988, in a 5-3 ruling, stating that public settings may differ by locale. With regard to a school, the nature of the public sector within publically-funded institutions - such as public schools - is defined with regard to the nature of the respective form of media, its adherence to legislation, and the discretion of school administration. As a result, schools are not entitled to the breadth of the 1st Amendment as is entitled to jurisdictions existing outside of publically-funded educational facilities.

*--Hazelwood School District et al. v. Kuhlmeier et al.*

   a. Identify the constitutional clause that is common in both *Hazelwood v. Kuhlmeier* (1988) and *Tinker v. Des Moines* (1969)

   ▪ Free Speech as defined by the First Amendment.

   b. Based on the constitutional clause identified in part a, explain why the holdings in these two cases are different.

   ▪ In the *Tinker* case, the Court ruled it was "pure speech" of the student and was protected by the First Amendment. In the *Hazelwood* case, the Court ruled it was "school sponsored" speech and could be censored by the administration.

   c. Describe actions that can be taken by the members of the public who might disagree with the ruling in *Hazelwood v. Kuhlmeier.*

   ▪ Members of the community can peacefully protest and even bring further "test cases" before the Court.

3. The graph shows the proportion of the civilian, noninstitutionalized population, age 18 and over voting in various elections. Using this information and your knowledge of U.S. politics:

   a. Briefly describe two trends depicted in this graph.

   ▪ Two of the trends on the graph can be described as moving slightly downward over time.

   b. Identify two factors that may have produced the trends you describe.

   ▪ Identifying a decline in trust in government or a decline in partisan identification or an increase in the proportion of the electorate composed of racial/ethnic minorities who generally have lower turnout rates are creditable responses.

c. Explain why there are differences between the levels of voting for presidential and congressional elections.

- More people vote in presidential elections than in congressional elections because they are drawn out to vote for a higher-level office for which there is a better-financed and more high-visibility campaign.

d. Explain why there are differences based on educational attainment.

- People with higher levels of education tend to vote at higher levels because they have higher levels of political knowledge and higher incomes, both of which are associated with greater political participation.

4. The Framers of the Constitution were concerned that power would be too concentrated in government. Some citizens today complain that government cannot get anything done.

Develop a thesis that responds to the prompt and establish a line of reasoning.

Identify three mechanisms that the Framers adopted to make sure power was not too concentrated in government. Identification of any of the following would qualify for credit:

- Federalism
- Separation of Powers ("Separate Institutions Sharing Power")
- Bicameralism
- Differing Terms
- Differing Means of Selection, ergo Differing Constituencies
- Differing Formal Qualifications
- Checks & Balances
- The Formal Amendment Process

Explain how each of these mechanisms was meant to make sure power was not too concentrated in government.

- For the chosen mechanisms, the student needs to communicate that this mechanism deconcentrates power "BY …."

Identify one mechanism used today to try to make sure government accomplishes something.

- Political parties

Explain how this mechanism used today is meant to make sure government accomplishes something.

- Political parties are meant to organize political interests to achieve policy goals.